PRACTICAL USAGE OF REXX

Abramsky, S. & Hankin, C.J.	ABSTRACT INTERPRETATION OF DECLARATIVE LANGUAGES
Alexander, H.	FORMALLY-BASED TOOLS AND TECHNIQUES FOR HUMAN–COMPUTER DIALOGUES
Atherton, R.	STRUCTURED PROGRAMMING WITH BBC BASIC
Atherton, R.	STRUCTURED PROGRAMMING WITH COMAL
Baeza-Yates, R.A.	TEXT SEARCHING ALGORITHMS
Bailey, R.	FUNCTIONAL PROGRAMMING WITH HOPE
Barrett, R., Ramsay, A. & Sloman, A.	POP-11
Berztiss, A.	PROGRAMMING WITH GENERATORS
Bharath, R.	COMPUTERS AND GRAPH THEORY
Bishop, P.	FIFTH GENERATION COMPUTERS
Bullinger, H.-J. & Gunzenhauser, H.	SOFTWARE ERGONOMICS
Burns, A.	NEW INFORMATION TECHNOLOGY
Carberry, J.C.	COBOL
Carlini, U. & Villano, U.	TRANSPUTERS AND PARALLEL ARCHITECTURES
Chivers, I.D.	AN INTRODUCTION TO STANDARD PASCAL
Chivers, I.D.	MODULA 2
Chivers, I.D. & Sleighthome, J.	INTERACTIVE FORTRAN 77
Clark, M.W.	PC-PORTABLE FORTRAN
Clark, M.W.	TEX
Cockshott, W. P.	A COMPILER WRITER'S TOOLBOX: How to Implement Interactive Compilers for PCs with Turbo Pascal
Cockshott, W. P.	PS-ALGOL IMPLEMENTATIONS: Applications in Persistent Object-Oriented Programming
Colomb, R.	IMPLEMENTING PERSISTENT PROLOG
Cope, T.	COMPUTING USING BASIC
Curth, M.A. & Edelmann, H.	APL
Dahlstrand, I.	SOFTWARE PORTABILITY AND STANDARDS
Dongarra, J., Duff, I., Gaffney, P., & McKee, S.	VECTOR AND PARALLEL COMPUTING
Dunne, P.E.	COMPUTABILITY THEORY
Eastlake, J.J.	A STRUCTURED APPROACH TO COMPUTER STRATEGY
Eisenbach, S.	FUNCTIONAL PROGRAMMING
Ellis, D.	MEDICAL COMPUTING AND APPLICATIONS
Ennals, J.R.	ARTIFICIAL INTELLIGENCE
Ennals, J.R.	BEGINNING MICRO-PROLOG
Ennals, J.R., *et al.*	INFORMATION TECHNOLOGY AND EDUCATION
Filipič, B.	PROLOG USER'S HANDBOOK
Ford, N.	COMPUTER PROGRAMMING LANGUAGES
Grill, E.	RELATIONAL DATABASES
Grune, D. & Jacobs, C.J.H.	PARSING TECHNIQUES: A Practical Guide
Guariso, G. & Werthner, H.	ENVIRONMENTAL DECISION SUPPORT SYSTEMS
Harland, D.M.	CONCURRENCY AND PROGRAMMING LANGUAGES
Harland, D.M.	POLYMORPHIC PROGRAMMING LANGUAGES
Harland, D.M.	REKURSIV
Harris, D.J.	DEVELOPING DEDICATED DBASE SYSTEMS
Henshall, J. & Shaw, S.	OSI EXPLAINED, 2nd Edition
Hepburn, P.H.	FURTHER PROGRAMMING IN PROLOG
Hepburn, P.H.	PROGRAMMING IN MICRO-PROLOG MADE SIMPLE
Hill, I.D. & Meek, B.L.	PROGRAMMING LANGUAGE STANDARDISATION
Hirschheim, R., Smithson, S. & Whitehouse, D.	MICROCOMPUTERS AND THE HUMANITIES: Survey and Recommendations
Hutchins, W.J.	MACHINE TRANSLATION
Hutchison, D.	FUNDAMENTALS OF COMPUTER LOGIC
Hutchison, D. & Silvester, P.	COMPUTER LOGIC
Koopman, P.	STACK COMPUTERS
Kenning, M.-M. & Kenning, M.J.	COMPUTERS AND LANGUAGE LEARNING: Current Theory and Practice
Koskimies, K. & Paaki, J.	AUTOMATING LANGUAGE IMPLEMENTATION
Koster, C.H.A.	TOP-DOWN PROGRAMMING WITH ELAN
Last, R.	ARTIFICIAL INTELLIGENCE TECHNIQUES IN LANGUAGE LEARNING
Lester, C.	A PRACTICAL APPROACH TO DATA STRUCTURES
Lucas, R.	DATABASE APPLICATIONS USING PROLOG
Lucas, A.	DESKTOP PUBLISHING
Maddix, F.	HUMAN–COMPUTER INTERACTION: Theory and Practice
Maddix, F. & Morgan, G.	SYSTEMS SOFTWARE
Matthews, J.L.	FORTH
Millington, D.	SYSTEMS ANALYSIS AND DESIGN FOR COMPUTER APPLICATIONS
Moseley, L.G., Sharp, J.A. & Salenieks, P.	PASCAL IN PRACTICE
Moylan, P.	ASSEMBLY LANGUAGE FOR ENGINEERS
Narayanan, A. & Sharkey, N.E.	AN INTRODUCTION TO LISP
Parrington, N. & Roper, M.	UNDERSTANDING SOFTWARE TESTING
Paterson, A.	OFFICE SYSTEMS
Phillips, C. & Cornelius, B.J.	COMPUTATIONAL NUMERICAL METHODS

Series continued at back of book

PRACTICAL USAGE OF REXX

ANTHONY S. RUDD B.Sc., M.Sc.
Technical Consultant, DATEV, West Germany

ELLIS HORWOOD
NEW YORK LONDON TORONTO SYDNEY TOKYO SINGAPORE

First published in 1990
and Reprinted in 1991 by
ELLIS HORWOOD LIMITED
Market Cross House, Cooper Street,
Chichester, West Sussex, PO19 1EB, England

A division of
Simon & Schuster International Group
A Paramount Communications Company

Printed and bound in Great Britain
by Hartnolls, Bodmin, Cornwall

British Library Cataloguing in Publication Data

Rudd, Anthony S.
Practical usage of REXX. —
Ellis Horwood series in computers and their applications).
1. Computer systems. Operating systems.
I. Title
005.43
ISBN 0–13–682790–X

Library of Congress Cataloging-in-Publication Data

Rudd, Anthony S., 1945–
Practical usage of REXX/Anthony S. Rudd
p. cm. — (Ellis Horwood series in computers and their applications)
Includes bibliographical references and index.
ISBN 0–13–682790–X
1. REXX (Computer program language) I. Title. II. Series: Computers and their
applications.
QA76.73.R24R83   1990
005.2′25–dc20   90–44160
                                                                          CIP

For information about our audio products, write to us at:
Newbridge Book Clubs, 3000 Cindel Drive, Delran, NJ 08370

Table of contents

Preface   13

1. Introduction
    1.1   What is REXX?   15
    1.2   REXX features   16
    1.3   Origin of REXX   16
    1.4   Where can REXX be used?   17

2. REXX concepts
    2.1   REXX components   18
    2.2   Statement format   18
    2.3   REXX items   20
      2.3.1   Number   22
      2.3.2   Literal   23
      2.3.3   Symbol   24
      2.3.4   Operator   26
    2.4   REXX syntax   27
      2.4.1   Character operators   29
      2.4.2   Arithmetic operators   30
      2.4.3   Comparison operators   31
      2.4.4   Logical (Boolean) operators   32
      2.4.5   Operator priority   33
    2.5   Invocation of a REXX exec   34

3. Parsing
    3.1   Introduction   35
    3.2   Processing of words   35
    3.3   Processing of character strings   36

3.3.1	Parsing at a particular position	36
3.3.2	Parsing at a delimiter	37
3.3.3	Parsing at words	38
3.3.4	Parsing at a relative position	39
3.3.5	Parsing using placeholders	39
3.3.6	Parsing of arguments	39
3.3.7	Composite parsing	40
3.3.8	Dynamic parsing	40

4. REXX program elements

4.1	Introduction	41
4.2	Routines	42
4.2.1	Subroutine	43
4.2.2	Procedure	44
4.2.3	Function	45
4.2.4	Search order	46
4.2.5	Invocation	46
4.2.6	Parameters	47
4.2.7	Return	48
4.3	Do-group	49
4.3.1	Simple Do	50
4.3.2	Repetitive Do	51
4.3.3	Endless Do	51
4.3.4	Controlled repetitive Do	51
4.3.5	Iteration condition	52
4.3.6	Modification of processing within a Do-loop	53
4.4	SELECT - Select one condition from a series of conditions	55
4.5	CALL - Invoke subroutine or procedure	56
4.6	SIGNAL - Control processing flow	57
4.7	Assignment (=)	58
4.8	Stack (queue) processing	59
4.8.1	Stack as terminal input buffer	60
4.8.2	Stack for general data storage	61
4.8.3	Stack for passing data between programs	61
4.8.4	Stack as file buffer	63
4.9	Special variables	63
4.10	Debugging	63

5. Arithmetic

5.1	Introduction	65
5.2	Precision and representation	65
5.3	Sequence of operations	66

6. Input/Output
6.1	Introduction	68
6.2	Data buffering	69
6.3	Opening and closing the data files	69
6.4	Terminal operations	69
6.5	Character-mode operations	70
6.6	Line-mode operations	70
6.7	File-mode operations	70

7. Debugging
7.1	Introduction	72
7.2	Exception conditions	73
7.3	Tracing options	73
7.3.1	ALL - Display expressions before execution	74
7.3.2	COMMANDS - Display commands before execution	74
7.3.3	ERROR - Display commands which return an error condition	74
7.3.4	FAILURE - Display commands which return a negative error condition	74
7.3.5	INTERMEDIATE - Display expressions (with intermediate results) before being executed	75
7.3.6	LABELS - Display labels as they are reached	75
7.3.7	RESULTS - Display expressions (with end results) before being executed	75
7.3.8	SYNTAX - Check syntax without processing the statements	75
7.4	Trace output	75
7.4.1	Trace data prefixes	76
7.4.2	Trace intermediate data prefixes	76
7.4.3	Trace output example	76
7.5	Interactive debug	78
7.5.1	Interactive debugging example	79

8. Programming practices
8.1	Introduction	81
8.2	Readability	82
8.3	Reliability	82
8.4	Maintainability	83
8.5	Compatibility	83
8.6	Performance	84

9. REXX instructions
9.1	Introduction	85
9.2	Instruction definitions	86
9.2.1	= (assignment)	86
9.2.2	ADDRESS - Set environment	86

9.2.3	ARG - Fetch argument	89
9.2.4	CALL - Invoke routine	90
9.2.5	DO - Define start of block	91
9.2.6	DROP - Free variable	93
9.2.7	EXIT - Terminate exec	93
9.2.8	IF - Condition execution	94
9.2.9	INTERPRET - Interpret statement	95
9.2.10	ITERATE - Terminate current cycle in Do-loop	95
9.2.11	LEAVE - Terminate Do-loop	96
9.2.12	NOP - No-operation	96
9.2.13	NUMERIC - Define numeric formats	97
9.2.14	OPTIONS - Pass parameters to language processor	98
9.2.15	PARSE - Assign data	98
9.2.16	PROCEDURE - Define internal procedure	101
9.2.17	PULL - Fetch data element from the head of the stack	102
9.2.18	PUSH - Set data element at the head of the stack	103
9.2.19	QUEUE - Set data element at the tail of the stack	103
9.2.20	RETURN - Return from routine	104
9.2.21	SAY - Display	104
9.2.22	SELECT - Conditional execution of one statement from a group of statements	105
9.2.23	SIGNAL - Enable (disable) exception condition, or cause control to be passed to a routine	106
9.2.24	TRACE - Set debugging options	109
9.2.25	UPPER - Transform lower case characters to upper case	111

10. REXX built-in functions (SAA)

10.1	Introduction	112
10.2	Function definitions	113
10.2.1	ABBREV - Test whether string is an abbreviation	115
10.2.2	ABS - Return absolute value	115
10.2.3	ADDRESS - Return name of current environment	116
10.2.4	ARG - Return argument	116
10.2.5	BITAND - Logical And	117
10.2.6	BITOR - Logical Or	118
10.2.7	BITXOR - Logical Exclusive-Or	119
10.2.8	CENTRE (CENTER) - Centralise data	119
10.2.9	COMPARE - Compare	120
10.2.10	CONDITION - Return condition	121
10.2.11	COPIES - Duplicate data	122
10.2.12	C2D - Convert character data to decimal	122
10.2.13	C2X - Convert character data to hexadecimal	123
10.2.14	DATATYPE - Determine data type	124
10.2.15	DATE - Return current date	125

10.2.16	DELSTR - Delete substring	127
10.2.17	DELWORD - Delete words	127
10.2.18	DIGITS - Return the NUMERIC DIGITS setting	128
10.2.19	D2C - Convert decimal data to character	129
10.2.20	D2X - Convert hexadecimal data to character	130
10.2.21	ERRORTEXT - Return message text	130
10.2.22	FORM - Determine NUMERIC FORM setting	131
10.2.23	FORMAT - Format numeric value	131
10.2.24	FUZZ - Determine NUMERIC FUZZ setting	132
10.2.25	INSERT - Insert substring	132
10.2.26	LASTPOS - Determine last position of phrase	133
10.2.27	LEFT - Left-align string	133
10.2.28	LENGTH - Determine length of string	134
10.2.29	MAX - Determine the maximum of a series of numeric values	135
10.2.30	MIN - Determine the minimum of a series of numeric values	135
10.2.31	OVERLAY - Overlay part of a string with a phrase	136
10.2.32	POS - Search for substring	137
10.2.33	QUEUED - Determine the number of entries in the queue	138
10.2.34	RANDOM - Generate a (pseudo-)random number	138
10.2.35	REVERSE - Reverse the sequence of data	139
10.2.36	RIGHT - Right-align string	139
10.2.37	SIGN - Determine numeric sign	140
10.2.38	SOURCELINE - Return "program line"	141
10.2.39	SPACE - Insert fill-character between words	141
10.2.40	STRIP - Remove padding-characters at the start or end of a string	142
10.2.41	SUBSTR - Extract substring	143
10.2.42	SUBWORD - Extract series of words from word-string	144
10.2.43	SYMBOL - Determine the status of a symbol	144
10.2.44	TIME - Return the current time-of-day	145
10.2.45	TRACE - Return (and set) current trace mode	147
10.2.46	TRANSLATE - Translate	149
10.2.47	TRUNC - Truncate numeric value	151
10.2.48	VALUE - Return the content of a symbol	151
10.2.49	VERIFY - Test whether only characters in a phrase are present in string	152
10.2.50	WORD - Fetch word	153
10.2.51	WORDINDEX - Determine the character position of a word in a string of words	153
10.2.52	WORDLENGTH - Determine word length	154
10.2.53	WORDPOS - Determine word-number of word in word-string	154
10.2.54	WORDS - Determine number of words in word-string	155
10.2.55	XRANGE - Define a range of hexadecimal values	155
10.2.56	X2C - Convert hexadecimal to character	156

10.2.57   X2D - Convert hexadecimal to decimal   157

11. REXX built-in functions (non-SAA)
11.1   Introduction   158
11.2   Function definitions   158
11.2.1   CHARIN - Read a string of characters   159
11.2.2   CHAROUT - Write a string of characters   160
11.2.3   CHARS - Interrogate the status of the input stream
            (character mode)   161
11.2.4   FIND - Search for word   161
11.2.5   INDEX - Search for substring   161
11.2.6   JUSTIFY - Justify string of words   162
11.2.7   LINEIN - Read a line (record)   163
11.2.8   LINEOUT - Write a line (record)   164
11.2.9   LINES - Interrogate the status of the input stream (line mode)   165
11.2.10   LINESIZE - Return the (maximum) width of a terminal line   165
11.2.11   USERID - Return Userid   166

12. Host REXX commands
12.1   Introduction   167
12.2   Host REXX command definitions   167
12.2.1   DELSTACK - Delete stack   168
12.2.2   DROPBUF - Release buffer   168
12.2.3   EXECIO - Perform input/output operation   168
12.2.4   EXECUTIL - Specify execution environment for REXX program   171
12.2.5   HI (Halt Interpretation)   173
12.2.6   HT (Halt Typing)   173
12.2.7   MAKEBUF - Create new buffer in the stack   173
12.2.8   NEWSTACK - Create a new stack   174
12.2.9   QBUF (Query Buffer) - Return the number of buffers in the
            current stack   174
12.2.10   QELEM (Query Elements) - Return the number of elements
            in the current buffer   175
12.2.11   QSTACK (Query Stack) - Return the current number of stacks   175
12.2.12   RT (Resume Typing)   175
12.2.13   SUBCOM - Confirm the host environment   176
12.2.14   TE (Trace End)   177
12.2.15   TS (Trace Start)   177

13. MVS command functions
13.1   Introduction   178
13.2   MVS command function calls   178
13.2.1   LISTDSI - List (obtain) dataset information   180
13.2.2   MSG - Set (interrogate) CLIST CONTROL MSG option   182

13.2.3	OUTTRAP - Trap TSO display output	183
13.2.4	PROMPT - Set (interrogate) CLIST CONTROL PROMPT option	185
13.2.5	STORAGE - Set (interrogate) main storage content	186
13.2.6	SYSDSN - Request dataset status	186
13.2.7	SYSVAR - Fetch TSO system variable	187
13.2.8	Invocation of other TSO commands	188

14. REXX implementations

14.1	Introduction	190
14.2	MVS-TSO/E implementation	191
14.2.1	Invocation	191
14.2.2	Linkage to host (MVS-TSO) environment	194
14.2.3	Linkage to programs	195
14.2.4	Interface with ISPEXEC (ISPF Dialog Manager)	196
14.2.5	Interface with ISREDIT (ISPF/PDF Edit macro)	196
14.2.6	Interface with DB2 (Database 2)	197
14.2.7	Interface with QMF (Query Management Facility)	198
14.2.8	Interface from programs to REXX	200
14.3	REXX/2 (OS/2) implementation	200
14.3.1	REXX/2 invocation	200
14.3.2	Linkage to host (OS/2) environment	200
14.4	Personal REXX (DOS) implementation	201
14.4.1	Personal REXX invocation	202
14.4.2	Linkage to host (DOS) environment	203
14.4.3	Interface from programs to Personal REXX environment	203

15. Worked examples

15.1	Introduction	205
15.2	Worked example 1	205
15.3	Worked example 2	209

16. System interfaces

16.1	Introduction	217
16.2	General conditions	217
16.3	Invocation of a REXX exec	219
16.3.1	Interface from programs to batch REXX (IRXJCL service)	219
16.3.2	Invocation of a REXX exec using the TSO Service Facility (IJKEFTSR service)	220
16.3.3	Interface from programs to REXX processor (IRXEXEC service)	223
16.4	Program access to REXX variables (IRXEXCOM service)	226
16.5	Stack processing (IRXSTK service)	228
16.6	Function interface	230
16.7	Function package	236
16.7.1	Function Directory	237

16.8   Load routine - IRXLOAD service   240
16.9   Initialisation routine - IRXINIT service   242
16.10   Get result - IRXRLT service   243
16.11   Control blocks   245
    16.11.1   Argument List   245
    16.11.2   EFPL (External Function Parameter List)   245
    16.11.3   ENVBLOCK (Environment Block)   246
    16.11.4   EVALBLOCK (Evaluation Block)   248
    16.11.5   EXECBLK (Exec Block)   248
    16.11.6   INSTBLK (In-storage Control Block)   250
    16.11.7   SHVBLOCK (Shared Variable (Request) Block)   251
    16.11.8   VEEP (Vector of External Entry Points)   253

Appendix A. REXX instructions syntax summary   254
Appendix B. REXX built-in functions syntax summary   258
Appendix C. Host REXX commands syntax summary   264
Appendix D. MVS commands syntax summary   266
Appendix E. Syntax notation   267
Appendix F. Bibliography   271
Appendix G. Glossary   273
Appendix H. ASCII-EBCDIC code table   278
Appendix I. Compatibility   281

Index   285

Preface

The title of this book *PRACTICAL USAGE OF REXX* reveals the purpose I had in writing it: a concise, complete, source of information necessary for the development of applications using the REXX language.

Practical means that the information is presented in such a form so as to be easy to find and use - lists and diagrams are used where possible.

This means that the book does not read like a novel. My personal experience is that books on such topics are not read from cover to cover, rather only those items of interest are read. With this in aim I have structured the book with numbered sections and used self-contained syntax diagrams.

The widespread acceptance of REXX in many different environments is good for the language but creates difficulties for an author. Which implementation should be described? Unfortunately, each implementation has its differences. If all implementations were described in detail, the book would no longer be a compact reference. I have adopted the policy of taking one popular implementation, namely for MVS-TSO/E Version 2 (subsequently referred to as MVS-TSO), and describing it in detail. I have augmented the description of this implementation with those features commonly found in the other implementations - in particular, REXX/2 and Personal REXX are also discussed. In this way *PRACTICAL USAGE OF REXX* is hopefully of use to the widest possible range of readers.

And who should these readers be? The answer - both beginners and experts. Beginners are lead through the steps required to develop REXX applications; complete worked examples, large enough to be practical but devoid of superfluous detail that enable the REXX novice to see what is necessary to write a simple application. Experts have a compact reference.

At this point I would like to thank Mike Ellis, Detlef Insel and Syed Mohomed, and the Ellis Horwood staff for their efforts in helping me prepare this book and their suggestions for improvements.

The following terms are either trade marks or registered trade marks of IBM:

Database 2
DB2
IBM
MVS
PC-DOS
Operating System/2
OS/2
QMF
SAA
Systems Application Architecture
VM

The following terms are registered trade marks of Microsoft:

Microsoft
MS-DOS

1

Introduction

1.1 WHAT IS REXX?

REXX is the name of IBM's Systems Application Architecture (SAA) procedural language, and is the acronym derived from **Re**structured **Ex**tended E**x**ecutor. The name REXX gives a number of clues as to its origin. Extended Executor - an extension of the EXEC procedure language implemented for the VM/CMS operating system; Restructured - as the word says. REXX, as with all good acronyms, has itself a meaning - the Latin word *rex, regis* (king) - REXX is namely the King of Programming Languages.

Procedural language in this context means a language used to create **procedures** or **commands**; a procedure being a named series of statements to perform some particular task. REXX procedures are known as **execs**, which are synonymous with **programs**.

Such procedures are common in data processing, although they may be given different names. Examples from various environments are:

- DOS or OS/2, a batch file (extension `.BAT` or `.CMD`);
- VM/CMS, an EXEC or EXEC2 procedure;
- MVS-TSO, a CLIST (command procedure).

The above definition of a procedure is essentially that of a program. Indeed, REXX can be used for programming tasks. However, REXX offers more, as it also interfaces with other system components. For example, in the TSO environment, a REXX program can use TSO facilities to allocate files and ISPF (Dialog Manager) to display panels. This can be compared to the use of JCL (job control language) statements in batch mode.

1.2 REXX'S ORIGIN

REXX was originally implemented for the IBM VM/CMS environment. Those readers interested in the historical background to the development of the REXX language should read the book *The Rexx Language, A Practical Approach to Programming* written by M.J.Cowlishaw, the original author of the language.

A number of experimental versions followed the VM/CMS implementation. However, these implementations were only of limited general interest. More important implementations were the porting of the language to the IBM Personal Computer (PC) in the form of Mansfield Software Group's Personal REXX, and IBM's implementations for MVS TSO/E Version 2 and OS/2 Version 1.2.

1.3 REXX FEATURES

REXX is a structured language with a relatively limited number of basic **instructions**. These instructions are supplemented by a library of **functions**. The library functions are especially suited to character-string processing. These standard (SAA) REXX components (instructions and functions) are supplemented by routines particular to the operating environment: **host commands** and **operating system command functions** - these extensions are implementation dependent. Fig. 1.1 illustrates the scope of a REXX implementation - Appendix I contains tables showing the degree to which the various implementations are compatible with each other.

The standard components can be augmented by user routines (written in REXX or a conventional programming language). REXX also interfaces with host components (e.g. TSO or ISPF in the MVS environment). The language is further simplified by removing the need to perform housekeeping functions, for example, field definition.

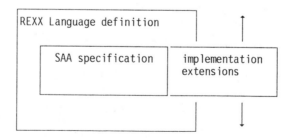

Fig. 1.1 - Scope of a REXX implementation

To summarise:

- The limited repertoire of components makes REXX an easy language to learn.
- The extensive library of powerful functions greatly reduces the amount of coding necessary to write applications.
- Implementations in a wide range of environments simplifies the writing of applications to run under different hardware and operating systems.

1.4 WHERE CAN REXX BE USED?

REXX is a general purpose language. The unified syntax simplifies the porting of applications between the various operating environments. Unfortunately, the host environment extensions are often needed for input/output operations, and these extensions are not always identical in all operating environments.

REXX is an interpreted language and so is not suited to be used for long-running applications, although it may well be used to create a prototype for such an application.

The interfaces from REXX with other components (in particular, dialogue components), make it well suited to be used as a front-end for dialogue applications, e.g. as an intelligent link between the various components.

REXX parsing facilities make it especially suited to string processing applications.

To summarise, REXX is especially useful for:

- prototyping;
- front-end for dialogue applications;
- one-off jobs.

However, it is by no means limited to such tasks. Its power will often avoid the necessity of having to write conventional programs to perform the required processing.

2

REXX concepts

2.1 REXX COMPONENTS

REXX programs are called **execs**, and, like most programs, are comprised of **statements**. These statements comprise of:

- **keyword instructions**;
- **host REXX commands**;
- **host environment command functions**.

These statements can in turn use **REXX built-in functions**. Both keyword instructions and REXX built-in functions are part of the SAA definition, and so standard to all REXX implementations. Although host REXX commands are available in each implementation they do not necessarily have the same syntax and semantics. The availability of host environment command functions depends on the **host environment** being used, e.g. the MVS implementation supports both TSO and non-TSO address spaces; however, TSO host command functions can only be used within a TSO address space.

Statements which are not recognised as being keyword instructions are passed to the current host environment.

2.2 STATEMENT FORMAT

REXX statements can generally be written in a free format manner (cases where this is not so will be explained explicitly).

Free format means:

• Individual terms of a statement are separated by one or more term delimiters (normally a blank, but may be any non-alphanumeric character allowed in the expression).

Example:
```
a = b * 12;
a  =  b  *  12;
a=b*12;
```
are all equivalent.

Note: In character expressions, terms separated by one or more blanks are concatenated together with a single blank between each term, e.g.
```
SAY "alpha"    "beta";
```
displays
```
alpha beta
```

• The terms in a REXX statement are in general case-insensitive. This means that the terms may be written in either upper case or lower case, or mixed. This rule does not apply to character literals, which are case-sensitive. Despite the flexibility that REXX allows, it helps to make programs easier to read and understand if some convention is adopted - for example, I have used upper case notation in this book to denote instructions and non-internal functions.

• The end-of-statement (clause) delimiter (;) is usually optional and is only needed when the meaning would otherwise be ambiguous. The end of the line implies the end of the statement, unless continuation is implied from the syntax of the statement.

Example:
```
IF a = b THEN SAY "equal"; ELSE SAY "not equal"
```
requires a semicolon at the end of the THEN clause when the statement is written in a single line, ELSE SAY "not equal" would otherwise be taken as part of the text to be displayed when the condition is satisfied.

Note: It is good programming practice to end each statement with an end-of-statement delimiter - this can avoid certain program errors caused by inadvertent continuations.

• Statements can be written on one or more lines (a comma (,) must be used to indicate a non-implicit continuation).

Example:
```
IF a = b
  THEN SAY "equal"
  ELSE SAY "not equal";
```
does not require a continuation comma (,) at the end of each line because the continuation is implicit (IF is followed by THEN which may itself be followed by ELSE);
```
a = b,
* c;
```
requires an explicit continuation at the end of the first line, as the line in itself is complete (and so no continuation is expected).

* A line can contain one or more statements.
  Example:
  ```
  a = b; SAY "this is a second statement";
  ```

2.3 REXX ITEMS

REXX statements are comprised of the following items:

* number;
* literal;
* symbol;
* operator (delimiter).

These items occur either singly or in combination.

This book, and indeed most books on programming languages, uses syntax diagrams to define the language elements. Although syntax diagrams may at first appear complex, they are easier to understand than long-winded prose. Familiarity with syntax diagrams is a prerequisite to understanding this book. Three simple examples to define elementary concepts are used as an introduction to syntax diagrams (Appendix E contains a detailed explanation on how to read syntax diagrams):

* digit;
* integer;
* signed integer.

Figure 2.1 defines a digit as being one (and only) of the characters 0, 1, 2, 3, 4, 5, 6, 7, 8, 9. Figure 2.2 defines an integer as being a string of one or more of the characters 0, 1, 2, 3, 4, 5, 6, 7, 8, 9; the arrow indicates that the character can be repeated. The individual characters are written without any intervening blanks.

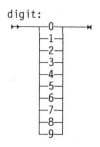

Figure 2.1 - Syntax diagram for the definition of a digit

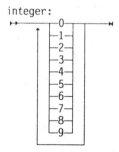

Figure 2.2 - Syntax diagram for the definition of an integer

The syntax diagram for an integer could also have been simplified to use the previous definition of a digit, as follows:

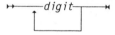

Digit written in italics indicates that it is defined elsewhere.

Figure 2.3 specifies the syntax for a signed integer. The sign here is optional; the underlined operand (+) is the default.

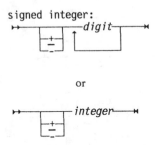

Figure 2.3 - Syntax diagram for the definition of a signed integer

2.3.1 Number

REXX has the concept only of **number**, there is no explicit subdivision into integers, floating-point numbers, etc. The **precision** of numbers is determined by the value specified in the NUMERIC DIGITS instruction (the default precision is 9 digits). Numbers larger or smaller than the precision are automatically converted to REXX floating point representation (the default format is SCIENTIFIC, but this may be changed with the NUMERIC FORM instruction).

The form of a number is shown in Fig. 2.4, which is somewhat simplified, in that the following two conditions are omitted:

- a number can contain only a single ".";
- the exponent 0 is not allowed, e.g. 1.2E0 is invalid.

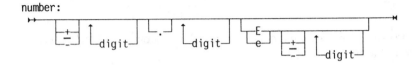

Figure 2.4 - Syntax diagram for the definition of a number

Examples of numbers:
```
123
12.3
12.3E-2
.123
0.123
-0.123
```

2.3.2 Literal
A literal is a string of characters contained within single quotes (') or double quotes
("); these are called the **delimiting quotes**. An individual literal has a maximum length
of 250 characters; this maximum length does not apply to literals which are
concatenated together.

Example:
```
'alpha BETA gamma'
"alpha BETA gamma"
```
are equivalent and define the 16 characters alpha BETA gamma.

If the delimiting quotes are required within the literal, then they must be paired. For
example,
```
'O''Brien'
```
represents O'Brien.

However, it is usually better to use the other delimiter, which is then not paired, for
example,
```
"O'Brien"
```

Data within a literal are case sensitive. For example,
```
"alpha"
"ALPHA"
"Alpha"
```
are three distinct literals representing alpha, ALPHA and Alpha, respectively.

Alphanumeric literals have a special operator, the X (or x) **suffix operator** - this
specifies that the preceding alphanumeric literal has a hexadecimal value, and so
defines a **hexadecimal literal**. The suffix operator must be written immediately following the terminating '. The individual characters in the literal may only be valid
hexadecimal digit - 0 through 9, A through F, a through f. For example,
```
"C1C2F0F1F2"x
```
defines the literal containing the hexadecimal digits, C1, C2, F0, F1 and F2, i.e. the
EBCDIC string "AB012".

To improve the readability, pairs of hexadecimal digits can be separated by one or more blanks. For example, the previous hexadecimal string could have been written as:

```
"C1 C2 F0 F1 F2"x
```

A literal can be continued onto the next line in one of two ways:
*   By placing a comma after the literal to be continued. Both the literal to be continued and the continuation literal must be enclosed within quotes. For example,

```
"alpha beta",
      "gamma"
```

defines the literal "alpha beta gamma".

If the continuation literal is to be placed immediately after the first literal, i.e. without the intervening blank, then the abuttal operator (||) must precede the continuation comma. For example,

```
"alpha beta"||,
      "gamma"
```

defines the literal "alpha betagamma".

*   By simply writing the literal over the lines. The initial literal delimiter (' or ") is placed at the start of the literal in the first line and final literal delimiter (' or ", as used for the initial literal delimiter) placed in the last line. For example,

```
"alpha beta
      gamma"
```

defines the literal "alpha beta   ...   gamma". The ... represent the blanks up to the end of the record.

2.3.3 Symbol
REXX has two types of symbol:

*   simple symbol;
*   compound symbol.

A symbol name has a maximum length of 250.

```
simple-symbol:
```
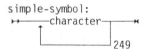

Character must be one of the following:
- a - z
- A - Z
- 0 - 9
- @ # $ ¢ ! ? _

Note: The first character of simple symbol may not be a digit.

Tip

For compatibility with other components restrict the characters used in symbols to alphanumerics (A through Z, upper or lower case, and 0 through 9), the three national characters: #, $ and @, and the underscore character (_). Some components have also a restriction on the maximum length of symbols, for example, symbols in ISPF have a maximum length of 8 characters.

Important: A **simple symbol** has initially its own name (upper case) as content, e.g.
```
alpha   contains   ALPHA
a1      contains   A1
```

```
compound-symbol:
 ►► ─ simple-symbol. ┬───────────────────┬ ──►◄
                     └─ simple-symbol ─┘
                  ┌──────────────────┐
                  └──────────────────┘ .
```

A **compound symbol** is a special form of symbol which consists of one or more simple symbols each separated by a period. The first part of a compound symbol is called the **stem**. The stem is always an alphanumeric literal, i.e. even if the simple symbol has been assigned a different value the stem remains unchanged.

Example:
```
        alpha = "BETA";
        alpha.alpha = "GAMMA";
```
assigns the value GAMMA to the compound symbol ALPHA.BETA (BETA has been assigned to the second alpha in the compound symbol alpha.alpha, the stem (first alpha) remains unchanged).

The stem can be used to assign a value to all compounds of that stem, e.g.
```
        alpha. = 0;
```
assigns 0 to all compounds having alpha. as stem. This applies even to compound variables which have not yet been used.

2.3.3.1 Declaration of symbols

Symbols are not declared. Each symbol has its own name (in upper case) as initial content, for example, the symbol Alpha has initial content ALPHA. Similarly, symbols have no implicit attribute (numeric, character, etc.) - the attribute is determined by the current content and may change during the course of execution.

2.3.3.2 Length of symbol data

Symbols, with the exception of those containing numeric data, have no explicit length - the length of data which can be stored in a symbol is limited only by the amount of main-storage available.

The length (precision) of numeric data is determined by the NUMERIC DIGITS setting - the default is 9, which means that a number is stored with a precision of 9 digits. The NUMERIC DIGITS setting does not necessarily apply to the whole program, rather it may be set where required.

2.3.3.3 Array

An array is a special form of a compound symbol. The indices are the second, third, etc. variables in the compound symbol. These indices are not restricted to being numeric. There is no limit to the number of dimensions.

Example:
The PL/I array ALPHA(I,J) could be written as the REXX compound variable alpha.i.j, or using self-explanatory terms, alpha.month.day.

2.3.4 Operator (delimiter)

The **operator** is the item which operates on the item coming immediately before and after it. *Important*: The operators used in an expression determine the type of the expression. There are four classes of operators:

* character;
* arithmetic;
* comparison;
* logical (Boolean).

These operators are described in section 2.4.

Example:
a||b   is a character expression ("||" is a character operator);

a+b   is a numeric expression ("+" is an arithmetic operator);
a=b   is a comparison expression ("=" is a comparative operator);
a&b   is a logical expression ("&" is a logical operator).

A single expression cannot contain mixed operators, although an expression can be comprised of sub-expressions, which themselves contain different classes of operator; sub-expressions are expressions contained within parentheses.

Example:
        x=2+(b>c)-(d&1);
is a valid numeric expression; the second sub-expression (b>c) evaluates to either 1 or 0, depending on whether the expression is true or false, respectively; the third sub-expression (d&1) is the value of performing a Logical Or with 1 on the content of the symbol d (d must contain either 0 or 1).
Note: This is an example of what *can* be done, it is not necessarily an example of how an expression *should* be written.

2.4 REXX SYNTAX

The general syntax for REXX statements is shown in Fig. 2.5. The particular syntax for each statement is shown when the statement is described in detail.

statement:

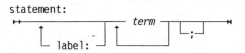

Figure 2.5 - Syntax diagram for the definition of a statement

term:

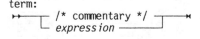

Figure 2.6 - Syntax diagram for the definition of a term

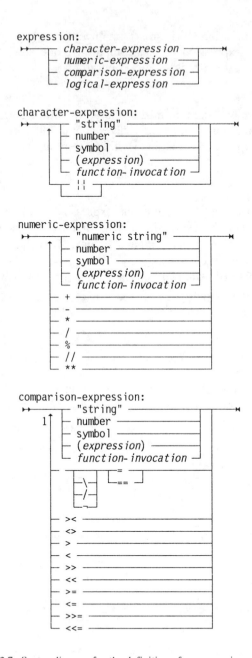

Figure 2.7 - Syntax diagram for the definition of an expression, part 1 of 2

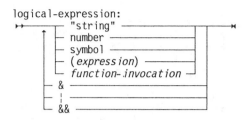

Figure 2.7 - Syntax diagram for the definition of an expression, part 2 of 2

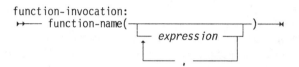

Figure 2.8 - Syntax diagram for the definition of a function invocation

2.4.1 Character operators

There is only one character operator, **concatenation**. REXX has two forms of concatenation:

- implicit
- explicit

Those operands (terms) in a character expression separated by one or more blanks will be concatenated together with one blank between each term, this is **implicit concatenation**. Those operands (terms) in a character expression which are not separated will be concatenated together without any intervening blanks, this is **abuttal concatenation**; this requires that the terms are distinguishable as such, e.g. a symbol followed by a literal. The **explicit concatenation** operator (||) is also an abuttal operator. Table 2.1 illustrates concatenation.

Note: a is assumed to contain alpha, b is assumed to contain beta.

operation	result
a b	alpha beta
"c"b	cbeta
a ¦¦ b	alphabeta

Table 2.1 - Concatenation

2.4.2 Arithmetic operators

Arithmetic operators are used to define the processing to be performed on the operands of a numeric expression. A numeric expression yields a numeric result; the precision of this result is determined by the value set with the instruction NUMERIC DIGITS (default is nine digits precision). Table 2.2 illustrates the results of various arithmetic operations.

The arithmetic operators are:

+   add
-       subtract
*   multiply
/   divide
%   divide (return integer quotient)
//   divide (return integer remainder)
**   power (may only be an integral value)

"+" and "-" may also be used as prefix operators.

2.4.3 Comparison operators

Comparison operators are used to compare two operands with each other. A comparison expression is processed from left to right and yields a numeric result: 1 - the comparison condition is **true**; 0 - the comparison condition is **false**. The operands being compared will be padded if necessary. The accuracy of the comparison of numeric operands is determined by the NUMERIC FUZZ instruction, which specifies how many least-significant digits are to be ignored from the comparison (default 0 - the complete operands are used). Table 2.3 illustrates the results of various comparison operations.

operation	result
5 + 2	7
5 - 2	3
5 * 2	10
5 / 2	2.5
5 % 2	2
5 // 2	1
5 ** 2	25
5 ** -2	0.04

Table 2.2 - Typical arithmetic operations

The comparison operators are:

==	strictly equal
=	equal (padded, if necessary)
/==	strictly not equal
/=	not equal
><	greater or less than (unequal)
<>	less or greater than (unequal)
>	greater than
<	less than
>>	strictly greater than
<<	strictly less than
>=	greater than or equal
<=	less than or equal
>>=	strictly greater than or equal
<<=	strictly less than or equal

The adverb *strictly* includes padding characters (non-significant blanks and 0's) in the comparison, refer to Table 2.3 for examples.

Prefix ¬ and \ both mean *not*, e.g. \= means not equal. Refer to the syntax diagram in Figure 2.7 for the allowed uses of the not prefix-operator.

Tip
Use \ or / rather than ¬ if applications are to be ported, as ¬ is not an operator in the ASCII character set.

operation	result
"5 " == "5" "5 " = "5"	false true
"5 " \== "5" "5 " \= "5"	true false
"6 " > "5" "5 " > "5" "5 " >> "5"	true false true
"6 " < "5"	false

Table 2.3 - Typical comparison operations

2.4.4 Logical (Boolean) operators

Logical operators are used to perform a Boolean operation on two 'binary' operands. The operands may contain only either 0 or 1, operations on operands containing any other value will cause an error - the built-in functions: BITAND, BITOR and BITXOR can be used to perform a bit-by-bit logical operation. Table 2.4 illustrates the results of various logical operations, the second operand operates on the first operand.

The Boolean operators are:

  &   And
  | Inclusive Or
  &&   Exclusive Or

operation	result
"0" & "0" "1" & "0" "0" & "1" "1" & "1"	"0" "0" "0" "1"
"0" | "0" "1" | "0" "0" | "1" "1" | "1"	"0" "1" "1" "1"
"0" && "0" "1" && "0" "0" && "1" "1" && "1"	"0" "1" "1" "0"

Table 2.4 - Result of logical operations

2.4.5 Operator priority

As a general rule statements are processed from left to right. This priority can be overridden in two ways:

- by the explicit use of parentheses, which divide the statement into one or more sub-statements contained within parentheses, the innermost sub-statement is evaluated first, then the next innermost, etc.;
- by the inherent processing sequence of operators (see Table 2.5).

Within a priority level the operators have the same priority, and are evaluated from left to right.

Examples:

```
      1 - 6 * -2 / 3
```
yields 5.
```
      6 * -2 -> -12 (the "-" in -2 is a prefix operator)
      -12 / 3 -> -4
      1 - -4 -> 5 (the "-" in -4 is an implicit prefix operator)

      (1 + 5) * 2 / 3
```
yields 4.
```
      1 + 5 -> 6
      6 * 2 -> 12
      12 / 4 -> 3
```

priority	operator	comment
1	+ - ¬ \	prefix operator
2	**	exponential (power) operator
3	* / % //	multiplication, division
4	+ -	addition, subtraction
5	¦¦	concatenation (also implicit)
6	= == > < etc.	comparison
7	&	And
8	¦ &&	Or, Exclusive Or

Table 2.5 - Operator precedence

2.5 INVOCATION OF A REXX EXEC

The invocation of a REXX exec is dependent on the host environment and on the particular implementation. Chapter 14 contains a description of the particular aspects of the various implementations.

3

Parsing

3.1 INTRODUCTION

Parsing (list analysis) is one of the most powerful REXX facilities. There are two forms of parsing:

- lists of words;
- strings of characters;

Words, in the REXX sense, are strings of characters delimited by one or more blanks; these strings of characters are known as **words**. Strings of characters can be parsed in the following ways:

- at a particular position;
- at a particular delimiter;
- at words.

The parsing pattern is known as the **template**. The parsed data are assigned to variables or to a **placeholder**; the placeholder, represented by . (period) takes the place of a variable. The same variable may appear more than once in the list of variables.

3.2 PROCESSING OF WORDS

REXX has a collection on functions concerned with the processing of words:
- SUBWORD   extracts the specified number of words from a list of words;
- WORD   extracts the specified word (number) from a list of words;

- WORDINDEX   returns the character position of the specified word (number) from a list of words;
- WORDLENGTH   returns the length of the specified word (number) from a list of words;
- WORDPOS   returns the word number of the specified word in a list of words;
- WORDS   returns the number of words in a list of words.

These functions are described in detail in Chapter 10.

3.3 PARSING OF CHARACTERS

character strings to be parsed have several sources:

- arguments passed to a REXX exec or procedure;
- data obtained from the input device (terminal);
- data from the queue;
- data contained in a variable;
- various control data (e.g. current REXX version).

REXX has three instructions concerned with parsing:
- ARG   process the argument (string) passed to the REXX exec or internal routine;
- PARSE   process the specified string;
- PULL   process the next entry from the queue (or standard input device).

PARSE is the most powerful parsing instruction; the ARG and PULL instructions are subsets of the PARSE instruction.

3.3.1 Parsing at a particular position
This processing is equivalent to the extraction of a substring from the specified data source and is shown in Figure 3.1.

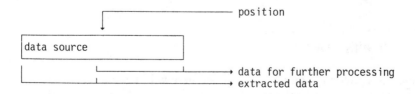

Figure 3.1 - Parsing using position as parameter

Example:

```
     a = 'alpha, beta  gamma';
     PARSE VAR a b 4 c;
```

splits the content of variable a at position 4; alp is set into the variable b and the remainder of the input (ha, beta gamma) is set into variable c.

3.3.2 Parsing at a particular delimiter

The source data is scanned, starting at the left, for the specified delimiter; the data before this delimiter are set into the specified variable and the data after the delimiter further processed. The delimiter is not restricted to being a single character. The delimiter may be either a literal or a character expression (specified within parentheses). Figure 3.2 illustrates this processing.

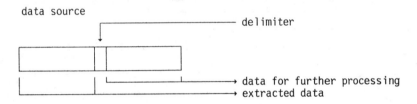

Figure 3.2 - Parsing using delimiter as parameter

Example:

```
     a = "alpha, beta  gamma";
     PARSE VAR a b ',' c;
```

and

```
     dlm = ",";
     a = "alpha, beta  gamma";
     PARSE VAR a b (dlm) c;
```

are equivalent, and use ',' as delimiter; alpha is set into the variable b and the remainder of the input (beta gamma) set into variable c.

3.3.3 Parsing at words

The words in the source data are delimited by one or more blanks. The processing of
words and blanks depends on their position in the source data:

- any blanks preceding the first word are ignored;
- for the last word in the source data only the *first* blank preceding the word is used
  as delimiter, any blanks following this first blank and any blanks following the last
  word are assigned to the specified variable;
- blanks between words (except for the last word) are not passed to the output variables;
- if only one word is present it is processed as a last word, i.e. all leading and trailing blanks are passed to the output variable.

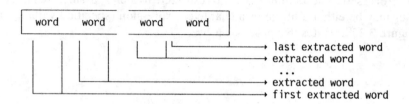

Figure 3.3 - Word parsing

Example 1:
```
a = "alpha, beta  gamma";
PARSE VAR a b c;
```
The word alpha, is set into the variable b and the remainder of the input (beta   gamma)
set into variable c.

Example 2:
```
a = " alpha,  beta   gamma  ";
PARSE VAR a b c d;
```
The word alpha, is set into the variable b, the word beta is set into the variable c and
the last word ' gamma ' set into variable d. *Note*: beta and gamma are separated by
three blanks, the first blank serves as word delimiter, and the other two blanks are
passed with the following word to the specified variable.

3.3.4 Parsing at a relative position

A variation of positional parsing (section 3.3.1) is the use of a relative position. The relative position is addressed by specifying the plus or minus sign (+ or -) followed by the numeric displacement from the last parsing operand which was located.

This option yields meaningful results only when it is used after either positional parsing (section 3.3.1) or parsing with a delimiter (section 3.3.2). When used after a delimiter, the parsing delimiter is assigned to the specified variable - this is illustrated in the following example.

Example:

```
a = " alpha, beta   gamma ";
PARSE VAR a b ',' c +4 d;
```

The string alpha is assigned to b (',' is the parsing delimiter), the next parsing position is at displacement 4 from the comma, the string starting at the comma and having length 4 (the displacement) is assigned to c, the remainder is assigned to d.

3.3.5 Parsing using placeholders

If not all parsing results are required as variables a **placeholder** may be used instead of a variable. A placeholder is indicated by using a period (".") insted of a variable name.

Tip

Use placeholders when the number of parsing elements is not known or could be increased.

Example:

```
a = " alpha, beta   gamma ";
PARSE VAR a . b .;
```

The word beta is set into the variable b; the first and last words are parsed as usual but are not assigned to any variables.

3.3.6 Parsing of arguments

Normally parsing is performed on a single expression. The processing of multiple arguments (parameters) passed to a routine is simplified by allowing the PARSE ARG (or ARG) instruction to parse the individual arguments; the names of the variables to contain the parsed items are separated by commas.

Example:
```
     CALL alpha beta, "gamma";
        ...
     alpha:
       PARSE ARG b, c;
         ...
       RETURN;
```
assigns beta to b and 'gamma' to c.

3.3.7 Composite parsing
The parsing described in sub-sections 3.3.1 through 3.3.3 can be combined to form a composite parsing on an input source string. The form of the symbol following the current output variable determines the current parsing to be performed, e.g. is a variable followed by a number, then parsing by position is to be performed for that variable.

Example:
```
     a = " alpha, beta   gamma   ";
       PARSE VAR a b 5 c ',' d;
```
assigns ' al' to b , 'pha' to c and ' beta   gamma   ' to d.

3.3.8 Dynamic parsing
A flexible form of parsing is to use information from the parsed string to alter the subsequent parsing of the string. In particular, data extracted from the input string can be used as delimiter for the following data.

Example:
```
     alpha = "%abc % ghi";
     PARSE VAR alpha dlm 2 b (dlm) c;
     SAY "dlm b c" b c;
```
The first character of the input string (alpha) is the delimiter to be used for subsequent parsing, i.e. the input string is to be split at the second character. This delimiter character is parsed into the variable dlm, which is then used as delimiter for the next operands. The following result is displayed:
```
     abc   ghi
```

4

REXX program elements

4.1 INTRODUCTION

The REXX programming language has statements for:
- structured programming constructions;
  - DO
  - ITERATE
  - LEAVE
  - SELECT
- sequence control;
  - IF - THEN - ELSE
- subroutine control and invocation;
  - CALL
  - EXIT
  - PROCEDURE
  - RETURN
- assignment;
  - =
- error processing;
  - SIGNAL
- stack (queue) processing;
  - PULL
  - PUSH
  - QUEUE
- parsing;
  - PARSE
- debugging;
  - TRACE
- miscellaneous instructions;

- ADDRESS[*]
- ARG[*]
- DROP
- INTERPRET
- NOP
- NUMERIC[*]
- SAY
- UPPER[*] (only available in the MVS-TSO implementation)

[*] indicates that this instruction (largely) duplicates a REXX function.

These basic program elements are augmented by a library of powerful functions, and statements appropriate for the host environment (e.g. input/output processing routines). This chapter describes the use (semantics) of the instructions; the detailed syntax is described in Chapter 9.

4.2 ROUTINES

A series of REXX statements can be grouped together and assigned a name, these groups of statements are referred to as a **routine**. A routine may have one of the following forms:

- subroutine
- procedure
- function.

There are three kinds of functions:

- built-in functions;
- internal functions;
- external functions.

Built-in functions are the standard functions belonging to the REXX repertoire; they are described in Chapter 10 and Chapter 11. **Internal functions** are defined in the current REXX exec. **External functions** are defined external to the current REXX exec, and do not need to be written in the REXX language.

Each explicitly invoked routine receives the standard environment (ADDRESS, NUMERIC, SIGNAL and TRACE, and elapsed time) settings on entry. The original settings are restored on return to the point of invocation. However, the stack is common to all routines in the current environment. The invoking routine can isolate the stack by using the following statements (TSO implementation only):

```
'NEWSTACK'              /* create a new stack */
invoke routine
'DELSTACK'              /* delete the stack previously created */
```

Such coding should be used if the invoked routine could leave unwanted entries in the stack. Section 4.8 describes stack processing.

Parameters (arguments) can be passed to routines using the following methods:

- explicit
- implicit
- stack.

Explicit parameters are passed at the point of invocation. Implicit parameters are those parameters referred to by name in the routine - for procedures such parameters must be declared with the EXPOSE clause. Implicit parameters should be avoided if possible, as there is the increased danger of modifications to the program affecting the processing. Section 4.2.6 describes the use of arguments.

4.2.1 Subroutine
A subroutine can be invoked with the CALL instruction or as a function or by being dropped through to.

```
name:
    statements

RETURN;
```

Fig. 4.1 - Subroutine

Example:
```
CALL alpha beta gamma;
    ...
EXIT;
alpha:
    PARSE ARG parml parm2;
    SAY "subroutine 'alpha' called with:" parml parm2 "parameters";
RETURN;
```
The subroutine alpha is called with two parameters (variables): beta and gamma. The
subroutine displays the contents of these two parameters.

4.2.2 Procedure

A procedure is a routine identified with the PROCEDURE instruction, and is invoked in
the same way as a subroutine. A procedure has the following differences compared
with a subroutine:

- global variables used in a procedure must be explicitly declared with the EXPOSE
  clause in the PROCEDURE instruction - this is the concept of **information hiding**;
- a procedure can only be invoked with the CALL instruction or as a function.

```
name: PROCEDURE [EXPOSE parameters]
     statements

     RETURN;
```

The square brackets ([ ]) indicate an optional entry.

Fig. 4.2 - Procedure

Example:
```
CALL alpha;
    ...
EXIT;
alpha: PROCEDURE EXPOSE beta gamma;
    SAY "subroutine 'alpha' called with:" beta gamma "parameters";
RETURN;
```
The procedure alpha is called with two global parameters (variables): beta and gamma.
The procedure displays the contents of these two parameters.

4.2.3 Function

A function may be either a subroutine or a procedure. Functions must always return a value in the RETURN instruction, even if this is the null value. This returned value replaces the explicit function invocation (e.g. function()) or is set into the RETURN special variable if invoked with the CALL instruction (e.g. CALL function). Functions make be invoked recursively, see Example 2.

```
                    name: [PROCEDURE]
                      statements

                    RETURN expression;
```

The square brackets ([ ]) indicate an optional entry.

Fig. 4.3 - Function

Example 1:
```
    x = alpha(beta,gamma);
    ...
    EXIT;
    alpha:
      PARSE ARG parm1,parm2;
      SAY "function 'alpha' called with:" parm1 parm2 "parameters";
    RETURN "";
```
The function alpha is called with two parameters (variables): beta and gamma. The function displays the contents of these two parameters, and returns the null value to the point of invocation.

Example 2 (recursive function):
```
    PARSE ARG x;
    SAY "fact" x fact(x);
    EXIT;
    fact:
    PARSE ARG n;
    IF n < 1 THEN RETURN 1;
    RETURN n * fact(n-1);
```
The function fact is called recursively to calculate the factorial of the number passed as parameter.

4.2.4 Search order
Routines are searched in the following order:

- internal routine (except if the routine name is specified within quotes, in which case it is assumed to be either a built-in function or an external routine);
- built-in function;
- external routine.

External routines are subject to the following search order:

- DBCS routines (the DBCS package is not discussed in this book);
- function package routines (described in section 16.6) - contact your system support personnel for details of any system functions available at your installation;
- the load library;
- the procedure library.

Note: The search sequence of load library and the procedure library may have been reversed at your installation - contact your system support personnel for details.

4.2.5 Invocation
Procedures and subroutines are invoked using the CALL instruction.

Example:
```
CALL alpha;
```
invokes the routine with the name alpha.

Functions can be invoked in two ways:

- directly using the function name;
- indirectly using the CALL instruction with the function name as routine name.

A function call is not a REXX instruction and so must be embedded in an instruction.

Example:
```
x = alpha();
```
The function name must be immediately followed by parentheses, without any intervening blanks. Parameters (arguments) to be passed to the function are included within these parentheses, the individual arguments are separated by a comma. A maximum of 20 parameters can be passed to a function. The parentheses must always be written, even when no arguments are passed to the function.

4.2.6 Parameters (arguments)

Routines may be passed parameters (**arguments**) in two ways:

- explicit parameters at the point of invocation, parameters for a function invocation are set within the parentheses;
- parameters contained in variables (such variables for a procedure or procedural function must be defined with the EXPOSE keyword).

Either a single parameter or multiple parameters, separated by commas, may be passed. The individual parameters may have subparameters.

Example:
Passing a single parameter (which consists of two subparameters) to a subroutine or procedure -

```
CALL alpha "beta" gamma;
```

Passing two parameters to a subroutine or procedure -

```
CALL alpha "beta", gamma;
```

Passing two parameters to a function

```
x = alpha("beta", gamma);
```

The parameters are retrieved in the invoked routine using the ARG function, or the ARG or PARSE ARG instruction:
- the function ARG( ) returns the number of parameters;
- the function ARG(n) returns the nth parameter.

The ARG function has the advantage in that it returns explicitly the number of parameters. The usual parsing operations can be used to obtain the subparameters.

Example 1:

```
CALL alpha "beta" gamma;
...
alpha:
   n_parm = ARG();
   parm1 = ARG(1);
   ...
RETURN;
```

yields the following results:

```
n_parm                    1
parm1                     'beta' gamma
```

Example 2:

```
CALL alpha "beta", gamma;
...
alpha:
  n_parm = ARG();
  parm1 = ARG(1);
  parm2 = ARG(2);
  ...
RETURN;
```

yields the following results:

```
n_parm                    2
parm1                     'beta'
parm2                     gamma
```

Example 3 (using the PARSE ARG instruction):

```
CALL alpha "beta", gamma;
...
alpha:
  PARSE ARG parm1, parm2;
  ...
RETURN;
```

yields the following results:

```
parm1                     'beta'
parm2                     gamma
```

4.2.7 Return

Routines use the RETURN instruction to return to the statement following the point of invocation. If a routine is not invoked with the CALL instruction, or implicit call in case of a function, the RETURN instruction is processed as an EXIT instruction, i.e. the REXX exec is terminated.

Functions must return a value in the RETURN instruction, even if it is not required by the invoking statement. This value is used in place of the function invocation in the invoking statement.

The value of the expression specified in the RETURN instruction is set into the RESULT special variable. The RESULT variable is non-initialised if no expression is specified.

Example:
```
x = alpha();
SAY x;
   ...
alpha:
RETURN 4;
```
and
```
CALL alpha;
SAY RESULT;
   ...
alpha:
RETURN 4;
```
both display 4.

4.3 DO-GROUP

The DO instruction introduces one or more statements terminated by the END instruction; these statements are known as a **Do-group**. The DO instruction has several forms:

- simple Do;
- repetitive Do;
- endless Do;
- controlled repetitive Do.

A Do-group can itself contain other Do-groups, such a Do-group is called a **nested Do-group**. The nested Do-groups constitute a **hierarchy** of Do-groups; the DO and END statements of a Do-group are at a **hierarchy level**, this is illustrated in Fig. 4.4.

The forms of a Do-group other than the simple Do (repetitive Do, endless Do, and controlled repetitive Do) constitute a **Do-loop**.

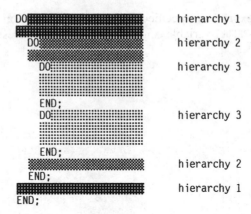

```
DO                              hierarchy 1
    DO                          hierarchy 2
        DO                      hierarchy 3

        END;
        DO                      hierarchy 3

        END;
                                hierarchy 2
    END;
                                hierarchy 1
END;
```

Fig. 4.4 - Do hierarchy example

There are two conditions which control as to whether the Do-loop is performed:

- An **iteration condition** is specified. The iteration condition has a **control variable**, which is assigned an **initial value** and is incremented on each pass through the loop. An **end value** (limit) must be specified for the control variable. The **increment** to be added to the control variable for each pass through the loop is optional, the default value is 1. The initial value, end value and increment can be negative. Any changes made within the Do-loop to the end value or increment have no affect on the loop control.
- A **conditional expression**, which determines whether the loop is terminated. The conditional expression can be influenced from within the Do-loop.

These two conditions may be specified in combination.

4.3.1 Simple Do
A **simple Do** is a group of statements which belong together, and can be used instead of a single statement, e.g. in the WHEN clause of a SELECT instruction.

Example:
```
DO;
    alpha = 1;
    SAY alpha "beta";
END;
```

4.3.2 Repetitive Do
A **repetitive Do** is a group of statements performed a fixed number of times.

Example:
```
DO 3;
  alpha = 1;
  SAY alpha "beta";
END;
```
performs the two statements between the DO and END three times.

4.3.3 Endless Do
The **endless Do** is a special form of the repetitive Do; the FOREVER operand is used instead of a number. Some means must be provided to leave the Do-group, otherwise a unending loop will result.

Example:
```
DO FOREVER;
  alpha = 1;
  SAY alpha "beta";
END;
```
performs the two statements between the DO and END an unlimited number of times.

4.3.4 Controlled repetitive Do
A **controlled repetitive Do** has a variable, called the **control variable**, which is assigned an initial (= keyword) value and end (TO keyword) value, and an increment (BY keyword) value. The control variable is incremented by this increment value each time the Do-group is performed. The Do-group is terminated when the control value is greater than the end value (for a positive increment) or less than the end value (for a negative increment). Alternatively, the BY keyword may be replaced by the FOR keyword, which specifies the number of times the Do-group is to be performed. The control variable can be specified in the corresponding END instruction, this can help avoid having unbalanced DO-END instructions and to help in the writing of robust programs.

Example:
```
DO i = 1 TO 4 BY 2;
  SAY i;
END i;
```
displays: 1 and 3.

Note: The END instruction contains the control variable associated with it (in this case i); this is not strictly necessary, but it clarifies the structure within nested Do-groups.

4.3.5 Iteration condition

The iteration condition can also be augmented with a conditional expression, which is used to specify under which conditions the iteration is to be performed. There are two forms of conditional expression:

- Do-group is performed while the condition is satisfied, the test is made at the start of the Do-group (WHILE keyword).
- Do-group is performed until the condition is satisfied, the test is made at the end of the Do-group (UNTIL keyword) - this means that a Do-group controlled by UNTIL is performed always at least once.

Example:
```
      j = 0;
      DO i = 1 TO 10 WHILE j < 21;
         j = i * 7;
         SAY i j;
      END;
```
performs three cycles. *Note*: The variable j should be initialised before the loop, otherwise the initial condition (j < 21) may fail.

Whereas:
```
      j = 0;
      DO i = 1 TO 10 UNTIL j > 21;
         j = i * 7;
         SAY i j;
      END;
```
performs four cycles.

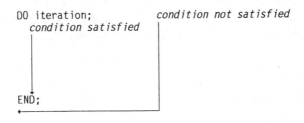

Fig. 4.5 - WHILE processing

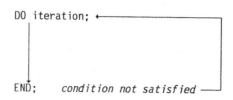

Fig. 4.6 - UNTIL processing

4.3.6 Modification of processing within a Do-loop

The processing within Do loops can be modified in the following ways:

- the current cycle is terminated (ITERATE instruction), i.e. an implicit branch is made to the END instruction;
- the current Do-group is terminated (LEAVE instruction), i.e. an implicit branch is made to the statement following the END instruction;
- the program is terminated (EXIT instruction);
- the program is terminated (EXIT instruction);
- the current Do-group is exited by passing control to some routine outside the Do-group (CALL or SIGNAL instruction), this is 'dirty' programming and is not recommended as it results in an unstructured program.

4.3.6.1 ITERATE - Terminate cycle of a Do-loop

The ITERATE instruction terminates the current cycle in the Do-loop having the same hierarchy; all statements following the ITERATE instruction up to the next END instruction at the same hierarchy are bypassed. The control variable is incremented and the iteration condition tested as usual.

```
DO iteration;

    ITERATE;  ————————┐
                      │
                      │
    END;  ←———————————┘
```

Fig. 4.7 - ITERATE processing

Example:
```
      DO i = 1 TO 4;
        IF i = 3 THEN ITERATE;
         SAY i;
      END;
```
displays 1, 2 and 4.

4.3.6.2 LEAVE - Terminate a Do-loop

The LEAVE instruction terminates the Do-loop; processing continues at the statement following the next END instruction at the same hierarchy.

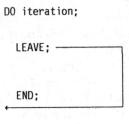

```
            DO iteration;

              LEAVE;

              END;
```

Fig. 4.8 - LEAVE processing

Example:
```
      DO i = 1 TO 4;
        IF i = 3 THEN LEAVE;
         SAY i;
      END;
```
displays 1 and 2.

4.3.6.3 Modification of the conditional expression from within the Do-loop

The conditional expression controlling a Do-loop can be changed from within the Do-loop.

Example:
```
    j = 5;
    DO i = 1 TO j WHILE j = 5;
      SAY i j;
      IF i = 2 THEN j = 3;
    END;
```
This example performs two cycles.

4.4 SELECT - SELECT ONE CONDITION FROM A SERIES OF CONDITIONS

The SELECT instruction is used to perform one (and only one) statement from a series of conditions defined with the WHEN keyword. The THEN statement applying to the first satisfied WHEN condition is executed.

A Do-group can be used if more than one statement is to be performed in the THEN-clause. Processing always continues after the END instruction, even if a subsequent condition would have been satisfied.

The statements introduced by the OTHERWISE keyword are performed if none of the conditions are satisfied.

A SELECT instruction must have at least one WHEN-THEN clause. An error results if no OTHERWISE clause is present for the case that none of the WHEN conditions has been satisfied. The NOP instruction can be used for the WHEN-THEN clause if no processing is to be performed; the OTHERWISE clause does not require any statements. Fig. 4.9 illustrates SELECT processing.

```
SELECT
   WHEN condition;
     THEN statement;
      ...
     WHEN condition;◄──────── first condition satisfied
       THEN statement;─┐
     WHEN condition;   │
      ...              │
     WHEN condition;   │
       THEN statement; │
     OTHERWISE;◄───────┼── no condition satisfied
       statement;      │
       statement;      │
      ...              │
       statement;      │
   END;────────────────┘
◄──────────────────────┘
```

Fig. 4.9 - SELECT processing

Example 1:
```
    a = 2;
    SELECT
      WHEN a < 2;
        THEN SAY "a lt 2";
      WHEN a > 1;
        THEN SAY "a gt 1";
      OTHERWISE
        SAY "a not gt 1";
    END;
```
displays the message "a gt 1".

Example 2:
```
    a = 2;
    SELECT
      WHEN a < 2;
        THEN SAY "a lt 2";
      WHEN a > 1;
        THEN DO;
          SAY "a gt 1";
        END;
      OTHERWISE;
        SAY "a not gt 1";
    END;
```
uses a Do-group to display the message "a gt 1".

4.5 CALL - INVOKE SUBROUTINE OR PROCEDURE

The CALL instruction invokes a subroutine or procedure. The invoked subroutine or procedure returns to the statement following the CALL instruction with the RETURN instruction. If the subroutine or procedure is not invoked with a CALL instruction, then the RETURN instruction is processed as an EXIT instruction, i.e. the REXX exec is terminated. The calling instruction can pass parameters (arguments) to the called routine; these parameters are retrieved with the ARG function, or the ARG (or PARSE ARG) instruction.

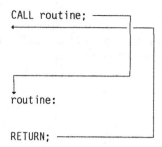

```
CALL routine;
routine:
RETURN;
```

Fig. 4.10 - CALL processing

Example:
```
CALL alpha;
SAY "beta";
...
alpha:
SAY "gamma";
RETURN;
```
displays beta and gamma, in that sequence.

4.6 SIGNAL - CONTROL PROCESSING FLOW

The SIGNAL instruction can be used in one of three ways:

- enable a trap to be taken should the specified condition arise (ON parameter);
- disable a trap (OFF parameter);
- pass control to a specified label.

The statement number of the statement which caused the SIGNAL to be *invoked* (not the statement number where the SIGNAL instruction was enabled) is set into the SIGL special variable.

The CALL instruction in the MVS-TSO implementation can be used to a large extent in the same way, except that the conditions which can be trapped are limited compared to the SIGNAL instruction.

Tip
Reserve the CALL instruction for invoking routines, unless the RETURN instruction is used to return control to the point of invocation.

Example:
```
SIGNAL ON NOVALUE;
  ...
NOVALUE:
SAY "novalue exit taken at statement" SIGL;
EXIT
```
displays the text 'novalue' exit taken at statement nnnn if a non-initialised variable has been used (nnnn is replaced by number of the statement in error).

4.7 ASSIGNMENT (=)

Unfortunately, the REXX language does not entirely conform to good software engineering principles of having a unique meaning for all operators. In particular, the = operator is used in several ways:

- assignment;
- assignment of initial value for the control variable in a Do-group;
- comparison for equality.

This potential conflict is resolved by the following rule.

Rule
The sequence:
- symbol
- =

as the first two items in a statement (ignoring any labels) is interpreted as being an assignment of the expression following this = operator to the symbol preceding the = operator.

Example:
```
alpha = (a = "b") + 1;
```
→ equality (comparison) operator
→ assignment operator

4.8 STACK (QUEUE) PROCESSING

One of the most useful features of the REXX language is **stack processing**. The stack is also referred to as the **queue**. The stack can be used for the following purposes:

- terminal input buffer;
- general data storage (intra-program communication);
- passing data between programs (inter-program communication);
- file buffer (EXECIO command).

There are three instructions used for explicit operations on the queue:

- PARSE PULL or PULL (obtain entry from head-of-queue);
- PUSH (put entry at head-of-queue);
- QUEUE (put entry at tail-of-queue).

PUSH and QUEUE processing are also referred to as **LIFO** (last-in / first-out), **FIFO** (first-in / first-out) processing, respectively. However, these terms lead to confusion when the operations are used in combination in the same stack. It is better to visualise where each entry is to be stored. Queue processing is illustrated in Fig. 4.11.

Example (illustrated in Fig. 4.12):
```
QUEUE "alpha";
PUSH "beta";
QUEUE "gamma";
n_elements = QUEUED();
DO i = 1 TO n_elements;
  PARSE PULL x;
  SAY x;
END;
```
displays (in this order):
```
beta
alpha
gamma
```

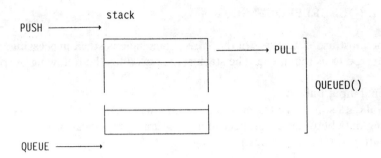

Fig. 4.11 - Queue processing

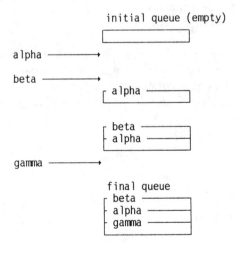

Fig. 4.12 - Queue processing from the previous example

4.8.1 Stack as terminal input buffer
The stack is the primary buffer for terminal input. This has two consequences:

- data for programs or commands awaiting terminal input can be stored in the stack;
- any data remaining in the stack after the completion of the program will be used as terminal input, i.e. commands for the **command processor**.

Tip

Clear the stack before the program terminates, unless the remaining entries in the stack are to be used as commands for the command processor. The QUEUED() function can be used the obtain the number of entries in the stack.

4.8.2 Stack for general data storage

The stack can be used for the storage of data items, for example, to pass data to a routine.

Tip

Use the stack for data which are to be processed sequentially. Compound symbols are more suitable for data which are to be accessed in a random manner.

4.8.3 Stack for passing data between programs

The stack can be used to pass data items between programs running in the same host environment. This facility is related to the use of the stack to pass commands to the command processor described in section 4.8.1. The other use is in a multi-tasking environment, for example, MVS-TSO.

4.8.3.1 MVS-TSO stack processing

The MVS-TSO environment has a number of extensions to better support the use of the stack in a multi-tasking environment. These facilities are also useful for normal processing. Fig. 4.13 illustrates the organisation of MVS-TSO stacks.

- A new stack is created when the TSO session is initiated. This stack is deleted when the TSO session terminates.
- Sub-stacks can be created. Each of these sub-stacks can be used in the same way as the original stack. The NEWSTACK (New Stack) command creates a new stack, which becomes the **current stack**. The DELSTACK (Delete Stack) command deletes the current stack and all entries contained within it, the previous stack becomes the current stack. The QSTACK (Query Stack) command returns the number of stacks.
- The current stack is the stack used when the REXX exec terminates. REXX execs initiated within the same TSO session can access any higher-level stacks which have been created using the usual stack commands.
- A stack can be sub-divided into one or more buffers. The MAKEBUF (Make Buffer) command creates a new buffer in the current stack, this buffer then becomes the **current buffer**. The DROPBUF (Drop Buffer) command deletes the specified buffers

and all entries contained within them. The QBUF (Query Buffer) command returns the number of buffers in the current stack which have been created with the MAKEBUF command and have not been deleted. The QELEM (Query Elements) command returns the number of entries buffers in the current buffer.

- Buffers are only a conceptual subset of a stack, and have no fundamental significance. The entries in the various buffers of a stack can be directly processed as entries of the stack.
- A stack or buffers in a stack, together with all their elements, can be explicitly deleted.

ISPF performs its own stack processing, and creates a new original stack for each invocation - screen splitting counts as a new invocation. This means that the stack cannot be used to pass data between ISPF screens. The original TSO stacks are restored when the ISPF session terminates.

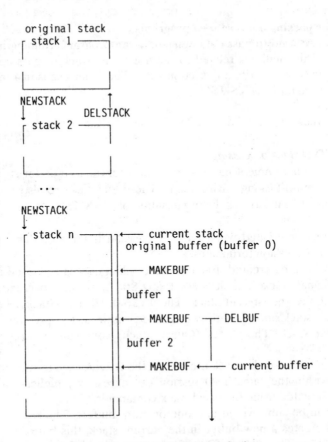

Fig. 4.13 - MVS-TSO stack organisation

Example (passing data between programs, tasks):
```
/* REXX - pass message between programs */
"NEWSTACK";  /* create new stack */
PUSH "this is a message" TIME();  /* set message into stack */
"NEWSTACK"  /* protect stack - create (new) empty stack */

/* REXX- retrieve message */
"DELSTACK";  /* point to previous stack */
PARSE PULL msg;  /* retrieve message from stack */
SAY "this is the message" msg;
```
The first REXX exec sets a single message (with the time of day) into a new stack,
and then creates a further stack, which at this point is empty. This means that the
previous stack contains a single entry. The second REXX exec deletes the empty
stack, i.e. the current stack is now the previous stack, which contains the passed message. This message is fetched with the PARSE PULL instruction.
Note: This method is not restricted to passing a single message.

4.8.4 File buffer
The current stack can be used as buffer for the EXECIO command.

4.9 SPECIAL VARIABLES

REXX has three reserved words for use as control variables:
- RC   The return code set by commands.
- RESULT   The value of the expression set in the RETURN instruction.
- SIGL   The number of the source line which caused the current exception to
                be raised.

4.10 DEBUGGING

The REXX language offers many facilities for debugging:

- trace statements;
- trace intermediate results;
- trace final results;

- trace statements causing an error return;
- trace labels;
- perform syntax check (without execution);
- disable the execution of host commands;
- pause after the execution of selected types of statement (equivalent to single-step).

The required level of debugging can be made in the REXX exec or set interactively after interrupting the execution. Chapter 7 describes debugging in detail.

5

Arithmetic

5.1 INTRODUCTION

The concepts of a number and of arithmetic operators were introduced in section 2.3.1 and 2.4.2, respectively.

The processing of arithmetic expressions in REXX follows the general rules which one expects. Although, as in all programming languages, there are certain rules with regard to:

- precision;
- representation;
- sequence of operations.

5.2 PRECISION AND REPRESENTATION

Precision is determined by the value specified in the NUMERIC DIGITS instruction or the DIGITS function. The default precision is 9 digits.

The DIGITS function specifies how many digits are to be retained as the result of a numeric operation, and is also directly concerned with how the result is represented in external format, e.g. how the number is displayed with the SAY function.

Tip
Do not set the precision higher than it need be:
- increasing the precision also increases the storage allocated, even when the higher precision is not used;
- increasing the precision increases the computation time.

Rule

If the number of digits before the decimal place is greater than the value specified for DIGITS, then the number is represented in exponential format. If the number of digits after the decimal place is greater than twice the value specified for DIGITS, then the number is represented in exponential format.

This rule is best illustrated with an example. If DIGITS has been set to 2 (e.g. x = DIGITS(2);), then the following results of multiplying 12.5 by 3 (to various numbers of decimal places) are displayed:

```
30 * 12.5              3.8E2
3 * 12.5               38
0.3 * 12.5             3.8
0.03 * 12.5            .38
0.003 * 12.5           .038
0.0003 * 12.5          .0038
0.00003 * 12.5         3.8E-4
```

Exponential format is a mathematical way of representing both very large and very small numbers. The "E" (or "e") represents in REXX the power ten, and the number following is the exponent.

Example:

E2 represents $10^2 = 100$

E-2 represents $10^{-2} = 1/100 = 0.01$

The mantissa, the number preceding the "E", is multiplied by this power of ten to give the end result.

Example:

3.8E2   represents $3.8 * 10^2 = 3.8 * 100 = 380$

3.8E-2   represents $3.8 * 10^{-2} = 3.8 * 0.01 = 0.038$

5.3 SEQUENCE OF OPERATIONS

General mathematics has the rule that multiplicative (which includes division) operations are performed before additive (which includes subtraction) operations. This rule is also adhered to in REXX.

Example:

    x = 10 + 4*2;

assigns 18 to x.

As in general mathematics, the order of performing operations can be determined by using parentheses; the expression in parentheses is calculated first.

Example:

    x = (10 + 4)*2;

assigns 28 to x.

If the parenthesised expression itself contains parentheses, then the innermost parentheses are resolved first.

Example:

    x = (2+(10 + 4)*2);

is calculated in the following manner:
10 + 4 = 14; 14 * 2 = 28; 2 + 28 = 30

Table 2.5 in Chapter 2 contains the order of precedence of the arithmetic operators.

6

Input/output

6.1 INTRODUCTION

Input/output (I/O) statements, other than simple terminal operations, are not part of the SAA implementation of REXX. Procedures using REXX may well be able to be written without using I/O statements. However, most practical REXX programs will require I/O operations.

Most REXX implementations have their own repertoire of I/O instructions. These instructions tend to be similar in each implementation, however, there are often subtle differences.

There are two sources on which the definitions for the I/O statements in the REXX implementations are based:
* the original VM implementation, which uses the EXECIO command based on the VM/CMS command;
* the definition of the REXX language contained in M.F.Cowlishaw's book *The Rexx Language, A Practical Approach to Programming* - the CHARIN, CHAROUT, CHARS, LINEIN, LINEOUT and LINES functions.

The I/O facilities can be classified into four groups:
* simple terminal operations (PULL and SAY instructions);
* operations at the character (byte) level (CHARIN, CHAROUT and CHARS functions);
* operations at the line (record) level (LINEIN, LINEOUT and LINES functions);
* operations at the file level (EXECIO command) - although the EXECIO command can also be used to process single records.

This chapter describes the general I/O facilities. The following chapters contain detailed descriptions of the I/O operations:
* Chapter 9 - I/O terminal instructions;

- Chapter 11 - I/O functions;
- Chapter 12 - EXECIO command.

6.2 DATA BUFFERING

The data buffering is related to the level (character, line or file) at which the I/O operation is performed. Input terminal data can be buffered in the stack. For character and line operations REXX variables are used to contain the data. For operations at the file level either the stack or stem variables are used as the data buffer.

6.3 OPENING AND CLOSING THE DATA FILES

REXX files are automatically opened when they are first used. They are also automatically closed when the REXX exec terminates. For processing at the file level, i.e. with the EXECIO command, files can be explicitly closed with the FINIS operand. This can be used to reprocess a file from the start (in certain operating system environments, e.g. MVS, the disposition specifies how a file is to be reprocessed).

In general a file should be closed when it is no longer needed. This has two advantages:
- main-storage is freed;
- if the file has been reserved for exclusive use by the processing exec, it is then available for use by other programs.

6.4 TERMINAL OPERATIONS

The PULL and SAY instructions are used to perform basic transfer from and to the terminal, respectively. However, the I/O functions (CHARIN, LINEIN, etc.) can also be directed to the terminal.

Terminal input is taken by default from the stack - this means that a request for terminal input is first satisfied by taking data from the stack; if the current stack is empty, then the program awaits input from the terminal.

This use of the stack has two consequences:

- responses can be pre-stored with the PUSH or QUEUE instruction - this can be useful to provide information for host environment commands and functions;

- when the REXX terminates, any entries remaining in the stack will be interpreted as being commands (the DELSTACK command can be used to remove the stack).

Tip
Always precede a request for terminal input data with a message to the terminal. This avoids the application program seeming to wait for no apparent reason.

6.5 CHARACTER-MODE OPERATIONS

Character-mode I/O operations are performed with the CHARIN, CHAROUT, and CHARS functions. In character-mode the input data stream is read character by character (including any delimiters for end-of-line, end-of-file, etc.).

Either permanent (disk) files or temporary (terminal) files can be processed. A **current position pointer** is maintained for permanent files. Character-mode and line-mode processing can be combined for permanent files.

6.6 LINE-MODE OPERATIONS

Line-mode I/O operations are performed with the LINEIN, LINEOUT, and LINES functions. In line-mode the input data stream is read line by line (any delimiters for end-of-line, end-of-file, etc. are ignored on input and generated for output).

Either permanent (disk) files or temporary (terminal) files can be processed. The same **current position pointer** as for character-mode operations is maintained for permanent files. Character-mode and line-mode processing can be combined for permanent files.

6.7 FILE-MODE OPERATIONS

The EXECIO command is used for file-mode I/O operations. Although it is neither part of the SAA definition nor described in *The Rexx Language*, the EXECIO command is the only I/O operation available in all REXX implementations.

The EXECIO command as implemented in REXX is based on the VM/CMS EXECIO command. However, not all the parameters are supported in each implementation. This book describes the MVS/TSO implementation.

The MVS/TSO implementation supports only the following record formats:

- fixed length records;
- variable length records.

The records may be either blocked or unblocked; data being written is formatted as appropriate, e.g. fixed length records are automatically padded on the right with blanks.

Warning

The EXECIO command is optimised. This has the consequence that an output file is opened only when data are to be written. However, a null variable contains no data - this also means that such a file is not closed on termination of the exec, normally the end-of-file marker would have been written.

7

Debugging

7.1 INTRODUCTION

Debugging described in this chapter deals with the mechanics involved, i.e. the tools which REXX makes available. The techniques used for debugging are largely an art, which can only be learnt to a limited degree - a good "debugger" (the person who debugs) does it largely by intuition. For those people who do not fall into this category, the best help is information. This chapter describes the REXX facilities available to supply this information.

REXX supports two forms of debugging:
* signal processing to be performed if a specified exception condition occurs;
* trace statement execution.

REXX offers two means of obtaining information:
* statically;
* dynamically (interactively).

Static means build the debugging statements into the REXX exec. **Dynamic** or **interactive** means interrupt the REXX exec while it is executing and invoke the appropriate debugging statements from the terminal. All REXX statements are available in interactive debugging mode.

7.2 EXCEPTION CONDITIONS

Exception conditions are:

- **error** - a non-zero return code from a host command;
- **failure** - a negative return code from a host command;
- **halt** - the interpretation of the REXX exec is halted, for example, with the HI command;
- **no value** - a symbol has been used which has not been initialised (i.e. has not received data);
- **syntax** - an invalid REXX statement has been invoked (this can have invalid syntax, or an operand contains invalid data (e.g. non-numeric data in an arithmetic expression, etc.)).

These exception conditions are trapped by the SIGNAL instruction. If exception conditions are not trapped, then messages are displayed only under the following circumstances:
- a host command returns the failure condition;
- syntax error (and processing is terminated).

Tip
To avoid unexpected processing occurring, the NO VALUE exception condition should always be set, even though this may increase the program coding to some extent.

   One of the features of the REXX language which makes coding easier is that each symbol is initialised by default to have its own name as content (in upper case). The hidden danger is that when such symbols are used as parameters, rather than using explicit literals, their value may be altered somewhere in the program - possibly when modifications are made at some later point in time.

7.3 TRACING OPTIONS

One of the following tracing options can be set:

- all
- commands
- error
- failure
- intermediate
- labels
- results
- syntax.

These options specify what tracing is to be performed, i.e. under what circumstances a trace message is to be displayed. Only one tracing option can be active at any one time. However, the setting of the trace option may be altered during the course of running the REXX exec.

There are also two prefix operators:
- ?
- !

one of which may be prefixed before any of the options specified above.

? invokes interactive debugging, which means that execution pauses when the set option occurs, e.g. TRACE '?ALL' stops before each statement is executed, and is equivalent to operating in single-step mode.

   ! suppresses the execution of host commands. The return code is set to 0 for each host command which would have been executed. This can be useful for testing a REXX exec when the required host commands are not available.

The two prefix operators (? and !) are binary switches (toggles). Each setting reverses the previous setting.

7.3.1 ALL - Display all expressions before execution
The ALL option is used to display all expressions before they are executed.

7.3.2 COMMANDS - Display all commands before execution
The COMMANDS option is used to display all commands before they are executed.

7.3.3 ERROR - Display all commands which return an error condition
The ERROR option is used to display all commands which return a non-zero code after being executed.

7.3.4 FAILURE - Display all commands which return a negative error condition
The FAILURE option is used to display all commands which return a negative code after being executed. This is the default setting.

7.3.5 INTERMEDIATE - Display all expressions (with intermediate results) before being executed

The INTERMEDIATE option is used to display all expressions before being executed, intermediate results are also displayed. This is the option usually used for general debugging.

7.3.6 LABELS - Display all labels as they are reached

The LABELS option is used to display the names of labels as they are reached. This option is useful for tracing the program flow. The displayed labels are automatically nested, i.e. each hierarchy is indented.

7.3.7 RESULTS - Display all expressions (with end results) before being executed

The RESULTS option is used to display all expressions before being executed, the end results are also displayed.

7.3.8 SYNTAX - Check syntax without processing the statements

The SYNTAX option is used to check the syntax of the complete program. The program is not executed. SYNTAX cannot be invoked in the following circumstances:
- from within a construction (Do-group or Select-block);
- from the interactive debugging mode.

Tip

REXX programs are interpreted. This means that in most implementations the statements are first processed when they are to be executed, with the result that erroneous statements may be hidden in parts of the program which are not normally executed, e.g. error handling routines. TRACE SYNTAX detects such errors, and so should be used before important applications are put into production.

7.4 TRACE OUTPUT

Trace output is prefixed with a three-character code which identifies the content of the following trace line. There are two forms of prefix:

- those used for trace data;
- those used for (intermediate) results.

7.4.1 Trace data prefixes
Prefixes used for trace data:

-   the program source line;

+++   trace message;

>>>   result;

>.>   value assigned to a placeholder.

7.4.2 Trace intermediate data prefixes
The following prefixes are used only when TRACE INTERMEDIATES has been specified:

>C>   data are the name of a compound variable;

>F>   data are the result of function invocation;

>L>   data are a literal;

>O>   data are the result of an operation;

>P>   data are the result of a prefix operation;

>V>   data are the contents of a variable.

The displayed data are shown in character form within double quotes, "?" denotes non-character data.

7.4.3 Trace output example

Sample REXX exec
```
1        /* REXX trace */
2        TRACE "I";
3        i = 1;
4        PARSE VALUE DATE('E') WITH day.i '/' .;
5        x = day.1 * -2;
6        SAY x;
7        BETA();
```

The corresponding (annotated) output follows - the number in the left-hand column refers to the statement number in the REXX exec. Annotations are written in italics and immediately follow the trace output to which they refer.

```
    3 *-* i = 1
source statement 3
      >L>    "1"
content of numeric literal
    4 *-* PARSE VALUE DATE('E') WITH day.i '/' .
source statement 4
      >L>    "E"
content of character literal, parameter for DATE function
      >F>    "12/04/90"
result of evaluating the DATE function
      >C>    "DAY.1"
resolved name of compound variable, "1" has been substituted for "i" in
"day.i"
      >>>    "12"
first parsed operand from the evaluated DATE('E'), "/" has been used as
delimiter
      >.>    "04/90"
remainder after parsing to the "/" delimiter, this has been assigned to a
placeholder
    5 *-* x = day.1 * -2
source statement 5
      >V>    "12"
content the variable "day.1"
      >L>    "2"
content of numeric literal
      >P>    "-2"
result of performing the prefix operator (-) on 2
      >O>    "-24"
result of the operation of multiplying 12 by -2
    6 *-* SAY x
source statement 6
      >V>    "-24"
content the variable "x"
-24
output from the SAY instruction
    7 *-* BETA()
source statement 7
    7 +++ BETA()
trace message
IRX0043I Error running RXTRACE, line 7: Routine not found
```

REXX error message IRX0043I, specifies that the routine (function) BETA()
has not been found, i.e. invalid.

7.5 INTERACTIVE DEBUG

Interactive debug mode is invoked in one of two ways:

- with the TRACE ?option instruction - (option is one of the trace options, e.g. TRACE
  '?ALL');
- by interrupting the REXX exec while it is executing, for example, by pressing the
  PA1 key (in MVS/TSO).

On entry to interactive debug mode a message similar to the following is displayed:
    +++ Interactive trace. 'Trace off' to end debug

In interactive debug mode one of the following actions can be performed:

- Enter a null line (i.e. press the Enter key without having entered any input data).
  This causes the REXX exec to proceed to the next trace point, when it will again
  pause. For example, the TRACE '?COMMAND' will stop at the next command.

  Tip
  TRACE '?ALL' stops at each statement, i.e. causes single-stepping through the
  REXX exec.

- Enter a single equals sign ("=") to re-execute the last statement traced. Processing
  will pause after this statement has been re-executed, irrespective of the setting of
  trace option.

- The TRACE 'OFF' instruction terminates interactive tracing. This is a special case of
  processing described in the following action.

- The EXIT instruction terminates the REXX exec.

- Any other input data will be interpreted as being a REXX statement and will be
  immediately processed as if it were contained within a Do-End group. This means
  that the input can be multiple REXX statements, each separated by ";"
  (semicolon).

7.5.1 Interactive debugging example

Sample REXX exec to invoke interactive debug when an error condition arises. Note that the statement numbers at the start of each line are for identification purposes only, and are not present in the actual code.

```
1       /* REXX debug */
2       SIGNAL ON SYNTAX;
        ...

3       EXIT;
        ...
4       SYNTAX:
5       SAY "debug invoked";
6       SAY "condition" CONDITION('C');
7       TRACE '?a';
8       SAY "source line" SIGL " " SOURCELINE(SIGL);
9       SAY "debug end"
10      EXIT;
```

2   The SIGNAL instruction specifies that the SYNTAX exception condition is to be set.

3   Terminate normal processing.

4   The entry point for the interactive debug routine.

5   Display a message to the user indicating that an exception condition has arisen.

6   Display the name of the condition which has arisen. The CONDITION built-in function with operand 'C' supplies this information.

7   Activate interactive trace. This enables the user to input his own debugging commands, if required. The text specifying that interactive trace has been invoked is displayed after the next text line is output.

8   Display the line number (contained in the SIGL special variable) and source data (obtained with the SOURCELINE built-in function) in error.

9   Display a message to indicate that debugging has terminated.

10   Terminate error processing.

Typical output arising from a syntax error using the above interactive debug processing follows.

```
debug invoked
condition SYNTAX
    9 *-* SAY "source line" SIGL " "SOURCELINE(SIGL)

source line 3   x = beta();
IRX0100I +++ Interactive trace.  TRACE OFF to end debug, ENTER to continue.

   10 *-* SAY "debug end"
debug end
```

8

Programming practices

8.1 INTRODUCTION

Good programming practices are related to the debugging discussed Chapter 7. A well written program can, to a large extent, avoid the need to debug it.

This discussion of good programming practices is of necessity subjective. Such recommendations as the use of structured programming techniques can, but need not, assist in the **readability, reliability** and **maintainability** of a program. However, they cannot guarantee that the program is free from errors. An example from one of my courses serves to show that a structured program is more than just a theoretical nicety - the results of my putting structure into a non-structured program (the functionality was not changed) are shown in Table 8.1.

The aspects of **performance** and **compatibility** can also be of importance for a program.

	original version	revised version
lines of code	299	241
GoTos	87	0
labels	44	0
errors	3	0

Table 8.1 - Example of the benefits of a structured program

The programming practices discussed in this chapter are principally concerned with their use with REXX. A specialised text should be consulted for the more general aspects of 'good programming'.

The REXX language allows much flexibility, how this flexibility is used is up to the programmer. In many cases it is advantageous not to use all the facilities which are available.

8.2 READABILITY

Readability, as the word says, is ease with which a program can be read, i.e. a physical characteristic. A program which is not easy to read is not easy to understand; however, the converse does not necessarily apply - a program which is easy to read may not also be easy to understand.

Readability can be influenced in a number of ways:

- Do not use upper case exclusively. It is well known that text written in upper case is more difficult to read than text written in mixed case. I use the convention: instructions, non-internal functions and keywords are written in upper case, all other entries are written in lower case. Similarly, double quotes (") are used for normal literals and single quotes (') are used to delimit parametric operands - unless a quote-delimited operand is to be passed to some environment or the literal itself contains the delimiting quote, for example, "O'Brien".

- Format the program in a logical (structured) manner. Devise some consistent method to format structured constructions (Do-groups, Select-blocks, etc.). For example, indent at least two positions for each hierarchy in a Do-group, start related Then and Else clauses in the same column. My first recommendation to colleagues with a program which does not function correctly is to first structure the program - in many cases the errors resolve themselves.

- The actual conventions adopted are not so significant, consistency is more important.

8.3 RELIABILITY

A program can be regarded as being reliable when it behaves in a controlled fashion under both normal and exception conditions. Certain features which make it easy to write REXX programs pose potential problems, as they conflict with the aims of reliability.

- A non-initialised symbol has its name (in upper case) as content, for example, the symbol Alpha has ALPHA as its initial content. Although this simplifies the writing of alphanumeric literals there is the danger that the content of the symbol is inadvertently altered in the program. This potential problem can be solved as follows:
  - write alphanumeric literals explicitly, e.g. "ALPHA";
  - set the SIGNAL ON NOVALUE instruction to trap the use of non-initialised symbols.

- A REXX program is interpreted. For some implementations the syntax is only checked when the statement is executed. This means that latent syntax errors may be present in sections of the code which are not normally executed, for example, error processing routines. The TRACE SCAN instruction can be used to perform a syntax scan of the complete program, and should be used before a program is put into productive use. The TRACE SCAN instruction also detects such errors as missing or excessive END statements. *Note*: This is no longer an SAA instruction.

- Input data should be checked for validity if there is the possibility that they may be invalid, for example, numeric data entered from the keyboard. As a general rule, error messages should be displayed as near as possible to the source of error.

- Terminate a program with an explicit EXIT instruction.

- Terminate each statement (clause) with a ";" (semicolon). This can avoid unexpected continuations being made.

- Use control variables on END statements. This can help in the detection of unbalanced blocks.

8.4 MAINTAINABILITY

Maintainability is the ease with which a program can be maintained. Maintenance is not restricted to removing errors but also includes extensions to include new functions and facilities.

Observance of readability and reliability is a necessary requirement for a maintainable program.

8.5 COMPATIBILITY

The major significance of compatibility is when a REXX program is to be used in various environments, for example, in MVS/TSO and OS/2. Full compatibility is only possible for those applications which do not use components specific for the particular host environment - such components include input/output (other than simple terminal operations using the SAY and PULL instructions). The porting of applications can be simplified by isolating environment-specific features in subroutines. Appendix I contains a table of the compatibilities between the various implementations.

Certain implementations demand a commentary as first line in a REXX program, in some cases this comment must also include the word REXX - this is necessary to be able to distinguish REXX execs from other procedures. It is any case a good practice to begin every REXX exec with a comment briefly describing its function.

8.6 PERFORMANCE

REXX programs are interpreted. An interpreted program has advantages such as flexibility, ease of debugging (errors can be corrected on the spot), speed of implementation (compilation, etc. is not required). However, the execution time of a REXX program will of necessity be longer than a compiled program. The size of this time-overhead is influenced by optimising measures built into the REXX interpreter (for example, certain REXX implementations can use preprocessed intermediate code as input, which saves the conversion of the source program to this code), and how the REXX program is written.

The best way to influence the speed of execution is not to execute unnecessary statements. For example, use a SELECT instruction rather than a series of IF statements, when not more than one condition can apply.

9

REXX instructions

9.1 INTRODUCTION

The REXX instructions constitute the framework with which a REXX program is written.

- = (assignment)
- ADDRESS - Set environment
- ARG - Fetch argument
- CALL - Invoke routine
- DO - Define start of block
- DROP - Free variable
- EXIT - Terminate exec
- IF - Conditional execution
- INTERPRET - Interpret statement
- ITERATE - Terminate the current cycle in the Do-loop
- LEAVE - Terminate Do-loop
- NOP - No-operation
- NUMERIC - Define numeric formats
- OPTIONS - Pass special parameters to the language processor
- PARSE - Assign data
- PROCEDURE - Define internal procedure
- PULL - Fetch data element from the head of the stack
- PUSH - Set data element at the head of the stack
- QUEUE - Set data element at the tail of the stack
- RETURN - Return from routine
- SAY - Display
- SELECT - Conditional execution of one statement from a group of statements

- SIGNAL - Enable (or disable) an exception condition, or cause control to be passed to a routine
- TRACE - Set debugging options
- UPPER - Transform lower case characters into upper case (MVS-TSO only)

9.2 INSTRUCTION DEFINITIONS

9.2.1 = - Assignment
The assignment instruction, represented by the = keyword, assigns the expression to the specified symbol.

```
►►─── symbol = expression ; ───►◄
```

symbol
>Name of the target variable.

expression
>Expression which, after evaluation, is assigned to **symbol**.

Example:
```
alpha = beta;
alpha = "beta";
alpha = 3*4;
```

9.2.2 ADDRESS - Set environment
The ADDRESS instruction sets the system component environment to which the non-REXX statements are to be passed.

The ADDRESS instruction without a statement sets the global environment, which applies, until changed, to all subsequent non-REXX statements. The ADDRESS clause prefixed to a statement sets the local environment for that statement only.

The initial ADDRESS environment for the various implementations is shown in Table 9.1.

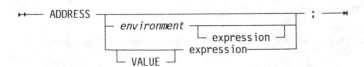

environment:

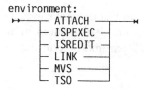

implementation	initial environment
MVS-TSO	TSO
MVS batch	MVS
Personal REXX	DOS
REXX/2	CMD

Table 9.1 - Initial ADDRESS environment

expression
> statement which is to be passed to the specified local **environment**.

VALUE expression
> **expression** is a character expression which defines the global environment. The VALUE keyword can be omitted when **expression** is enclosed within parentheses.

If no operands are specified, then the global environment is set back to what it was before the last change was made - see Example 3.

ATTACH
> Non-REXX statements are to processed via ATTACH, i.e. invoked asynchronously as a sub-task. The first item is the program name (maximum 8 characters), subsequent items are passed to the invoked program using the REXX parameter convention (see section 14.2.2).

ISPEXEC
> Non-REXX statements are to be passed to ISPF (Dialog Manager).

ISREDIT
> Non-REXX statements are to be processed as ISPF/PDF Edit macros.

LINK

Non-REXX statements are to processed via LINK, i.e. invoked synchronously. The first item is the program name (maximum 8 characters), subsequent items are passed to the invoked program using the REXX parameter convention (see section 14.2.2).

MVS

Non-REXX statements are to be processed as MVS (native REXX) commands. The worked example shown in section 15.3 illustrates the use of this instruction. This parameter returns the address environment to its initial value.

TSO

Non-REXX statements are to be processed as TSO commands. The first item is the command name (maximum 8 characters), subsequent items are passed to the invoked command (see section 13.2.8).

Note: The environment is not checked for validity.

Example 1:
```
ADDRESS ISPEXEC;
ADDRESS ISPEXEC "VPUT (ALPHA) SHARED";
```
The first instruction sets the global environment for ISPEXEC. The second instruction passes the "VPUT (ALPHA) SHARED" statement to the local ISPEXEC environment.

Example 2:
```
env = "ISPEXEC";
ADDRESS (env);
```
This example has the same effect as the first instruction in example 1, namely to set the global environment to ISPEXEC.
Note: At least one blank must follow the ADDRESS keyword, otherwise the ADDRESS function would have been invoked.

Example 3:
```
SAY ADDRESS();           /* display current environment */
ADDRESS MVS;             /* set MVS environment */
SAY ADDRESS();           /* display current environment */
ADDRESS;                 /* set previous environment */
SAY ADDRESS();           /* display current environment */
```
This example displays: TSO, MVS and TSO, respectively.

9.2.3 ARG - Fetch argument

The ARG instruction parses the argument passed via the CALL instruction or function invocation. The ARG instruction is a subset of the PARSE ARG instruction.
Note: This instruction largely duplicates the ARG function.

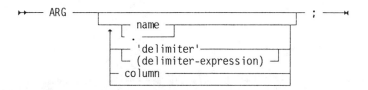

name

> Symbol to be assigned the parsed data.

> Placeholder, the data are parsed but no assignment is made.

'delimiter'

> Delimiter which is to be used as search argument for the source data. **Delimiter** is not restricted to being a single character.

(delimiter-expression)

> A character expression which is to be used as delimiter for the source data.

column

> Position at which the source data is to be split, 1 is the first position in the source data.
> If column is prefixed with either a ' + ' or '-' sign, then this column is relative to the last location parsed.

,

> Comma specifies that the next argument in the source data is to be processed.

Example:
```
    alpha = "beta ** gamma";
    CALL delta alpha;
    ...
    delta:
      ARG a b;
      ARG a '**' b;
      ARG a '*' b;
      ARG a 3 b;
    RETURN;
```

returns the following results:

a	b
"BETA"	"** GAMMA"
"BETA "	" GAMMA"
"BETA "	"* GAMMA"
"BE"	"TA ** GAMMA"

9.2.4 CALL - Invoke routine

The CALL instruction invokes the specified routine, and can optionally pass one or more arguments (parameters). The called routine returns with the RETURN instruction.

Tip

The MVS-TSO implementation allows trap conditions to be enabled or disabled using the CALL instruction. The SIGNAL instruction provides the same processing with more options for trap conditions, and, as it is part of the SAA implementation, should be used for such processing.

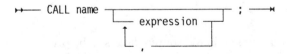

name

    Name of the routine to be invoked.

expression

    Argument (parameter) to be passed to the called routine. The individual arguments are separated by commas. Each argument may contain subparameters, which can be parsed in the usual way.

Example:
```
    CALL alpha beta;
    SAY RESULT;
    ...
    alpha:
    gamma = ARG(1);              /* fetch argument */
    SAY gamma;
    ...
    RETURN delta;
```
The routine alpha is invoked with argument beta.

9.2.5 DO - Define start of block
The DO instruction defines the start of a block; the block is terminated with the END instruction.

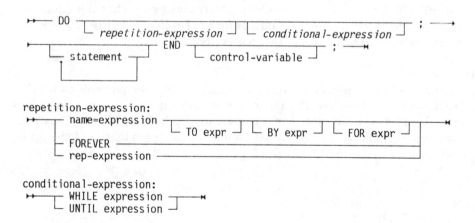

```
repetition-expression:
  ⊢⊢─┬── name=expression ─┬── TO expr ─┬── BY expr ─┬── FOR expr ─┬──────⊣
     ├── FOREVER ─────────────────────────────────────────────────────┤
     └── rep-expression ───────────────────────────────────────────────┘

conditional-expression:
  ⊢⊢─┬── WHILE expression ──┬──⊣
     └── UNTIL expression ──┘
```


name = expression

> Assignment of the initial value (**expression**) to the control variable (**name**) used for the Do-loop.

TO to-expr

> Definition of the final value (**to-expr**) of the control variable used for the Do-loop.

BY by-expr

> Definition of the increment value (**by-expr**) to be added to the control variable for each cycle through the Do-loop. The increment may be either positive or negative. Default: 1

FOR for-expr

    Definition of the number of cycles (**for-expr**) to be performed in the Do-loop. The **for-expr**, if present, takes priority over any other loop counts which are specified.

FOREVER

    This keyword specifies that an endless Do-loop is to be performed. Normally the Do-loop will be terminated using the LEAVE or EXIT instruction on some condition.

rep-expression

    Assignment of the repetitive expression (**rep-expression**) to be used for the Do-loop. This expression specifies the number of cycles to be performed.

WHILE expression

    Definition of the expression (**expression**) used as additional condition for the execution of the Do-loop. The Do-loop is performed only when this condition in conjunction with any other conditions for the Do-loop is satisfied. The WHILE condition is tested before the Do-loop is performed.

UNTIL expression

    Definition of the expression (**expression**) used as additional condition for the execution of the Do-loop. The Do-loop is performed only until this condition in conjunction with any other conditions for the Do-loop is satisfied. The UNTIL condition is tested at the end of the Do-loop; this means that the Do-loop is always performed at least once.

Example 1:

```
DO i = 1 TO 10;
...
END;
```

performs 10 iterations.

Example 2:

```
J = 3
DO i = 1 TO 10 FOR J;
...
END;
```

performs 3 iterations.

Example 3:
```
    DO FOREVER;
      ...
    END;
```
performs an endless iteration.

9.2.6 DROP - Free variable

The DROP instruction frees the specified variables. This means that the said variables no longer have any value and revert to their uninitialised state. The NOVALUE condition is signalled if a dropped variable is used without having been assigned a value.

Tip

The DROP instruction can be used to release storage which has been allocated to a variable. The storage allocated to arrays can be extensive.

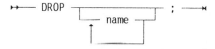

name

    Name of the variable to be freed.

Example:
```
    alpha = "beta";
    DROP alpha;
```

9.2.7 EXIT - Terminate exec

The EXIT instruction terminates the execution (logical end) of the current REXX exec - control is returned to the invoking program, etc. A REXX exec may have more than one EXIT. An EXIT is automatically generated at the physical end of the REXX exec, i.e. after the last statement.

Tip

It is good programming practice to explicitly specify the program EXIT. This is especially true before subroutines, which could be inadvertently executed by being dropped through to.

```
►►── EXIT ──┬─────────────┬── ; ──►◄
            └─ expression ─┘
```

expression

> Value to be returned to the point of invocation.

Example:
```
    EXIT 8;
```

9.2.8 IF - Conditional execution

The IF instruction specifies the processing to be performed based on the result of the condition tested. The IF instruction has two branches; the Then-branch is taken when the condition is satisfied, the Else-branch, if present, is taken when the condition is not satisfied.

```
►►── IF expression; THEN statement; ──┬──────────────────────┬──►◄
                                      └─ ELSE statement; ─────┘
```

expression

> Condition to be tested. **expression** must evaluate to either 1 (true) or 0 (false).

THEN statement

> Statement to be performed if **expression** evaluates to 1 (true). The NOP instruction can be used as statement and so satisfy the syntax, if no processing is to be performed.

ELSE statement

> Statement to be performed if **expression** evaluates to 0 (false). The ELSE clause is optional. The NOP instruction can be used as statement if no processing is to be performed.

Note: **statement** may be a Do-group, if more than one statement is to be performed.

Example:
```
IF alpha < 2
  THEN NOP;
  ELSE DO;
    SAY "alpha ge 2";
    SAY "line 2";
  END;
```
This example uses a Do-group as Else clause.

9.2.9 INTERPRET - Interpret statement
The specified expression is interpreted at run-time.

```
►►── INTERPRET expression; ──►◄
```

expression
>   The statement to be performed. **expression** must be a valid REXX statement, the final semicolon (";") is not specified.

Example:
```
alpha = "SAY 'beta'"
INTERPRET alpha;
```
is equivalent to:
```
SAY 'beta';
```

9.2.10 ITERATE - Terminate the current cycle in the Do-loop
The ITERATE instruction causes control to be passed to the END instruction of the current Do-loop.

```
►►── ITERATE ┬─────────┬ ; ──►◄
             └─ name ──┘
```

name
>   The name of the control variable for the Do-loop. The use of the control variable assists in detecting unbalanced Do-groups.

Example:
```
DO i = 1 TO 4;
   IF i = 2 THEN ITERATE;
   SAY i;
END;
```
displays 1, 3 and 4. The example could also have been written as:
```
DO i = 1 TO 4;
   IF i = 2 THEN ITERATE i;
   SAY i;
END i;
```

9.2.11 LEAVE - Terminate Do-loop
The LEAVE instruction causes the current Do-loop to be terminated, i.e. control is passed to the statement following the END instruction of the current Do-loop.

```
►►── LEAVE ──┬──────────┬── ; ──►◄
             └─ name ──┘
```

name
> The name of the control variable for the Do-loop. The use of the control variable assists in detecting unbalanced Do-groups.

Example:
```
DO i = 1 TO 4;
   IF i = 2 THEN LEAVE;
   SAY i;
END;
```
displays 1.

9.2.12 NOP - No-operation
The NOP instruction serves as statement placeholder. It is principally used in the THEN clause, when no processing is required but the clause must be present to satisfy the syntax requirements.

```
►►── NOP ; ──►◄
```

Example:

```
SELECT;
  WHEN alpha < 2;
    THEN SAY "alpha lt 2";
  WHEN alpha = 2;
    THEN NOP;
  OTHERWISE
    SAY "alpha gt 2";
END;
```

In this example processing is required only when alpha is not equal to 2.

9.2.13 NUMERIC - Define numeric formats

The NUMERIC instruction is used to define the format of numeric values. The NUMERIC instruction duplicates the functions: DIGITS, FORM and FUZZ.

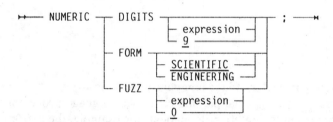

DIGITS expression

     expression is a numeric value which specifies the precision of numeric values. Default: 9.

FORM

     Specifies the external (display) form of numeric values whose size exceeds the DIGITS value. Such large, or very small, values are represented in exponential notation. There are two forms of exponential notation:

     SCIENTIFIC - only one non-zero appears before the decimal point of the mantissa, e.g. 1.2E+4.

     ENGINEERING - the exponent is always a power of three, e.g. 12E+3.

FUZZ expression

     expression is a numeric value which specifies the number of digits to be ignored during numeric comparisons.

     Default: 0.

Example 1:
```
n = 123456;
NUMERIC DIGITS 4;
NUMERIC FORM ENGINEERING;
SAY n*2; /* displays 246.9E+3 */
NUMERIC FORM SCIENTIFIC;
SAY n*2; /* displays 2.469E+5 */
NUMERIC DIGITS 6;
SAY n*2; /* displays 246912 */
```

Example 2:
```
NUMERIC DIGITS 4;
SAY 2.004 = 2; /* displays 0 (= false) */
NUMERIC FUZZ 1;
SAY 2.004 = 2; /* displays 1 (= true) */
SAY 1.998 = 2; /* displays 0 (= false) */
```

FUZZ is equivalent to:
```
ABS(value1-value2) = 0
```

9.2.14 OPTIONS - Pass special parameters to the language processor
The OPTIONS instruction is used to pass special parameters to the language processor. The form of these parameters is implementation dependent, for example, the OPTIONS instruction is used in the MVS-TSO implementation to set the DBCS environment.

```
►►─── OPTIONS expression; ───►◄
```

9.2.15 PARSE - Assign data
The PARSE instruction assigns the source data to the specified variables. The assignment is made according the following criteria:

• words;
• delimiter;
• position.

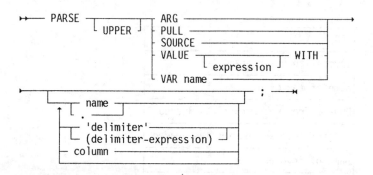

UPPER

The assigned data are converted to upper case.
Default: The case of the source data is retained.

ARG

The current argument is used as the source data. The argument is set in one of the following ways:
• argument passed to the REXX exec;
• argument passed to a routine (subroutine, procedure or function).

PULL

The entry at the head of the stack (or the input data stream, if the stack is empty) is fetched and used as the source data.

SOURCE

The current program source is used as the source data. Table 9.2 shows the program source format. Each entry is separated by a blank. "?" is set for entries where no information is available.

VAR name

name is the symbol containing the source data.

VALUE expr

The evaluation of **expr** is used as the source data.

name

Symbol to be assigned the parsed data.

Placeholder, the data are parsed but no assignment is made.

TSO
invocation of program
name of the exec
DDname from which exec was loaded
dataset from which exec was loaded
name of invoked exec
initial host environment
name of address space
user token

Table 9.2 - Program source

'delimiter'

Delimiter which is to be used as search argument for the source data. Delimiter is not restricted to being a single character.

(delimiter-expression)

A character expression which is to be used as delimiter for the source data.

column

Position at which the source data is to be split, 1 is the first position in the source data.

The column may also be a displacement, i.e. prefixed with either a ' + ' or '-' sign. This column is then relative to the last location parsed.

Comma specifies that the next argument in the source data is to be processed. This operand may only be used in conjunction with the ARG keyword.

The following non-SAA parameters are available in the TSO implementation

EXTERNAL

Data from the input data stream (terminal or input dataset) is used as the source data.

NUMERIC
The current numeric attributes (DIGITS, FORM, FUZZ) are used as the source data.

VERSION
The identifier containing REXX version information is used as the source data. Table 9.3 shows the version format (5 words).

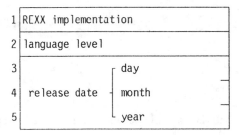

Table 5.3 - Version format

Examples:
```
CALL alpha "beta gamma";
EXIT;
alpha:
PARSE ARG a b;
SAY a b; /* displays alpha beta */
PARSE UPPER ARG a b;
SAY a b; /* displays ALPHA BETA */
RETURN;

alpha = "beta gamma";
PARSE VALUE alpha WITH a b;
SAY a b; /* display beta gamma */
```

9.2.16 PROCEDURE - Define internal procedure
The PROCEDURE instruction defines the start of an internal procedure. A procedure differs from a subroutine in that it can only be invoked explicitly and that global variables used in the procedure must be defined with the EXPOSE keyword.

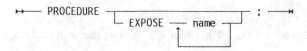

name
>   is a global variable.

Example:
```
beta = "gamma";
CALL alpha;
EXIT;
alpha: PROCEDURE;
   SAY beta; /* displays BETA */
RETURN;
```
BETA is displayed, because the variable beta is not initialised for the procedure alpha.

```
beta = "gamma";
CALL alpha;
EXIT;
alpha: PROCEDURE EXPOSE beta;
   SAY beta; /* displays gamma */
RETURN;
```
The variable beta has been exposed for procedure alpha, hence its content is available in the procedure.

9.2.17 PULL - Fetch data element from the head of the stack

The PULL instruction is equivalent to the PARSE UPPER PULL instruction. The entry at the head of the stack (or the input data stream, if the stack is empty) is fetched and used as the source data.

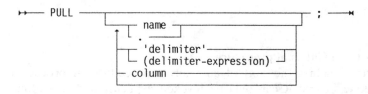

name
>   Symbol to be assigned the parsed data.

Placeholder, the data are parsed but no assignment is made.

'delimiter'

Delimiter which is to be used as search argument for the source data. Delimiter is not restricted to being a single character.

(delimiter-expression)

A character expression which is to be used as delimiter for the source data.

column

Position at which the source data is to be split, 1 is the first position in the source data.

If **column** is prefixed with either a ' + ' or '-' sign, then this column is relative to the last location parsed.

Example:
```
PULL . alpha .;
```
assigns the second word from the head of the stack to the variable alpha. Two placeholders (".") are used; one for the first word, and one for all words after the second word.

9.2.18 PUSH - Set data element at the head of the stack

The PUSH instruction places the specified data element at the head of the stack.

```
►►─── PUSH ─┬─────────────┬─ ; ───►◄
            └─ expression ─┘
```

expression

is the data element to be put into the stack.

Example:
```
PUSH "alpha";
PUSH "beta";
```
sets two entries into the stack.

9.2.19 QUEUE - Set data element at the tail of the stack
The QUEUE instruction places the specified data element at the tail of the stack.

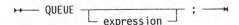

expression
> is the data element to be put into the stack.

Example:
```
QUEUE "alpha";
QUEUE "beta";
```
sets two entries into the stack.

9.2.20 RETURN - Return from routine
The RETURN instruction either:
- returns to the statement following the invoking statement; or
- exits from the exec, if the issuing routine was not invoked with CALL.

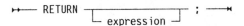

expression
> is the numeric value to be passed back to the point of invocation.

Example:
```
CALL alpha;
   ...
alpha:
   ...
   RETURN 4;
```
The value 4 is passed back to the statement following CALL alpha.

9.2.21 SAY - Display
The SAY instruction displays the specified data as terminal output.

```
►►── SAY ─┬───────────┬─ ; ──►◄
          └ expression ┘
```

expression
> is the data to be displayed. The **expression** is evaluated before being displayed.

Example:
```
    alpha = 10;
    SAY "value of alpha is:" alpha;
```
displays the message value of alpha is: 10.

9.2.22 SELECT - Conditional execution of one statement from a group of statements

The SELECT statement executes one (and only one) statement from a group of statements. A WHEN condition is specified for each statement in the group, the following THEN statement is executed if the condition is satisfied (yields a true result). The OTHERWISE group of statements is executed if none of the previous conditions has been satisfied. At least one WHEN condition must be specified. An error will be signalled if no OTHERWISE clause is present when none of the previous conditions has been satisfied.

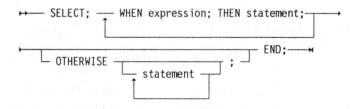

WHEN
> introduces a conditional clause.

expression
> Condition to be tested. **expression** must evaluate to either 1 (true) or 0 (false).

THEN statement
> is the statement to be performed if the WHEN **expression** evaluates to 1 (true). If more than one statement is to be performed, then a Do-group must be used. The NOP instruction can be used if no processing is to be performed.

OTHERWISE

> introduces the statements to be performed if none of the conditional clauses
> was true. The following **statements** (up to the Select END) are performed if the
> OTHERWISE clause is executed - this is an implicit Do.
> The OTHERWISE clause must be present if none of the previous WHEN clauses have
> been satisfied, even when no processing is to be done. However, the OTHERWISE
> does not need to have any entries - in such a case the NOP instruction can be
> used to emphasise that no processing is to be performed.

Example:
```
SELECT;
  WHEN alpha < 2;
    THEN SAY "alpha lt 2";
  WHEN alpha = 2;
    THEN NOP;
  OTHERWISE;
    SAY "alpha gt 2";
END;
```
This example performs processing only when alpha is not equal to 2.

9.2.23 SIGNAL - Enable (or disable) an exception condition, or cause control to be passed to a routine (or label)

The SIGNAL instruction can be used in one of three ways:

*   pass control to a routine or labelled statement;
*   enable an exception condition;
*   disable an exception condition.

If an exception condition has been enabled, then control is passed to the specified
routine should the particular exception condition occur; multiple exception
conditions can be active at any one point of time. The setting of any particular
exception condition overrides any previous setting for that condition.

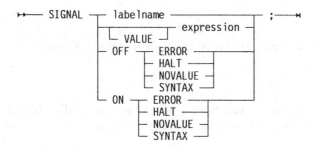

labelname

is the name of a label to which control is to be passed.

VALUE expression

specifies that the evaluated **expression** is the name of a label to which control is to be passed.

OFF

The following trap condition is disabled.

ON

The following trap condition is enabled. If the trapped condition is raised, then control is passed to the label having the condition name. For example, if the NOVALUE condition is enabled, then control is passed to the label NOVALUE if this condition is raised. A syntax error is signalled if the required label does not exist.

ERROR

The error condition (positive non-zero return from host command) is disabled or enabled according as to whether OFF or ON has been specified.

HALT

The halt condition is disabled or enabled according as to whether OFF or ON has been specified. The halt condition can be raised in several ways, for example, with the HI command.

NOVALUE

The no value condition (non-initialised variable used in a statement) is disabled or enabled according as to whether OFF or ON has been specified.

SYNTAX

The syntax condition is disabled or enabled according as to whether OFF or ON has been specified. The syntax-error condition can be raised in several ways, for example, a non-numeric value is used in an arithmetic expression.

The following additional exception condition can be enabled (disabled) in the MVS-TSO implementation.

FAILURE

> The failure condition (negative return from host command) is disabled or enabled according as to whether OFF or ON has been specified.

Example:

```
SIGNAL alpha;
SAY "beta";
alpha: SAY "gamma";
SIGNAL ON NOVALUE;
SAY delta;
EXIT;
NOVALUE: SAY "novalue raised";
EXIT;
```

displays:

```
gamma
no value raised
```

in this sequence. The **novalue** exception condition is raised by the statement SAY delta; (the variable delta has not been initialised).

9.2.23.1 SIGNAL used as GoTo

The SIGNAL instruction can be used as a GoTo, but it should not be used to cause a branch into a DO or SELECT construction - this will cause an error, see the following code segment.

```
DO i = 1 TO 5;
    IF i = 3 THEN SIGNAL a1;
a2: END;
    ...
a1: SIGNAL a2;
```

The first SIGNAL (to a1) functions correctly, the second SIGNAL (to a2) results in an error situation - the END is misplaced.

The SIGNAL target can also be a character expression - this is similar to a computed Goto.

Example:
```
target = "alpha";
SIGNAL (target||1);
```
causes control to be passed to the label alpha1.

Warning
The SIGNAL instruction having the function of an implicit branch should be used with caution. Where possible the SIGNAL instruction should be reserved for the setting (or disabling) of trap conditions.

9.2.24 TRACE - Set debugging options
The TRACE instruction is used to set the debugging option.

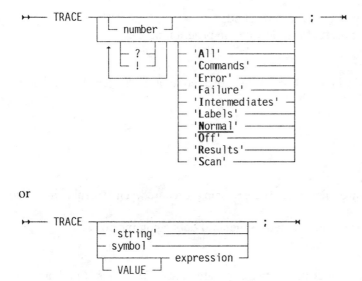

or

number
> 0 - this is the number of pauses to be bypassed;
< 0 - this is the number of trace outputs to be suppressed.

Only the first character of the following alphabetic keywords is significant.

'All'
All expressions are displayed before being executed.

'Commands'

Host commands are displayed before being executed.

'Error'

Host commands which return a non-zero code are displayed after being executed.

'Failure'

Host commands which return a negative code are displayed after being executed. This is the same as the **Normal** setting.

'Intermediate'

All expressions are displayed before being executed, intermediate results are also displayed.

'Labels'

Labels are displayed as they are reached.
Tip: This setting is useful for following the program paths.

'Normal'

Host commands which return a negative code are displayed after being executed. This is the default.

'Off'

Stop trace.

'Results'

All expressions are displayed before being executed, end results are also displayed.
Tip: This setting is recommended for general debugging purposes.

'Scan'

Check the syntax without processing the statements. *Note*: This is no longer an SAA parameter.

?

Turn on interactive debugging.

!

Suppress the execution of host commands. Return code is set to zero for each host command which would have been performed.
Tip: This setting is useful for testing a program when the host commands are either not available or erroneous.

Note: "?" and "!" are binary switches (toggles), i.e. each setting reverses the current setting of the option.

Example:
```
TRACE '?R';
```
single-steps through the program.

9.2.25 UPPER - Transform lower case characters into upper case (MVS-TSO only)

The UPPER instruction transforms the contents of the specified variables from lower case to upper case.

Note: This instruction duplicates the PARSE UPPER and TRANSLATE functions, and is available only in the MVS-TSO implementation.

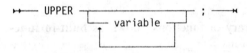

variable

     is the name of a variable which is to be transformed to upper case.

Example:
```
alpha = "beta";
SAY alpha; /* displays beta */
UPPER alpha;
SAY alpha; /* displays BETA */
```

Tip

The statement
```
UPPER alpha;
```
can be replaced with either
```
PARSE UPPER VAR alpha alpha;
```
or
```
alpha = TRANSLATE(alpha);
```

10

REXX built-in functions (SAA)

10.1 INTRODUCTION

The REXX language has an extensive library of functions known as **built-in functions**. There are two classes of built-in functions:

* those which are part of SAA (Systems Application Architecture);
* additional functions defined in the book *The Rexx Language* or in other implementations (e.g. MVS-TSO).

This chapter describes the SAA built-in functions. The non-SAA functions are described in Chapter 11.

Operands remain unchanged during the execution of the REXX function. This means that the same data field may be used as both an operand and as the result; the result is set only on completion of function. *Note*: This does not apply to exposed variables used in a user-written function.

Example:
```
alpha = COPIES(alpha,2);
```
creates an intermediate field containing two copies of alpha, and then assigns the content of this intermediate field to alpha, as depicted in the following diagram.

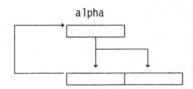

Many functions have keyword operands, of which only one letter, usually the initial letter, is significant - the significant letter is shown bold. These keyword operands may be written in either upper case or lower case. For example, the upper case operand for the DATATYPE function can be written as either 'Uppercase' or 'U', or even U. The last form (U) should not be used, as there is always the possibility that the symbol has been used as a variable somewhere else. This recommendation is not restricted to functions, all keyword operands should be written as literals.

The function invocation must include the parentheses, even when no arguments are to be passed to the function. This open-parenthesis ("(") must immediately follow the function name without any intervening blanks. If this requirement is not met, then the function name is interpreted as being a symbol.

In REXX the following conventions are adopted:
- the first position of a string is position 1;
- a word is a string of characters delimited by one or more blanks.

This book normally uses literals to simplify the examples, variables could also have been used. For example, the following three function calls are all equivalent:

```
alpha = "translate";
beta = "trans";
x = ABBREV(alpha,beta);
y = ABBREV(alpha,"trans");
z = ABBREV("translate",beta);
```

10.2 FUNCTION DEFINITIONS

- ABBREV - Test whether string is an abbreviation
- ABS - Return absolute value
- ADDRESS - Return name of current environment
- ARG - Return argument
- BITAND - Logical And
- BITOR - Logical Or
- BITXOR - Logical Exclusive-Or
- CENTRE (CENTER) - Centralise data
- COMPARE - Compare
- CONDITION - Return condition
- COPIES - Duplicate data
- C2D - Convert character data to decimal
- C2X - Convert character data to hexadecimal

- DATATYPE - Determine data type
- DATE - Return current date
- DELSTR - Delete substring
- DELWORD - Delete one or more words
- DIGITS - Return the NUMERIC DIGITS setting
- D2C - Convert decimal data to character
- D2X - Convert decimal data to hexadecimal
- ERRORTEXT - Return message text
- FORM - Determine NUMERIC FORM setting
- FORMAT - Format numeric value
- FUZZ - Determine NUMERIC FUZZ setting
- INSERT - Insert substring
- LASTPOS - Determine last position of phrase
- LEFT - Left-align string
- LENGTH - Determine length of string
- MAX - Determine the maximum of a series of numeric values
- MIN - Determine the minimum of a series of numeric values
- OVERLAY - Overlay part of a string with a phrase
- POS - Search for substring
- QUEUED - Determine the number of entries in the queue
- RANDOM - Generate a (pseudo-)random number
- REVERSE - Reverse the sequence of data
- RIGHT - Right-align string
- SIGN - Determine numeric sign
- SOURCELINE - Return "program line"
- SPACE - Insert fill-character between words
- STRIP - Remove padding-characters at the start or end of a string
- SUBSTR - Extract substring
- SUBWORD - Extract series of words from word-string
- SYMBOL - Determine the status of a symbol
- TIME - Return the current time-of-day
- TRACE - Return (and set) the current trace mode
- TRANSLATE - Translate
- TRUNC - Truncate numeric value
- VALUE - Return the content of a symbol
- VERIFY - Test whether only characters in a phrase are present in string
- WORD - Fetch word
- WORDINDEX - Determine the character position of a word in a string of words
- WORDLENGTH - Determine word length
- WORDPOS - Determine word-number of a word in word-string
- WORDS - Determine number of words in word-string
- XRANGE - Define a range of hexadecimal values
- X2C - Convert hexadecimal to character
- X2D - Convert hexadecimal to decimal

10.2.1 ABBREV - Test whether string is an abbreviation

The ABBREV function tests whether a substring is the abbreviation of a string, i.e. whether **substring** corresponds to the first characters of **string**.
The function returns:

* 1 - **substring** corresponds to **string**;
* 0 - **substring** does not correspond to **string**.

```
►►── ABBREV(string,substring ─┬──────────┬─) ──►◄
                              └ ,length ─┘
```

string
> is the string to be tested.

substring
> is the argument.

length
> is the minimum length which the argument must have.
> Default: The length of **substring**.

Example:
```
x = ABBREV("translate","trans");
y = ABBREV("translate","trans",4);
z = ABBREV("translate","transform");
```
sets x and y to 1, and z to 0.

10.2.2 ABS - Return absolute value

The ABS function returns the absolute (unsigned) value.

```
►►── ABS(number) ──►◄
```

number
> is the data to be converted.

Example:
```
x = ABS(-123);
y = ABS(4567);
```
sets x to 123 and y to 4567.

10.2.3 ADDRESS - Return the name of the current environment

The ADDRESS function returns the name of the current environment. The environment is either the default environment or that set with the ADDRESS instruction.

Note: The ADDRESS *instruction* and the ADDRESS *function* are distinguished from each other in that the function is written with parentheses.

```
►►── ADDRESS( ) ──►◄
```

Example:
```
     x = ADDRESS();
```
sets x to be the name of the current environment, e.g. TSO.

10.2.4 ARG - Return argument

The ARG function returns an argument passed to a routine. The ARG function can be used in one of four ways:
- return the number of arguments;
- return a specific argument;
- determine whether a specific argument is present;
- determine whether a specific argument is not present.

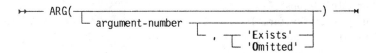

argument-number
> is the number of the argument to be returned.
> Default: The total number of arguments.

'Exists'
> Return 1 (true) if the specified argument exists.
> Return 0 (false) if the specified argument does not exist.

'Omitted'
> Return 1 (true) if the specified argument does not exist.
> Return 0 (false) if the specified argument exists.

Example:
```
    CALL alpha beta, gamma;

    ...
    alpha:
    x = ARG();
    y = ARG(1)
    z = ARG(3,'E')
```
sets

x	2	(the number of arguments)
y	beta	(the first argument)
z	0	(the third argument is not present).

10.2.5 BITAND - Logical And

The BITAND function performs a Logical And with the content of the second string on the content of the first string. The operation is performed bit by bit from left to right. The & operation (see section 2.4.4) performs a Logical And on the complete fields, which must have either 0 or 1 as content.

The following table describes the Logical And function:

```
    0 AND 0 -> 0
    0 AND 1 -> 0
    1 AND 0 -> 0
    1 AND 1 -> 1
```

string1

First string.

string2

Second string.
Default: The null string ('' or "").

pad-char

Padding character **pad-char**, if specified, is added to **string2**, if **string2** is shorter than **string1**.

Example:
```
    x = BITAND("123","22","4");
```
assigns '020' to x.

10.2.6 BITOR - Logical Or
The BITOR function performs a Logical Or with the content of the second string on the content of the first string. The operation is performed bit by bit from left to right. The | operation (see section 2.4.4) performs a Logical Or on the complete fields, which must have either 0 or 1 as content.
The following table describes the Logical Or function:

```
    0 OR 0 -> 0
    0 OR 1 -> 1
    1 OR 0 -> 1
    1 OR 1 -> 1
```

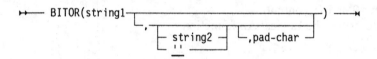

string1
> First string.

string2
> Second string.
> Default: The null string.

pad-char
> Padding character **pad-char**, if specified, is added to **string2**, if **string2** is shorter than **string1**.

Example:
```
    x = BITOR("123","22","4");
```
assigns '327' to x.

10.2.7 BITXOR - Logical Exclusive-Or (XOR)

The BITXOR function performs a Logical XOR (bit reversal) with the content of the second string on the content of the first string. The operation is performed bit by bit from left to right. The && operation (see section 2.4.4) performs a Logical Exclusive-Or on the complete fields, which must have either 0 or 1 as content.
The following table describes the Logical XOR function:

```
0 XOR 0 -> 0
0 XOR 1 -> 1
1 XOR 0 -> 1
1 XOR 1 -> 0
```

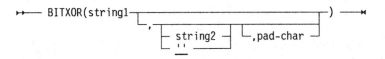

string1

    First string.

string2

    Second string.
    Default: The null string ('' or "").

pad-char

    Padding character **pad-char**, if specified, is added to **string2**, if **string2** is shorter than **string1**.

Example:
```
    x = BITXOR("123","0202"x,"04"x);
```
assigns '307' to x.

10.2.8 CENTRE (CENTER) - Centralise data

The CENTRE function centralises the specified data. The centralisation is made by filling the data to the specified length with equal numbers of padding characters on each side of the data.

Note: This function has two alternative spellings, CENTRE and CENTER, to cater for the British and American ways of spelling. The two functions are identical.

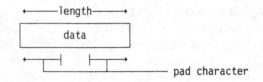

string1
>   Data to be centralised.

length
>   Length of the centralised data.

pad-char
>   Padding character.
>   Default: Blank.

Example:
>   x = CENTRE("alpha",9);
assigns ' alpha ' to x.

10.2.9 COMPARE - Compare
The COMPARE function compares two data fields. The two fields are compared character by character from left to right, a shorter field is padded on the right with the pad character. The position of the first non-equal character is returned, 0 indicates that the two data fields (padded, if necessary) are equal.

A character comparison is also made for numeric fields, e.g. COMPARE returns the not equal condition for the two numeric fields 1.2E+1 and 12, although these two fields are numerically equal).

```
▸▸──── COMPARE(string1,string2──────────────)──▸
                              └,─┬ pad-char ─┘
                                 └ ' ' ┘
```

string1
>   First data field.

string2

> Second data field.

pad-char

> Padding character.
> Default: Blank.

Example:

        x = COMPARE("translate","translation");

assigns 9 to x.

10.2.10 CONDITION - Return condition

The CONDITION function returns the specified condition. This function is usually used in an error exit to determine the cause of error.

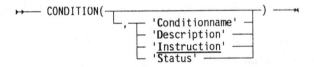

'Conditionname'

> returns the current condition, one from the list:
> * ERROR
> * FAILURE
> * HALT
> * NOVALUE
> * SYNTAX

'Description'

> returns the descriptive text associated with the condition. There may not necessarily be any descriptive text available.
>
> An example of descriptive text is the name of the symbol causing the condition.

'Instruction'

> returns the name of instruction invoking instruction, either CALL or SIGNAL. This is the default.

'Status'
> returns the status of the trapped condition, one from the list:
> - DELAY - any new occurrence is delayed;
> - OFF - the condition is disabled;
> - ON - the condition is enabled.
>
> *Note*: The status may change during the course of execution.

Chapter 7 (Debugging) contains an example of the use of the CONDITION function.

10.2.11 COPIES - Duplicate data

The COPIES function duplicates a data field.

```
►►─── COPIES(string,number) ───►◄
```

string
> Data field.

number
> is the number of copies to be created.

Example:
```
    x = COPIES("beta",2);
```
assigns 'betabeta' to x.

10.2.12 C2D - Convert character data to decimal

The C2D (character-to-decimal) function converts data to its decimal equivalent. The binary code for the data field is converted to a decimal number. The sign of the converted data is taken from the leftmost bit of the data field (padded or truncated).

Note: The C2D function is code-dependent, i.e. different results are returned in the mainframe (EBCDIC) and personal computer (ASCII) environments. For example, the upper case character 'A' has the ASCII code X'41' and the EBCDIC code X'C1'.

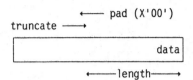

string

>   is the data field.

length

>   specifies the length of the data field. If necessary **string** will be padded on the left with hexadecimal zeros to achieve the required length. If **length** is less than the field length, **string** will be truncated from the left.

Example (EBCDIC):

```
    x = C2D("0");
    y = C2D("0",2);
```

assigns the value -240 to x (the leftmost bit of '0' (= 'F0'x) is set) and 240 to y (the leftmost bit of '0' padded to length 2 (= '00F0'x) is not set).

10.2.13 C2X - Convert character data to hexadecimal

The C2X (character-to-hexadecimal) function converts data to its hexadecimal equivalent. The hexadecimal code (two hexadecimal digits) for each character of the data field is assigned to the result field.

Note: The C2X function is code-dependent, i.e. different results are returned in the mainframe (EBCDIC) and personal computer (ASCII) environments.

```
    C2X(string)
```

string

>   is the data to be processed.

Example (EBCDIC):

```
x = C2X("0");
```

assigns F0 to x.

10.2.14 DATATYPE - Determine data type

The DATATYPE function can be used in two ways:
- return the form of the data (numeric or character, character is non-numeric);
- confirm (or otherwise) that the data is of a particular form.

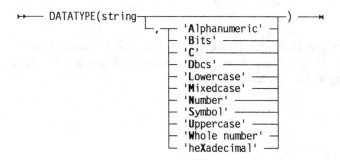

string

> The data field to be tested. The optional keyword specifies the class of data to be tested. If the data field being tested contains valid data for the specified class, 1 (true) is returned, otherwise 0 (false). If no class keyword is specified then the value NUM or CHAR is returned, depending on whether the field contains numeric data or not, respectively.
>
> Table 10.1 defines the data content for each class.

class	content	comment
'Alphanumeric'	a-z A-Z 0-9	
'Bits'	0 1	
'C'		SBCS/DBCS data
'Dbcs'		DBCS data
'Lowercase'	a-z	
'Mixedcase'	a-z A-Z	
'Number'		valid REXX number
'Symbol'		valid REXX symbol
'Uppercase'	A-Z	
'Whole number'		non-exponential number
'heXadecimal'	a-f A-F 0-9	

Table 10.1 - Class content

Example:
```
x = DATATYPE("ag",'X');
y = DATATYPE(1.2E4);
z = DATATYPE(1.2F4);
```
assigns 0 (false) to x ("g" is not a valid hexadecimal character), NUM to y, and CHAR to z (1.2F4 is not a valid number).

10.2.15 DATE - Return current date
The DATE function returns the current date in the specified format. Table 10.2 summarises the date formats.

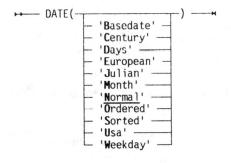

'Basedate'		days since January 1, 0001
'Century'		days since January 1, xx00
'Days'		days since January 1, xxxx
'European'	dd/mm/yy	
'Julian'	yyddd	
'Month'		month name
'Normal'	dd mon yyyy	
'Ordered'	yy/mm/dd	
'Sorted'	yyyymmdd	
'Usa'	mm/dd/yy	
'Weekday'		day name

Table 10.2 - Date formats

'Basedate'

    returns the number of days (including the current day) since January 1, 0001.

'Century'

    returns the number of days (including the current day) since January 1 of the start of the century.

'Days'

    returns the number of days (including the current day) since January 1 of the current year.

'European'

    returns the date in the European form dd/mm/yy.

'Julian'

    returns the date in the form yyddd.

'Month'

    returns the name (in English) of the current month, e.g. January.

'Normal'

    returns the date in default format: dd mon yyyy ("mon" is the 3-character English abbreviation for month, e.g. Jan for January.

'Ordered'

returns the date in the sortable format: yy/mm/dd.

'Sorted'

returns the date in the sortable format: yyyymmdd.

'Usa'

returns the date in the American form mm/dd/yy.

'Weekday'

returns the name (in English) of the current day of the week, e.g. Sunday.

Example (assuming the current date is February 2, 1990):

```
x = DATE();
y = DATE('J');
z = DATE('W');
```
assigns the following values:
```
x    '2 Feb 1990'
y    90033
z    'Friday'
```


10.2.16 DELSTR - Delete substring

The DELSTR function deletes a substring starting at the specified position from a data field.

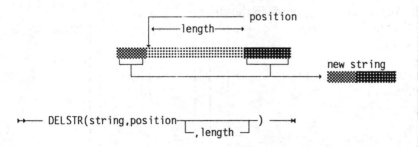

string

is the data field from which the substring is to be deleted.

position

is the starting position in the data field of the substring to be deleted. The first character in the field is at position 1.

length
>   is the length of the substring to be deleted.
>   Default: The complete data remaining in the string.

Example:
>   x = DELSTR("alpha",3,2);

returns 'ala' - position 3 = p, length 2 = ph, leaves ala.

10.2.17 DELWORD - Delete words
The DELWORD function deletes one or more words from a string of words.

```
►►─── DELWORD(string,word-number─┬──────────────┬─) ───►◄
                                 └─,word-count ─┘
```

string
>   is the data field from which the words are to be deleted.

word-number
>   is the starting position (word number) of the first word to be deleted.

word-count
>   is the number of words to be deleted.
>   Default: All the remaining words in the string.

Example:
>   x = DELWORD("a bb ccc",2,1);

returns 'a ccc'.

10.2.18 DIGITS - Return the DIGITS setting
The DIGITS function returns the current precision for numeric values, which is set using the NUMERIC DIGITS instruction.

```
►►─── DIGITS() ───►◄
```

Example:
```
    NUMERIC DIGITS 4;
    x = DIGITS();
```
assigns 4 to x.

10.2.19 D2C - Convert decimal to character

The D2C (decimal-to-character) function converts a decimal value to character
(internal code). This is equivalent to converting a decimal number to signed binary.
The sign of the binary number is propagated to the specified length.

Note: The D2C function is code-dependent, i.e. different results are returned in the
mainframe (EBCDIC) and personal computer (ASCII) environments.

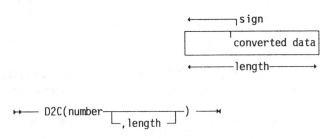

number
> is the data field.

length
> specifies the length (in characters) of the result. The sign of the input **number**
> will be propagated if necessary. An error results if no **length** is specified for a
> negative **number**.
> Default: If no **length** is specified, then the length of the result is such that no
> '00'x characters are present at the start of the result field.

Example (EBCDIC):
```
    x = D2C(240);
```
returns '0'.

10.2.20 D2X - Convert decimal to hexadecimal
The D2X (decimal-to-hexadecimal) function converts a decimal value to the hexadecimal digits representing its internal code (binary value). The sign of the binary number is propagated to the specified length.

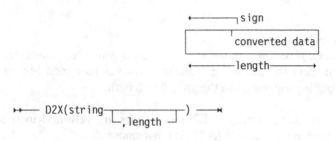

number
>   is the data field.

length
>   specifies the length (in characters) of the result. The sign of the input **number**
>   will be propagated if necessary. An error results if no **length** is specified for a
>   negative **number**.
>   Default: If no **length** is specified, then the length of the result is such that no
>   '00'x characters are present at the start of the result field.

Example:
>   x = D2X(240);
returns 'F0'.

10.2.21 ERRORTEXT - Return message text
The ERRORTEXT function returns the message text which applies to the specified message number. No text is returned for a non-existent message.

```
►►──── ERRORTEXT(error-number) ────►◄
```

Example:
>   SAY ERRORTEXT(40);
displays the message: Incorrect call to routine.

10.2.22 FORM - Determine NUMERIC FORM setting

The FORM function returns the current display form for numeric values, which is set using the NUMERIC FORM instruction.

```
►►── FORM() ──►◄
```

Example:
```
     NUMERIC FORM SCIENTIFIC;
     x = FORM();
```
returns SCIENTIFIC.

10.2.23 FORMAT - Format numeric value

The FORMAT function formats a numeric value for display. Default formatting is made when the FORMAT function is not used.

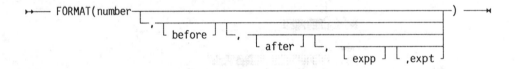

before

>　is the number of digits to be formatted before the decimal point; leading zeros (except for a single zero before the decimal point) are suppressed.

after

>　is the number of digits to be formatted after the decimal point.

expp

>　is the number of digits (places) to be used for the exponential. If omitted, the number of digits necessary to represent the exponent is used.

expt

>　is the number of digits to trigger the exponential representation.

Example:
```
     x = FORMAT("12.3",3,2)
     y = FORMAT("1234",,,2,2)
```
assigns ' 12.30', 1.234E+03 to x and y, respectively.

10.2.24 FUZZ - Determine NUMERIC FUZZ setting

The FUZZ function returns the current number of digits to be ignored for numeric comparisons, this value is set using the FUZZ function or the NUMERIC FUZZ instruction.

```
▸▸── FUZZ() ──◂
```

Example:
```
    NUMERIC FUZZ 2;
    x = FUZZ();
```
returns 2.

10.2.25 INSERT - Insert substring

The INSERT function inserts a substring into the specified position of a data field.

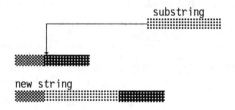

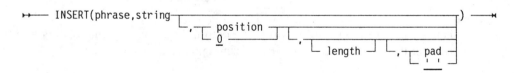

phrase

     is the data field which is to be inserted into the specified **string**.

string

     is the data field into which the **phrase** is to be inserted.

     Note: A copy, and not string itself, is altered.

position

     is the position in **string** after which **phrase** is to be inserted.

     Default. 0 (i.e. **phrase** is inserted before the start of **string**).

length

     is the length of the **phrase** to be inserted.

pad

     is the padding character to be used if the specified **length** is greater than the implicit length of phrase.

     Default: ' ' (blank)

Example:

```
x = INSERT("alpha","beta",3);
```
assigns 'beta**lpha**a' to x.

10.2.26 LASTPOS - Determine last position of phrase

The LASTPOS function determines the last position of a phrase in a string. This is done by searching backwards starting from the specified position.

0 is returned if the phrase is not found.

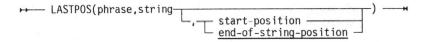

phrase

     is the data field which is to be used as search argument.

string

     is the data field to be searched.

start-position

     is the position from which the search is to started.

     Default: The last position in **string**.

Example:

```
x = LASTPOS("lt","deltaepsilon");
```
returns 3.

10.2.27 LEFT - Left-align string

The LEFT function left-aligns a string, padded if necessary.

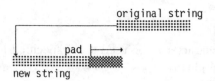

```
►►── LEFT(string,length─┬─────────┬─) ──►◄
                        └─,─┬─ pad ─┘
                            └─' '─┘
```

string

> is the data field containing the words to be aligned.
> *Note*: A copy, and not string itself, is altered.

length

> is the final length of the aligned **string**.

pad

> is the padding character to be used if the specified **length** is greater than the
> implicit length of **string**.
> Default: ' ' (blank)

Example:
```
        x = LEFT("alpha",8);
```
returns 'alpha   '.

10.2.28 LENGTH - Determine length of string

The LENGTH function returns the length of a string. The length includes any blanks at
the start or end of the string.

```
►►── LENGTH(string) ──►◄
```

string

> is the data field whose length is to be returned.

Example:
```
        x = LENGTH(" alpha  ");
```
returns 8 (includes one leading blank and two trailing blanks).

10.2.29 MAX - Determine the maximum of a series of numeric values

The MAX function returns the largest numeric (signed) value from a series of numbers. The maximum count of the numbers being processed is implementation dependent (for MVS the maximum count is 20). If more values are to be processed this can be done either by cascading or in a loop.

Cascading the MAX function:
```
      x = MAX(.,.,...);
      x = MAX(x,...);
etc.
```

Using the MAX function for an array of values:
```
      x = -999999999; /* set minimum value */
      DO i = 1 TO n;
        x = MAX(x,a.i);
      END;
```
This example assumes that the data values are in the array a. with n values.

```
►►─── MAX(─── number ──)  ──►◄
         └──── , ────┘19
```

number

        is a numeric value.

Example:
```
      x = MAX(1,-4,2);
returns 2.
```

10.2.30 MIN - Determine the minimum of a series of numeric values

The MIN function returns the smallest numeric (signed) value from a series of numbers. The maximum count of the numbers being processed is implementation dependent (for MVS the maximum count is 20). If more values are to be processed this can be done either by cascading or in a loop.

Cascading the MIN function:
```
      x = MIN(.,.,...);
      x = MIN(x,...);
etc.
```

Using the MIN function for an array of values:

```
x = 999999999; /* set maximum value */
DO i = 1 TO n;
    x = MIN(x,a.i);
END;
```

This example assumes that the data values are in the array a. with n values.

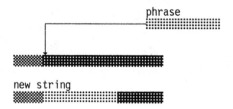

number

is a numeric value.

Example:

```
x = MIN(1,-4,2);
```

returns -4.

10.2.31 OVERLAY - Overlay part of a string with a phrase

The OVERLAY function overlays part of a string with a phrase (substring).

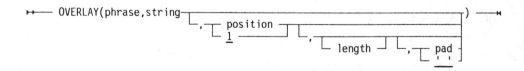

phrase

is the data field which is to overlay the specified **string**.

string

is the data field into which the **phrase** is to be overlayed.

Note: A copy, and not string itself, is altered.

position

>   is the position in **string** after which **phrase** is to be overlayed.
>   Default. 1 (i.e. **phrase** is overlayed at the start of **string**).

length

>   is the length of the **phrase** to be overlayed.
>   Default: The implicit length of **phrase**.

pad

>   is the padding character to be used if the specified **length** is greater than the
>   implicit length of phrase.
>   Default: ' ' (blank)

Example:
```
    x = OVERLAY("beta","epsilon",3);
```
returns 'ep**beta**n'

10.2.32 POS - Search for substring

The POS function searches for the first occurrence of a substring in a string.

  POS returns the first position of the substring in the searched string; 0 = substring
not found.

phrase

>   is the data field being searched for.

string

>   is the data field being searched.

start-position

>   is the starting position in **string**.
>   Default: 1.

Example:
```
    x = POS("ps","epsilonpsi",5);
```
returns 8.

10.2.33 QUEUED - Determine the number of entries in the queue (stack)

The QUEUED function returns the number of entries in the current queue.

```
►►── QUEUED() ──►◄
```

Example:
```
    "NEWSTACK";
    PUSH "alpha";
    PUSH "beta";
    x = QUEUED();
```
returns 2.

10.2.34 RANDOM - Generate a (pseudo-)random number

The RANDOM function generates a pseudo-random number (positive integer). The bounds of the generated number may be specified. A seed value may be specified for the initialisation of the random number generation process; if the same seed value is specified, then the same random number will be generated.

Tip

Even if no seed is specified the same pseudo-random number may, depending on the implementation, always be generated. If this is undesirable, then a seed value should be generated using some variable source, e.g. from the time-of-day clock.

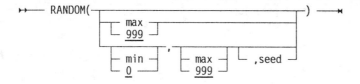

max

is a positive integer which specifies the upper limit for the generated value. Default: 999.

min

is a positive integer which specifies the lower limit for the generated value. Default: 0.

seed

is a positive integer used to initialise the random number generation process.

However, this is not the random number returned. The same random number is always generated if the same seed and bounds are specified.

Example:
```
x = RANDOM();
y = RANDOM(,,40);
```
returns two random numbers for x, and y. The random number generated for y is repeatable, i.e. the same number will always be generated.

10.2.35 REVERSE - Reverse the sequence of data
The REVERSE function reverses the sequence of data in a string, i.e. the first byte is returned as the last byte, etc.

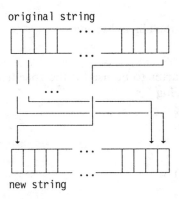

original string

new string

$\rightarrow\!\!\!\rightarrow$—— REVERSE(string) ——$\rightarrow\!\!\!\rightarrow$

string
    is the data being processed.

Example:
```
x = REVERSE("beta");
```
returns 'ateb'.

10.2.36 RIGHT - Right-align string
The RIGHT function right-aligns a string, padded if necessary.

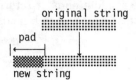

string
> is the data field containing the words to be aligned.
> *Note*: A copy, and not string itself, is altered.

length
> is the final length of the aligned **string**.

pad
> is the padding character to be used if the specified **length** is greater than the implicit length of **string**.
> Default: ' ' (blank)

Example:
> x = RIGHT("alpha",8);

returns ' alpha'.

10.2.37 SIGN - Determine numeric sign
The SIGN function returns the sign of a number:
- -1, if the number is less than 0;
- 0, if the number equals 0;
- +1, if the number is greater than 0;

```
►►── SIGN(number) ──►◄
```

number
> is the data field to be processed.

Example:
```
x = SIGN(-2);
y = SIGN(0);
z = SIGN(2);
```
returns -1, 0 and 1, respectively.

10.2.38 SOURCELINE - Return "program line"
The SOURCELINE function can be used in one of two ways:
- return the program (source file) line corresponding to the specified line number;
- return the last program line if no line number is specified.

Note: The SIGL special variable contains the source file number of the line from which a CALL or SIGNAL was invoked.

```
►►──── SOURCELINE(─┬─────────────┬─) ────►◄
                   └─ line-number ─┘
```

line-number
> specifies the line number to be retrieved from the source exec.

Chapter 7 (debugging) includes an example of the use of the SOURCELINE function.

10.2.39 SPACE - Insert fill-character between words
The SPACE function inserts the specified fill-character between words. The word-string is normalised (the string is delimited into its individual words) before the SPACE operation is performed.

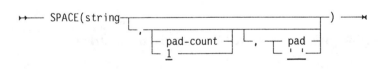

```
►►──── SPACE(string─┬──────────────────────────────────┬─) ────►◄
                    └─┬─ pad-count ─┬─ └─,─┬─ pad ─┬────┘
                      └─ 1 ─────────┘      └─' '───┘
```

string
> is the data field to be processed.

pad-count
> is the number of padding-characters (**pad**) to be placed between each word in the returned string.
> Default: 1.

pad
> is the padding-characters to be placed between each word in the returned string.
> Default: ' ' (blank).

Example:
```
    x = SPACE("a bb  c",3 ,'*');
returns 'a***bb***c'.
```

10.2.40 STRIP - Remove padding-characters at the start or end of a string
The STRIP function removes the specified fill-character at the start or end (or start and end) of a string.

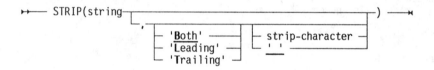

string
> is the data field to be processed.

'Both'
> The specified strip-character is removed from both the start and end of the **string**.

'Leading'
> The specified strip-character is removed from the start of the **string**.

'Trailing'
> The specified strip-character is removed from the end of the **string**.
> Default: 'Both'.

strip-character
> is the character to be removed from the **string**.
> Default: ' ' (blank).

Example:
```
    x = STRIP(" alpha  ",'L');
    y = STRIP(" alpha  ",'T');
    z = STRIP("(alpha)",,'(');
```
returns 'alpha ', ' alpha' and 'alpha)', respectively.

Tip

If parentheses (or similar paired, but non-equal, delimiters) are to be removed from string, then the STRIP function must be used twice; once on the original string to remove the leading delimiter and once on the intermediate result to remove the trailing delimiter. For example
```
    x = STRIP(alpha,'L',"(");
    x = STRIP(x,'T',")");
```
removes delimiting parentheses from the contents of alpha.

10.2.41 SUBSTR - Extract substring
The SUBSTR function extracts a substring from the specified position of a data field.

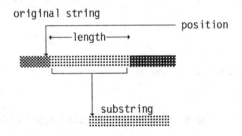

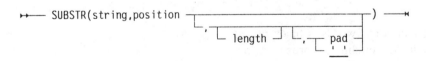

string
>   is the data field from which the substring is to be extracted.
>   *Note*: A copy, and not string itself, is altered.

position
>   is the position in **string** after which the substring is to be extracted.

length
>   is the length of the substring to be extracted.

pad
>   is the padding character to be used if the specified **length** is not entirely contained in **string**.
>   Default: ' ' (blank)

Example:
```
x = SUBSTR("alpha",3,2);
y = SUBSTR("alpha",3,4);
z = SUBSTR("alpha",3,4,'*');
```
returns 'ph' , 'pha' and 'pha*', respectively.

10.2.42 SUBWORD - Extract series of words from word-string
The SUBWORD function extracts the specified number of words from a word-string starting at the specified word number.

```
►►── SUBWORD(string,word-number ─┬──────────────┬─) ──►◄
                                 └─ ,word-count ─┘
```

string
>   is the data field to be processed.

word-number
>   is the number of the starting word in **string** from which the words are to be extracted.

word-count
>   is the number of words to be extracted.
>   Default: All remaining words in string.

Example:
```
x = SUBWORD("a bb cc ddd e",2,3);
```
returns 'bb cc ddd'.

10.2.43 SYMBOL - Determine the status of a symbol
The SYMBOL function returns the status of a symbol. This status is either:
* 'VAR' - the symbol has been assigned a value (and has not been dropped with the DROP function);

- 'LIT' - the symbol has not been assigned a value or has been dropped with the DROP function or is a literal (numeric or character);
- 'BAD' - the symbol is not a valid name. However, in many cases a REXX error (invalid expression) will be raised.

```
⊢─── SYMBOL(name) ───⊣
```

name

       is the symbol to be tested.

Example:
```
alpha = "beta";
x = SYMBOL("alpha");
y = SYMBOL(alpha);
```
returns 'VAR' and 'LIT', respectively.

10.2.44 TIME - Return the current time-of-day

The TIME function returns the current time-of-day. The time is returned in one of the specified formats. Table 10.3 summarises the time formats.

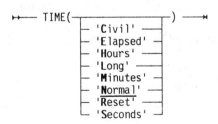

The time fields have the form:
- hh is the hour (00 through 23), except for 'Civil';
- mm is the minute (00 through 59);
- ss is the number of seconds (00 through 59);
- uuuuuu is the number of microseconds.

'Civil'	hh:mmxx	xx = AM or PM
'Elapsed'	sssssss.uuuuuu	elapsed-clock
'Hours'	hh	
'Long'	hh:mm:ss.uuuuuu	
'Minutes'	mmmm	since midnight
'Normal'	hh:mm:ss	
'Reset'	sssssss.uuuuuu	since elapsed-clock reset
'Seconds'	sssss	since midnight

hh = hours mm = minutes ss = seconds uu = microseconds

Table 10.3 - Time formats

'Civil'

returns the time of day in the form: hh:mmxx

hh is the hour (1 through 12, leading zeros are suppressed), xx is either am or pm, depending on whether the time is before midday (am) or after midday (pm). The minute is truncated, e.g. 10 minutes 59 seconds is returned as 10.

'Elapsed'

returns the time which has elapsed since the elapsed-clock was set. This time is returned in the form: sssssss.uuuuuu

The elapsed-clock is set by either the **Elapsed** or **Reset** operand.

'Hours'

returns the hours since midnight in the form: hh

'Long'

returns the time of day in the long form: hh:mm:ss.uuuuuu

'Minutes'

returns the minutes since midnight in the form: mmmm

'Normal'

returns the time of day in the default form: hh:mm:ss

'Reset'

returns the time which has elapsed since the elapsed-clock was set or reset, and resets the elapsed-clock to zero. This time is returned in the form: sssssss.uuuuuu

The elapsed-clock is set by either the **Elapsed** or **Reset** operand.

'Seconds'

returns the seconds since midnight in the form: sssss

Example:
```
x = TIME('E');
y = TIME('E');
SAY y-x;
```
displays the elapsed time since the two invocations of the TIME function, i.e. the processing time required for this function. This is equivalent to the following code (assuming the processing times for Elapsed and Reset are identical, which is probably not the case):
```
x = TIME('R');
x = TIME('E');
SAY x;
```

10.2.45 TRACE - Return (and set) the current trace mode

The TRACE function returns the current trace mode and sets the trace mode to the specified option. Chapter 7 (Debugging) contains a detailed description of the use of the TRACE function.

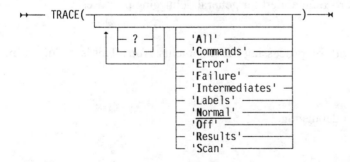

'All'

All expressions are displayed before being executed.

'Commands'

Host commands are displayed before being executed.

'Error'

>   Host commands which return a non-zero code are displayed after being executed.

'Failure'

>   Host commands which return a negative code are displayed after being executed. This is the same as the **Normal** setting.

'Intermediate'

>   All expressions are displayed before being executed, intermediate results are also displayed.

'Labels'

>   Labels are displayed as they are reached.
>   **Tip**: This setting is useful for following the program paths.

'Normal'

>   Host commands which return a negative code are displayed after being executed.

'Off'

>   Stop trace.

'Results'

>   All expressions are displayed before being executed, end results are also displayed.
>   **Tip**: This setting is recommended for general debugging purposes.

'Scan'

>   Check the syntax without processing the statements. *Note*: This is no longer an SAA parameter.

?

>   Turn on interactive debugging.

!

>   Suppress the execution of host commands. The return code is set to zero for each host command which would have been performed.
>   **Tip**: This setting is useful for testing a program when the host commands are either not available or erroneous.

Note: "?" and "!" are binary switches (toggles), i.e. each setting reverses the current setting of the option.

Example:
```
x = TRACE();
y = TRACE('0');
```
returns the current trace mode in x and y, respectively; the first invocation does not alter the trace mode, the second invocation disables tracing (option 'OFF').

10.2.46 TRANSLATE - Translate

The TRANSLATE function is used to transform the contents of the input data based on translation tables. The TRANSLATE function has two forms:
- translation tables present;
- translation tables not present.

The translation is performed character by character from left to right.

When translation tables are present, the entries in the input table (**input-table**) are replaced by the corresponding entries in the output table (**output-table**); entries which are not present remain unchanged. When translation tables are not present, the input is translated from lower case to upper case.

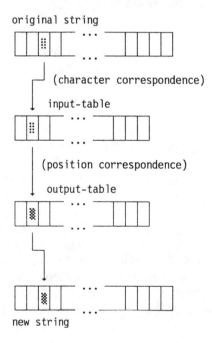

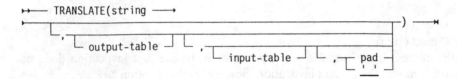

string
> is the data to be processed.

output-table
> defines the character to be substituted for the character in the same position of **input-table**.

input-table
> defines the characters to be translated. The position of the entries (characters) in this table is used as index to the entries in the **output-table**, e.g. the first entry in **input-table** indexes to the first entry in **output-table**. The first occurrence is used if the same character appears more than once.
> If a character from **string** is not present in the **input-table**, then it is passed unchanged to the function result field.

pad
> is the character to be used for padding, if **output-table** is shorter than **input-table**.
> Default: ' ' (blank).

Example:
```
x = TRANSLATE("alpha");
y = TRANSLATE("beta","34","ab");
```
returns 'ALPHA' and '4et3', respectively.

Tip
TRANSLATE is a powerful function which can often simplify processing by normalising data. For example, the TRANSLATE function is used in the following example to convert alphabetic data to upper case and replace non-alphabetic characters by an asterisk. The TRANSLATE function could be similarly used to normalise data strings to word-strings, i.e. separate words with blanks, which can then be processed using standard word-parsing functions.

```
fld = "abcIJK 123  QRS";
UpperCase = "ABCDEFGHIJKLMNOPQRSTUVWXYZ";
AllChars = UpperCase||XRANGE();   /* upper case + '00'x - 'FF'x */
fld = TRANSLATE(fld);             /* convert to upper case */
```

```
    fld = TRANSLATE(fld,UpperCase,AllChars,"*");
    SAY "fld" fld;
```
this code displays 'ABCIJK******QRS'.

10.2.47 TRUNC - Truncate numeric value

The TRUNCATE function is used to format a number to a specified number of decimal places. The NUMERIC DIGITS setting takes priority.

```
┌┼── TRUNC(number ─┬─────────────────────)──── ┤
                   └──,─┬─ decimal-places ─┘
                        └─ 0 ──────────────
```

number

      is the value to be processed.

decimal-places

      is the number of decimal (digits to the right of the decimal point) to be returned.
      Default: 0.

Example:
```
    x = TRUNC("123.45");
    y = TRUNC("123.45",3);
```
returns '123' and '123.450', respectively.

10.2.48 VALUE - Return the content of a symbol

The VALUE function returns the content of the specified symbol. This is equivalent to indirect addressing. The VALUE keyword is used in certain instructions, where it has the same meaning as this function.

```
┌┼── VALUE(name) ───┤
```

name

      is the symbol whose content is to be returned.

Example:
```
alpha = "beta";
beta = "gamma";
x = VALUE(alpha);
y = VALUE("alpha");
```
returns 'gamma' and 'beta', respectively.

10.2.49 VERIFY - Test whether only characters in a phrase are present in string

The VERIFY function returns either:

- the first position of a character in a string which is present in the specified phrase (option Match);
- the first position of a character in a string which is not present in the specified phrase (option Nomatch).

The processing is performed character by character from left to right.

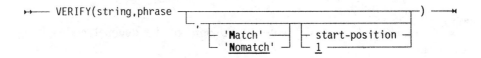

string
> is the data to be processed.

phrase
> is the data field which contains the characters to be tested.

start-position
> is the starting position.
> Default: 1.

'Match'
> The test is to be performed for the first matching character from **string** which also occurs in **phrase**.

'Nomatch'
> The test is to be performed for the first character from **string** which does not occur in **phrase**.
> Default: 'Nomatch'.

Example:
```
    x = VERIFY("beta","ab",'M');
    y = VERIFY("beta","ab",'N');
    z = VERIFY("abcabc","abcd",'N');
```
returns 1, 2 and 0, respectively.

10.2.50 WORD - Fetch word
The WORD function fetches the specified word from a word-string.

    0 is returned if the specified word number is not present in the word-string.

```
►─── WORD(string,word-number) ───►
```

string
> is the data field to be processed.

word-number
> is the number of the word in **string** to be fetched.

Example:
```
    x = WORD("a bb ccc dddd",3);
```
returns 'ccc'.

10.2.51 WORDINDEX - Determine the character position of a word in a string of words
The WORDINDEX function returns the character position of the start of the specified word number in a word-string.

    0 is returned if the specified word number is not present in the word-string.

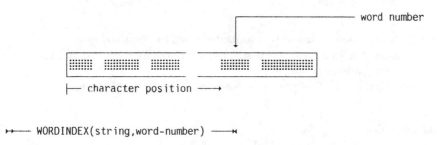

```
►─── WORDINDEX(string,word-number) ───►
```

string
>   is the word-string to be processed.

word-number
>   is the number of the word in **string** whose position is to be determined.

Example:
```
    x = WORDINDEX("a bb ccc dddd",3);
```
returns 6.

10.2.52 WORDLENGTH - Determine word length
The WORDLENGTH function returns the length of the specified word number in a word-string.
    0 is returned if the specified word number is not present in the word-string.


```
⊢⊢── WORDLENGTH(string,word-number) ──⊣
```


string
>   is the data field to be processed.

word-number
>   is the number of the word in **string** whose length is to be determined.

Example:
```
    x = WORDLENGTH("alpha beta gamma",2);
```
returns 4.

10.2.53 WORDPOS - Determine word-number of word in word-string
The WORDPOS function searches the word-string for the specified phrase and returns the corresponding word number.
    0 is returned if the specified phrase is not present in the word-string.

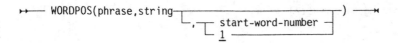

string

> is the data field to be processed.

phrase

> is the phrase to be used to search word-string.

start-word-number

> is the number of the word in **string** at which the search is start.
> Default: 1

Example:
```
    x = WORDPOS("ccc","a bb ccc dddd");
```
returns 3.

10.2.54 WORDS - Determine number of words in word-string

The WORDS function returns the number of words in a word-string.

```
►►── WORDS(string) ──►◄
```

string

> is the data field to be processed.

Example:
```
    x = WORDS("alpha beta gamma");
```
returns 3.

10.2.55 XRANGE - Define a range of hexadecimal values

The XRANGE function defines a string of character-codes lying in the range of values (including the bounds).

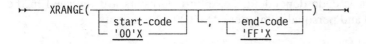

start-code
>   is the lower bound of the range.
>   Default: '00'x.

end-code
>   is the upper bound of the range.
>   Default: 'FF'x.

Note: If **end-code** is less than **start-code** wrap-around will occur.

Warning
Care should be taken with the definition of code tables, especially if the application is going to be ported to other hardware environments. The ASCII and EBCDIC codes are different, see Appendix H.
For example, the table of uppercase characters must be defined by specifying each character:

>   "ABCDEFGHIJKLMNOPQRSTUVWXYZ".

The shorter definition using the XRANGE function XRANGE('A','Z') is only valid for ASCII codes; the statement

>   XRANGE('A','I')XRANGE('J','R')XRANGE('S','Z')

would be required to yield the equivalent results in both ASCII and EBCDIC environments.

Example:

>   x = XRANGE('0','9');

defines 'F0F1F2F3F4F5F6F7F8F9'x (EBCDIC).

>   x = XRANGE('9','0');

defines 'F9FAFBFCFDFEFEFF00'x through 'F0F1F2F3F4F5F6F7F8F9'x (EBCDIC).

10.2.56 X2C - Convert hexadecimal to character

The X2C (hexadecimal-to-character) function converts a string of hexadecimal digits (0 through 9 and A through F) to the equivalent character data. The data is converted from left to right, two hexadecimal digits are used for each character.
     A 0 will be padded to the start of the input string if its length is not even.

Note: The X2C function is code-dependent, i.e. different results are returned in the mainframe (EBCDIC) and personal computer (ASCII) environments.

➤──── X2C(hex-string) ────➤

hex-string
>   is the string of hexadecimal digits to be processed.

Example (EBCDIC):
>   x = X2C("C1C2");

returns 'AB'.

10.2.57 X2D - Convert hexadecimal to decimal

The X2D (hexadecimal-to-decimal) function converts the binary representation of a string of hexadecimal digits (0 through 9 and A through F) to its equivalent decimal (numeric) value. The sign of the input hexadecimal string (truncated or padded, if necessary) is used for the result.

➤──── X2D(hex-string─┬──────────┬─) ────➤
　　　　　　　　　　　└ ,length ┘

hex-string
>   is the string of hexadecimal digits to be processed.

length
>   specifies the length (in hexadecimal digits) of the input data. The input **hex-string** is padded on the left with 0 or truncated to the specified **length**.

Example:
>   x = X2D("F0");

returns 240.

11

REXX built-in functions (non-SAA)

11.1 INTRODUCTION

The REXX language, as defined in the SAA (Systems Application Architecture) specification, omits a number of important functions, the most important being those for input/output operations. Some of these functions are defined in M.F.Cowlishaw's *The Rexx Language, A Practical Approach to Programming*. Other functions are defined for a particular implementation, sometimes these functions duplicate functions contained in the SAA specification, in other cases the function serves some purpose in the host environment.

This chapter describes the input/output functions and the other non-SAA functions found in most implementations. However, these functions are not always standardised, and so could possibly yield different results across the various REXX implementations.

The EXECIO command, although not part of the SAA specification, is more consistent than the input/output functions, which are not available in some IBM implementations.

If an equivalent SAA function is available, it should be used in preference to a non-SAA function, as for FIND and INDEX.

Appendix I summarises the functions available in each implementation.

11.2. FUNCTION DEFINITIONS

- CHARIN - Read a string of characters
- CHAROUT - Write a string of characters
- CHARS - Interrogate the status of the input stream (character mode)
- FIND - Search for word

- INDEX - Search for substring
- JUSTIFY - Justify string of words
- LINEIN - Read a line (record)
- LINEOUT - Write a line (record)
- LINES - Interrogate the status of the input stream (line mode)
- LINESIZE - Return the (maximum) width of a terminal line
- USERID - Return Userid.

11.2.1 CHARIN - Read a string of characters

The CHARIN function returns a string of characters read from the specified input stream. The characters are read byte by byte, and include any control characters (carriage-return, etc.) present.

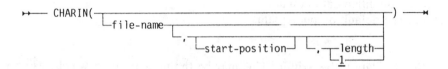

file-name

    identifies the file (dataset) from which the characters are to be read. The form of file-name is implementation-dependent, for example, in Personal REXX it is the fully qualified dataset name.

    Default: The default input stream.

start-position

    defines the position in the input stream from which the characters are to be read. 1 is the first position in the input stream.

    Default: The characters are read from the current position in the input stream.

length

    specifies how many characters are to be read. If **length** is 0, then the current pointer will be positioned according to the value specified by **start-position**, no data will be returned.

    Default. 1

Example:

    x = CHARIN("b:datafile.txt",,10);

reads 10 characters from the file B:DATAFILE.TXT starting at the current position.

11.2.2 CHAROUT - Write a string of characters

The CHAROUT function writes a string of characters onto the specified output stream. The characters are written byte by byte, and include any control characters (carriage-return, etc.) present. A non-zero value will be returned if not all the characters can be written.

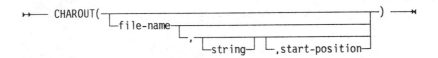

file-name

> identifies the file (dataset) on which the characters are to be written. The form of file-name is implementation-dependent, for example, in Personal REXX it is the fully qualified dataset name.
> Default: The default output stream.

string

> specifies the data to be written. This may be the null-string, in which case no data are written.

start-position

> defines the position in the output stream where the characters are to be written. The current contents will be overwritten. 1 is the first position in the output stream.
> Default: The characters are written at the current position in the output stream.

Note: If neither **string** nor **start-position** is specified, then the current position pointer will be set to the current end of the data stream.

Examples:

        x = CHAROUT("b:datafile.txt",alpha,10);

writes the contents of the variable alpha at position 10 in the file B:DATAFILE.TXT.

        x = CHAROUT("b:datafile.txt");

sets the current position pointer to the end of the file B:DATAFILE.TXT.

11.2.3 CHARS - Interrogate the status of the input stream (character mode)

The CHARS function returns the status of the specified input stream - status being whether data remain in the input stream. Certain implementations return the actual number of characters remaining. In all implementations 0 means that the input stream is empty.

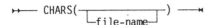

file-name
>identifies the file (dataset) from which the status is to be obtained.
>Default: The default input stream.

Example:
```
    x = CHARS("b:datafile.txt");
```
assigns a non-zero value to x if data in the file B:DATAFILE.TXT remain to be read.

11.2.4 FIND - Search for word

The FIND function searches for the first occurrence of a phrase in a string of words. FIND returns the first position of the phrase in the searched string; 0 = phrase not found.

Note: The SAA function WORDPOS is recommended.

>⊢⊢── FIND(string,phrase) ──►

string
>is the string being searched.

phrase
>is the phrase being searched for.

11.2.5 INDEX - Search for substring

The INDEX function searches for the first occurrence of a substring in a string. INDEX returns the first position of the substring in the searched string; 0 = substring not found.

Note: The SAA function POS is recommended.

```
►►── INDEX(phrase,string────────────────)──►◄
                        └,─┬ start-position ┤
                          └ 1 ─────────────
```

string
    is the string being searched.

phrase
    is the phrase being searched for.

start-position
    is the starting position in string.
    Default: 1.

Example:
```
    x = INDEX("epsilonpsi","ps",5);
```
returns 8.

11.2.6 JUSTIFY - Justify string of words
The JUSTIFY function adjusts the individual words in a string of words so that all the words are equally spaced, and the first and last words are justified to the specified bounds. The number of blanks separating words in the original string has no significance.

```
►►── JUSTIFY(string,length────────────)──►◄
                       └,─┬ pad ┤
                         └ ' ' ─
```

string
    is the string containing the words to be adjusted.
    Note: A copy, and not string itself, is altered.

length
    is the final length of the adjusted **string**.

pad
> is the padding character to be used if the specified **length** is greater than the implicit length of **string**.
> Default: ' ' (blank)

Example:
```
    x = ("a b   cc",8);
returns 'a  b  cc'.
```

11.2.7 LINEIN - Read a line (record)

The LINEIN function either returns a line (record) of character data read from the specified input stream or sets the current position pointer to the specified line (record). The line (record) is delimited according to the conventions of the host environment, any delimiting characters (e.g. carriage-return, line-feed) are not returned.

```
►►── LINEIN(─┬──────────────────────────────────┬──) ──►◄
             └─file-name─┬──────────────────────┬┘
                        '└─line-number─┘ └─,─┬─count─┬─
                                             └──1──┘
```

file-name
> identifies the file (dataset) from which the line is to be read. The form of file-name is implementation-dependent, for example, in Personal REXX it is the fully qualified dataset name.
> Default: The default input stream.

line-number
> defines the position in the input stream from which the line (record) is to be read. 1 is the first line (record) in the input stream.
> Default: The line (record) is read from the current position in the input stream.

count
> is either 0 or 1.
> • 1 - a line (record) is to be read;
> • 0 - the current position pointer is to be positioned to the start of the line identified by **line-number**.
> Default. 1

Example:
```
x = LINEIN("b:datafile.txt",10,0);
```
positions the current position pointer in the file B:DATAFILE.TXT at line 10.

11.2.8 LINEOUT - Write a line (record)

The LINEOUT function writes either a line (record) of character data onto the specified output stream or sets the current position pointer to the end of the specified output stream. A non-zero value will be returned if the line cannot be written. The line (record) will be delimited according to the conventions of the host environment, any necessary delimiting characters (e.g. carriage-return, line-feed) will be generated.

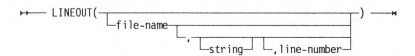

file-name
>   identifies the file (dataset) on which the line is to be written. The form of file-name is implementation-dependent, for example, in Personal REXX it is the fully qualified dataset name.
>   Default: The default output stream.

string
>   specifies the data to be written. This may be the null-string, in which case no data are written.

line-number
>   defines the position in the output stream at which the line (record) is to be written. 1 is the first line (record) in the output stream.
>   Default: The line (record) is written at the current position in the output stream.

Note: If neither **string** nor **start-position** is specified, then the current position pointer will be set to the current end of the data stream.

Example:
```
x = LINEOUT("b:datafile.txt",10,0);
```
positions the current position pointer in the file B:DATAFILE.TXT at line 10.

11.2.9 LINES - Interrogate the status of the input stream (line mode)

The LINES function returns the status of the specified input stream. The status is either:

    0   the input stream is empty; or

    >0   there are still lines (records) in the input stream. Certain implementations return the actual number of lines remaining.

```
┣━━ LINES(─────────────┬─) ───┫
              └─file-name─┘
```

file-name

    identifies the file (dataset) from which the status is to be obtained.

    Default: The default input stream.

Example:
```
x = LINES("b:datafile.txt");
```
assigns a non-zero value to x if lines in the file B:DATAFILE.TXT remain to be read.

11.2.10 LINESIZE - Return the (maximum) width of a terminal line

The LINESIZE function returns the maximum width of a terminal line.

```
┣━━ LINESIZE() ───┫
```

Example:
```
x = LINESIZE();
```
assigns the maximum width of a terminal line to the variable x.

11.2.11 USERID - Return Userid

The USERID function returns the job identifier. This identifier is dependent on the current environment:

- TSO - userid;
- MVS - userid (if present), or
     stepname (if present), or
     jobname (if present).
- Personal REXX - the value set to the USERID environmental value.

12

Host REXX commands

12.1 INTRODUCTION

Each REXX implementation has a number of extensions which do not belong to the SAA definition of the REXX language - these are known as **host REXX commands**. This chapter describes the MVS-TSO implementation.

The result or status of the host REXX command is set into the RC special variable.

12.2 HOST REXX COMMAND DEFINITIONS

- DELSTACK - Delete stack
- DROPBUF - Release buffer
- EXECIO - Perform input/output operation
- EXECUTIL - Specify execution environment for REXX program
- HI (Halt Interpretation)
- HT (Halt Typing)
- MAKEBUF - Create new buffer in the stack
- NEWSTACK - Create a new stack
- QBUF (Query Buffer) - Return the number of buffers in the current stack
- QUERY - Return number of elements in the current buffer
- QSTACK (Query Stack) - Return the current number of stacks
- RT (Resume Typing)
- SUBCOM - Confirm the host environment
- TE (Trace End)
- TS (Trace Start)

12.2.1 DELSTACK - Delete stack

The DELSTACK command deletes the most recently created stack. If no stack has been created (with the NEWSTACK command), then all elements from the original stack are deleted.

▸▸─── DELSTACK ───◂

Example:
```
"DELSTACK";
```

12.2.2 DROPBUF - Release buffer

The DROPBUF command deletes the specified buffer (and its elements) from the current stack. Buffers are created with the MAKEBUF command.

The RC special variable is set to contain the return code:
- 0   successful completion;
- 1   the buffer number is invalid;
- 2   the buffer number does not exist.

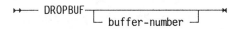

buffer-number
> is the number of the first buffer to be deleted. This buffer and all higher numbered (newer) buffers are deleted.
> Default: The most recently created buffer is deleted.

Example:
```
"DROPBUF 4";
```
deletes buffer number 4 and all newer buffers from the current stack.

12.2.3 EXECIO - Perform input/output operation

The EXECIO command performs the specified input/output operation. One of the following operations may be performed:
- read;
- read for update;
- write.

The read for update operation is not supported in some implementations.

The EXECIO command is primarily concerned with processing at the file level, although single records or groups of records can also be processed. The processed records are stored or taken from either:
• the current stack;
• a stem variable.

When records are read into the stack, these records may be placed either at the head (FIFO) or tail (LIFO) of the stack, or ignored (SKIP). Ignored records are read but not stored.

A record which has been read for update (DISKRU option) may be rewritten (updated) by an immediately following write operation (DISKW option). Only a single record may be stored for update. An option is available to close the dataset after the last record has been processed (FINIS parameter).

The dataset to be processed must have been previously allocated, using either the TSO ALLOC command or the JCL DD statement.

The record formats may be either:
• fixed (blocked);
• variable (blocked);
provided that such formats are supported in the host environment.

The RC special variable is set to contain the return code:

0	successful completion;
1	data was truncated during the DISKW operation;
2	end of file has been reached for a read operation;
20	a severe error has occurred.

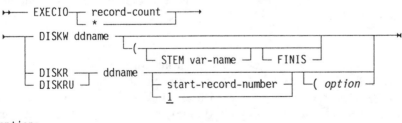

option:

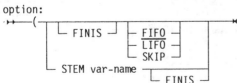

Note: The MVS implementation allows a right-parenthesis (")") at the end of the option list. This delimiter is invalid in other implementations, and should be omitted if compatibility is required.

record-count
> Number of records to be processed. Processing is also terminated when by a null entry.

*
> The complete dataset is read or the complete buffer is written, or until the first null entry is reached.

DISKW
> The dataset is to be written.

DISKR
> The dataset is to be read.

DISKRU
> The dataset is to be read for update. In update mode only a single record may be read. If this DISKRU operation is followed (without any intervening input/output operations for this file) by a DISKW operation, then this dataset record will be updated.

ddname
> identifies the dataset set to be processed. The **ddname** is the filename previously allocated with a TSO ALLOC statement or the DD-name specified by a JCL DD statement.

STEM var-name
> specifies that the records are read or written into or from stem variables, as appropriate. **var-name** appended with the entry number contains the record, e.g. for STEM alpha. the records are in alpha.1, alpha.2, etc. **var-name** does not necessarily need to be defined with a period, e.g. for STEM alpha the records are in alpha1, alpha2, etc. **var-name0** (e.g. alpha.0 for STEM alpha) is set to contain the number of stored records; **var-name0** is not used for output files.

FINIS
> specifies that the dataset is to be closed on completion of processing.

start-record-number
> specifies the first record which is to be written from the stem variables or stack. Default: 1.

FIFO

> specifies that the records are to be stored at the head of the stack (first-in first-out). This is the default.

LIFO

> specifies that the records are to be stored at the end (tail) of the stack (last-in first-out).

SKIP

> specifies that the specified number of records are to be skipped, i.e. read but not stored.

Example:
```
"EXECIO * DISKR FILEIN (STEM A.)";
```
In this the complete dataset with the file name (DDname) FILEIN is read, the records are stored in A.1, A.2 etc. A.0 is set to contain the number of records read.

12.2.4 EXECUTIL - Specify execution environment for REXX program

The EXECUTIL command specifies the execution (TSO) environment for the REXX exec. The EXECUTIL command can be:
* used in a REXX exec;
* used from TSO (or CLIST).

The EXECUTIL command can be used to:
* specify whether the system exec library is to be closed after the exec has been loaded;
* specify whether the system exec library is to be searched in addition to the system procedures library;
* specify whether tracing is to be started or stopped;
* specify whether terminal output is to be suppressed or resumed after having been stopped.

The two-character codes (e.g. HT) can be also invoked interactively.

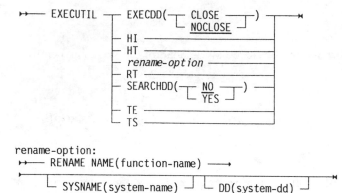

```
rename-option:
▸▸─── RENAME NAME(function-name) ───▸
 ▸─────────────────────────────────────────────────────────────────◂
        └ SYSNAME(system-name) ┘  └ DD(system-dd) ┘
```

EXECDD

specifies whether the system exec library is to be closed after the exec has been loaded.
(CLOSE) - close the system exec library.
(NOCLOSE) - do not close the system exec library.
Default: NOCLOSE.

HI

Halt Interpretation - terminate the execution of all execs that are currently running.

HT

Halt Typing - suppress SAY output.

RENAME

is used to change entries in the function package directory. This is a specialised function normally used only by system administrators, and is not described in this book.

RT

Resume Typing - restart SAY output.

SEARCHDD

specifies whether the system exec library is to be searched in addition to the system procedure library.
YES - the system exec library (SYSEXEC) is to be searched before the system procedure library (SYSPROC) is searched.
NO - the system exec library is to not be searched.
Default: NO.

TE

    Trace End - terminate tracing.

TS

    Trace Start - initiate tracing.

Example:
    "EXECUTIL SEARCHDD(YES)";
specifies that the system exec library (SYSEXEC) is to be searched for the exec.

12.2.5 HI (Halt Interpretation)
Terminate the execution of all execs that are currently running.

    ⊢⊢── HI ──⊣

Example:
    "HI";
terminates execution.

12.2.6 HT (Halt Typing)
Suppress SAY output.

    ⊢⊢── HT ──⊣

Example:
    "HT";
terminates typing.

12.2.7 MAKEBUF - Create new buffer in the stack
The MAKEBUF command creates a new buffer in the current stack. The stack initially contains one buffer, buffer 0. Each invocation of MAKEBUF increases the number of buffers in the current stack. Buffers are removed with the DROPBUF command. New stacks are created with the NEWSTACK command.

The number of the new buffer is returned in the RC special variable. The QBUF command can be used to obtain the number of buffers in the current stack.

⊢⊢─── MAKEBUF ───▸

Example:
```
"NEWSTACK";
"MAKEBUF";
x = RC;
"MAKEBUF";
y = RC;
```
assigns 1 and 2 to x and y, respectively.

12.2.8 NEWSTACK - Create a new stack

The NEWSTACK command creates a new stack, which then becomes the current stack. The DELSTACK command deletes the current stack (and all entries in it) and reverts the current stack to being the previous stack. The stack is only available to execs running in the environment which created it.

The QSTACK command can be used to obtain the number of entries in the current stack.

⊢⊢─── NEWSTACK ───▸

Example:
```
"NEWSTACK";
```
creates a new stack.

12.2.9 QBUF (Query Buffer) - Return the number of buffers in the current stack

The QBUF command returns the number of buffers created in the current stack with the MAKEBUF command. This number is returned in the RC special variable.

⊢⊢─── QBUF ───▸

Example:
```
"QBUF";
SAY RC;
```
displays the current number of buffers.

12.2.10 QELEM (Query Elements) - Return the number of elements in the current buffer

The QELEM command returns the number of elements in the buffer most recently created with the MAKEBUF command. This number is returned in the RC special variable.

```
>>── QELEM ──><
```

Example:
```
"QELEM";
SAY RC;
```
displays the number of elements (entries) in the current buffer.

12.2.11 QSTACK (Query Stack) - Return the current number of stacks

The QSTACK command returns the current number of stacks in existence. This number is returned in the RC special variable.

One stack always exists when the exec is invoked. Additional stacks are created with the NEWSTACK command. Stacks are deleted with the DELSTACK command.

```
>>── QSTACK ──><
```

Example:
```
"QSTACK";
SAY RC;
```
displays the number of stacks.

12.2.12 RT (Resume Typing)

Resume SAY output.

```
>>── RT ──><
```

Example:
>   "RT";
resumes SAY output.

12.2.13 SUBCOM - Confirm the host environment
The SUBCOM command sets the status as to whether the invoking exec is in the specified host environment.

The status is returned in the RC special variable:
>   0   the exec is running in the specified environment;
>   1   the exec is *not* running in the specified environment.

Warning
The value returned is not true (1) or false (0) as might be expected.

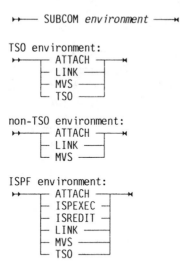

Example:
>   "SUBCOM TSO";
>
>   IF RC = 0 THEN SAY "TSO active";
displays the message TSO active if the TSO environment is active.

12.2.14 TE (Trace End)
Terminate tracing.

Example:
    "TE";
terminates tracing.

12.2.15 TS (Trace Start)
Initiate tracing.

   ⊷──── TS ────⊷

Example:
    "TS";
initiates tracing.

13

MVS command functions

13.1 INTRODUCTION

Each REXX implementation has a number of functions pertaining to the host environment. The MVS host environment commands described in this chapter are, with the exception of the STORAGE command, CLIST statements. Other host environment commands may be invoked in the normal (REXX) way, see section 13.2.8.

MVS command functions are called in the same way as REXX functions. All MVS command functions described in this chapter set a **function code**, which is returned to the point of invocation. The function code is either the status code or data returned by the command, as appropriate.

13.2 MVS COMMAND FUNCTION CALLS

- LISTDSI* - List (obtain) dataset information;
- MSG* - Set (interrogate) CLIST CONTROL MSG option;
- OUTTRAP* - Trap TSO display output;
- PROMPT* - Set (interrogate) CLIST CONTROL PROMPT option;
- STORAGE - Set (interrogate) main storage content;
- SYSDSN* - Request dataset status;
- SYSVAR* - Fetch TSO system variable;
- Invocation of other TSO commands.

* indicates that the MVS command function can only be used in the TSO environment.

Table 13.1 shows the equivalent TSO CLIST component.

LISTDSI		LISTDSI
MSG		CONTROL [NO]MSG
OUTTRAP	variable	&SYSOUTTRAP, &SYSOUTMAX
PROMPT		CONTROL [NO]PROMPT
STORAGE		-
SYSDSN	variable	&SYSDSN
SYSVAR	variable	see command description

[ ] indicate an optional item

Table 13.1 - Equivalent TSO CLIST components

Several MVS command functions used in the TSO environment require a dataset name. In TSO the dataset name has two possible forms:

- fully qualified, enclosed within quotes;
- user dataset, to which the user's prefix is appended as first qualifier.

To avoid fully qualified dataset names being processed as REXX literals, such dataset names must be enclosed within either paired single quotes (') or double quotes ("). This is illustrated in the following example:

```
x = SYSDSN("'sys1.maclib'");
```
specifies the fully qualified dataset name 'SYS1.MACLIB',
whereas
```
x = SYSDSN('sys1.maclib');
```
specifies the user's dataset SYS1.MACLIB.

Similarly, certain MVS command functions have parameters with subparameters contained within parentheses. Such terms must be defined as a REXX literal so that they themselves are not processed as a (non-existent) function. This is illustrated in the following example.

```
x = LISTDSI(alpha 'VOLUME(DISK00)');
```
If VOLUME(DISK00) were specified without the enclosing quotes it would be interpreted as the invocation of the function VOLUME with argument DISK00.

Arguments passed to MVS command functions are subject to the usual REXX syntax rules, e.g. terms not enclosed within quotes are processed as symbols. In the following example the dataset name passed to the LISTDSI command function is the contents of the variable alpha, i.e. beta.

```
alpha = 'beta';
x = LISTDSI(alpha);
```

The following statement is required to pass the dataset name alpha to the LISTDSI command function:

```
x = LISTDSI('alpha');
```

13.2.1 LISTDSI - List (obtain) dataset information
The LISTDSI command function returns information pertaining to a dataset as REXX variables. The LISTDSI command function can be used in one of two ways:

- using dataset name;
- using file (DD) name.

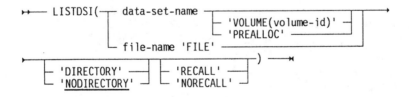

data-set-name
> is the name of the dataset to be processed. The form of **data-set-name** conforms to the usual TSO conventions, i.e. a dataset name written without enclosing quotes has the user's TSO prefix appended.

VOLUME(vol-id)
> This operand is only required for datasets which are not catalogued; **vol-id** is the name of the volume on which the dataset resides.

'PREALLOC'
> specifies that a preallocation of the dataset is to be used if possible.

file-name
> is the name of the file to be processed. File in this context is the DD statement. This **file-name** must have been previously allocated.

'FILE'

is the keyword denoting that the previous operand is the name of a file.

'DIRECTORY'

specifies that the directory of a partitioned dataset is to be read in order that directory information (SYSADIRBLK, SYSUDIRBLK and SYSMEMBERS) can be obtained. *Note*: This processing can be relatively time-consuming for large directories, and so should be specified only when the directory information is required.

'NODIRECTORY'

specifies that no directory information is to be returned.
Default: NODIRECTORY.

'RECALL'

specifies that a dataset migrated with DFHSM (Data Facility Hierarchical Storage Manager) is to be restored.

'NORECALL'

specifies that a dataset migrated with DFHSM is to not be restored.

If neither RECALL nor NORECALL is specified, then a dataset is restored only if it has been migrated to a direct access storage device.

The following variables are set:

SYSDSNAME	dataset name
SYSVOLUME	volume serial number
SYSUNIT	unit name
SYSDSORG	dataset organisation: PS, PSU, DA, DAU, IS, ISU, PO, POU, VS(am) ??? (= unknown)
SYSRECFM	record format: U, F[B][A|M], V[B][A|M] ? (= unknown)
SYSLRECL.	record length
SYSBLKSIZE	block length
SYSKEYLEN	key length
SYSALLOC	allocation (in space units)
SYSUSED	space used (in space units)
SYSPRIMARY	primary allocation (in space units)
SYSSECONDS	secondary allocation (in space units)
SYSUNITS	space unit: CYLINDER, TRACK, BLOCK, ? (= unknown)
SYSEXTENTS	number of extents
SYSCREATE	date created (yyyy/ddd)
SYSREFDATE	date last referenced (yyyy/ddd)
SYSEXDATE	expiry date (yyyy/ddd)

SYSUPDATED	dataset updated: YES or NO
SYSTRKSCYL	number tracks per cylinder
SYSBLKSTRK	number blocks per track
SYSADIRBLK	number of allocated directory blocks
SYSUDIRBLK	number of used directory blocks
SYSMEMBERS	number of directory members

Note:
- The directory information is returned only when the DIRECTORY parameter is specified.
- Only limited information is returned for VSAM datasets (the TSO LISTC command, invoked in REXX by the instruction ADDRESS TSO "LISTC", returns comprehensive information).

One of the following function codes is returned:

0	successful completion;
4	some dataset (directory) information is not available;
16	severe error.

Example:
```
x = LISTDSI('EX.ISPCLIB' 'DIRECTORY');
SAY "number of members" SYSMEMBERS;
```
displays the number of members which can be stored in the directory of the user's EX.ISPCLIB partitioned dataset. x is assigned the LISTDSI return code.

Note the usage of quotes used in the above example. The quotes for 'EX.ISPCLIB' and 'DIRECTORY' are used by REXX to denote alphanumeric literals. If an explicit dataset name, i.e. a dataset name which is not to be prefixed with the user's TSO prefix, then two levels of quotes are required. This is shown in the following example.

```
x = LISTDSI("'SYS1.MACLIB"');
```
or
```
x = LISTDSI('''SYS1.MACLIB''');
```

13.2.2 MSG - Set (interrogate) CLIST CONTROL MSG option
The MSG command function can be used in two ways:

- return the current CONTROL MSG status (as function code), and
- set the CONTROL MSG status (optional).

```
 ⊷── MSG(─┬──────┬─) ──⊶
          ├ 'OFF' ┤
          └ 'ON' ─┘
```

'OFF'

      sets the MSG status OFF, i.e. messages issued from TSO commands will be suppressed.

'ON'

      sets the MSG status ON, i.e. any messages issued by TSO commands will be displayed.

If no argument is specified, then the current MSG setting remains unchanged.

The function code is returned with the current MSG setting.

Example:

      x = MSG('ON')

x is assigned the current MSG status, and MSG is set ON (irrespective of the previous status).

13.2.3 OUTTRAP - Trap TSO display output

The OUTTRAP command function is used to trap the TSO output that would normally be displayed on the terminal. The OUTTRAP command function can be used in one of three ways:

- return the name of the stem variable in which the trapped output is to be stored (no arguments);
- disable trapping (OFF option), i.e. subsequent TSO output will be displayed normally;
- set the trapping options.

Note: Only TSO output issued with the PUTLINE macro using the OUTPUT keyword can be trapped.

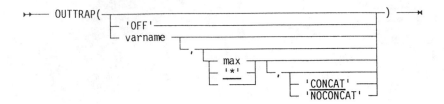

'OFF'

> The trapping of TSO display output is to be disabled, i.e. TSO display output is to be displayed normally.

varname

> is the name of the stem variable which is to contain the trapped TSO display output. The form of **varname** determines how the trapped data is accessed.

max

> is the maximum number of lines which can be trapped, any additional TSO output will be ignored.

'*' or blank

> The complete TSO output will be trapped. This is the default.

'CONCAT'

> The trapped output will be appended to the end of any output which has been previously trapped.

'NOCONCAT'

> The trapped output will overwrite any output which has been previously trapped, i.e. the first line of trapped output from each TSO command will be stored in the first stem variable, etc.
>
> Default: CONCAT

The OUTTRAP command function sets the following variables:

varname0   The number of lines that have been actually trapped.

varnameMAX   The maximum number of lines which can be trapped - this is a parameter passed to the OUTTRAP command function.

varnameTRAPPED   The number of lines which have been intercepted. The difference between **varname**TRAPPED and **varname**0 is the number of output lines which have been lost.

varnameCON   The status of the concatenation option, either CONCAT or NOCONCAT.

Examples:
```
x = OUTTRAP(alpha.,,'NOCONCAT');
ADDRESS TSO "TIME";
SAY alpha.0 alpha.1;
```
```
            │          └──────────→ 1st output line
            └──────────────────────→ actual number of trapped output lines
```

```
x = OUTTRAP();
```
returns the name of the stem variable to be used for trapping TSO display output; in the previous example this is alpha., the variable alpha.CON contains NOCONCAT.

```
x = OUTTRAP('OFF');
```
disables the trapping of TSO display output.

13.2.4 PROMPT - Set (interrogate) CLIST CONTROL PROMPT option

The PROMPT command function can be used in two ways:

- return the current CONTROL PROMPT status (as function code), and
- set the CONTROL PROMPT status (optional).

```
►►──── PROMPT(──────┬──────────┬──)  ────►◄
                    ├─ 'OFF' ──┤
                    └─ 'ON'  ──┘
```

'OFF'

sets the PROMPT status OFF, i.e. TSO commands cannot prompt for any missing information, a TSO command which needs additional information will fail.

'ON'

sets the PROMPT status ON, i.e. TSO commands can prompt for any missing information.

If no argument is specified, then the current PROMPT setting remains unchanged.

The function code is returned with the current PROMPT setting.

Example:
```
x = PROMPT('ON');
ADDRESS TSO "LISTC";
```
will prompt for the name of the dataset to be processed by the TSO LISTC command.

13.2.5 STORAGE - Set (interrogate) main-storage content
The STORAGE command function is used to interrogate (return) the contents of the specified main-storage address and to optionally change the content. This command function should only be used by specialists, and so is not described in this book.

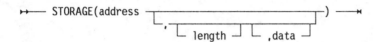

13.2.6 SYSDSN - Request dataset status
The SYSDSN command function is used to obtain the status of a catalogued dataset (or member).

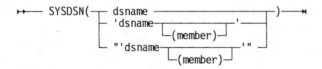

dsname
>   is the name of the dataset to be processed.

member
>   is the name of the member of the partitioned dataset (**dsname**) to be processed.

If the dataset name is fully qualified, then it must be written in the form shown in the following example:
```
x = SYSDSN("'sys1.maclib(alpha)'");
```
which tests whether the member ALPHA is present in the 'SYS1.MACLIB' partitioned dataset.

The function code is returned with text describing the status of the dataset (and member, if specified). The following text can be returned:

OK	**dsname** (and **member**, if specified) are present
DATASET NOT FOUND	dataset **dsname** is not present
MEMBER NOT FOUND	**member** is not present in **dsname**
MEMBER SPECIFIED BUT DATASET IS NOT PARTITIONED	a member name may not be specified for a non-partitioned dataset
ERROR PROCESSING REQUESTED DATASET	an error was detected during the processing of **dsname**
PROTECTED DATASET	the user is not authorised to process **dsname** (RACF protection)
VOLUME NOT ON SYSTEM	the volume containing the catalogued dataset is not currently mounted
INVALID DATASET NAME, **dsname**	the form of **dsname** is invalid
MISSING DATASET NAME	no dataset name has been specified
UNAVAILABLE DATASET	another user is currently processing **dsname**.

Example:

```
x = SYSDSN('jcl.cntl');
```

assigns x with the text describing the status of the user's dataset jcl.cntl (e.g. OK, DATASET NOT FOUND).

13.2.7 SYSVAR - Fetch TSO system variable

The SYSVAR command function is used to return a TSO system variable. Table 13.3 lists non-supported CLIST variables and how the equivalent information can be retrieved in REXX.

```
┣━━ SYSVAR(sysvarname) ━━┫
```

sysvarname
      is the name of the TSO system variable to be retrieved. Table 13.2 lists the

available TSO system variable names with their equivalent CLIST variable
name.

SYSPREF	&SYSPREF
SYSPROC	&SYSPROC
SYSUID	&SYSUID
SYSLTERM	&SYSLTERM
SYSWTERM	&SYSWTERM
SYSENV	&SYSENV
SYSICMD	&SYSICMD
SYSISPF	&SYSISPF
SYSNEST	&SYSNEST
SYSPCMD	&SYSPCMD
SYSSCMD	&SYSSCMD
SYSCPU	&SYSCPU
SYSLRACF	&SYSLRACF
SYSRACF	&SYSRACF
SYSSRV	&SYSSRV
SYSTSOE	TSO/E Level

Table 13.2 - TSO system variables

&SYSDATE	DATE('usa')
&SYSDLM	-
&SYSJDATE	DATE('julian')
&SYSSDATE	DATE('ordered')
&SYSSTIME	SUBSTR(TIME('normal'),1,5)
&SYSTIME	TIME()

Table 13.3 - Non-supported CLIST variables

13.2.8 Invocation of other TSO commands

Other TSO commands can be invoked from the TSO environment using the ADDRESS
TSO instruction.

```
►►─── ADDRESS TSO "tso-command" ───►◄
```

The RC special variable is set to contain the command return code (equivalent to the CLIST &LASTCC variable); -3 is returned if the command cannot be invoked.

Example:
```
        ADDRESS TSO "LISTDS (EX.ISPPLIB) MEMBERS";
```
invokes the TSO LISTDS command to return the members of the user's EX.ISPPLIB dataset.

14

REXX implementations

14.1 INTRODUCTION

The REXX language has been implemented in a number of hardware and software environments, both SAA and non-SAA. One of the strengths of REXX is the availability of interfaces to other components in the respective host environments. This chapter discusses these interfaces for the following implementations:

- MVS-TSO/E
- REXX/2 (Operating System/2)
- Personal REXX (DOS)

In all cases the control statements necessary to process the following REXX exec, called BETA, are used as example.

```
/* REXX */
PARSE ARG operand1 operand2;
PARSE PULL operand3;
x = operand1*operand2/operand3;
SAY x;
```

Two parameters, 12 and 4, are passed to BETA. BETA fetches one further data item from the terminal (or equivalent) with the PARSE PULL instruction. The SAY instruction is used to display the result of dividing the product of the two invocation parameters (operand1 and operand2) by the pulled operand (operand3).

14.2 MVS-TSO/E IMPLEMENTATION

The MVS-TSO/E implementation allows a REXX exec to run in several environments, both dialogue and batch. From within this invoking environment the ADDRESS instruction can be used to select a sub-environment for non-REXX statements. This sub-environment is the interface to other components, for example, the ISPEXEC sub-environment for ISPF Dialog Manager services.

REXX programs must have a commentary containing the word REXX in the first line to distinguish them from normal command procedures (CLISTs).

14.2.1 Invocation
A REXX program can be invoked from:

- TSO/ISPF dialogue
- TSO batch
- MVS batch.

The REXX program is stored as member of a partitioned dataset (library). The name of this dataset must be made available to the REXX interpreter.

14.2.1.1 TSO/ISPF dialogue invocation
REXX programs can be invoked from either TSO native mode or from ISPF. The REXX program to be invoked must have been stored as member in the library to be accessed.

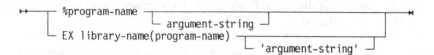

```
►►─┬──── %program-name ──┬────────────────────────┬───────────►◄
   │                     └── argument-string ──┘                │
   └── EX library-name(program-name) ─┬─────────────────────────┘
                                       └── 'argument-string' ──┘
```

EX

specifies that the library containing the REXX exec to be invoked is specified explicitly.

If EX is not specified, then the REXX program is loaded from either the SYSEXEC or the SYSPROC file - SYSEXEC takes precedence. In this case the **program-name** should be preceded by "%" to avoid searching the command (load) library.

library-name
> specifies the dataset name of the library containing the REXX exec. If the dataset name is not fully qualified (i.e. not enclosed within quotes), then the user's TSO prefix is set as first qualifier in front of the specified **library-name**, and CLIST is set as final qualifier (unless it has been specified).

program-name
> The name of the exec to be executed.

argument-string
> Arguments to be passed to the program.

Example:
```
%BETA 12 4
```
The REXX exec BETA is invoked from the library assigned to SYSEXEC or SYSPROC, and is passed the parameter "12 4".

14.2.1.2 TSO batch invocation

The TSO terminal monitor program (IKJEFT01) can also be invoked as a batch job. REXX programs can then be invoked in the normal manner. Terminal input and output is made from or to a file, respectively.

IKJEFT01 requires the following control statements:

- SYSEXEC or SYSPROC file (DDname), is the library containing the REXX program to be executed.
- SYSTSPRT file (DDname), is the dataset to contain TSO terminal output and output produced with the SAY instruction.
- SYSTSIN file (DDname), is the dataset which contains command input for batch TSO and the (terminal) input required by the PULL instruction. The command to invoke the REXX exec is contained in this dataset.

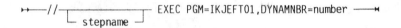

```
 ►──//─┬──────────┬─ EXEC PGM=IKJEFT01,DYNAMNBR=number ──►
       └ stepname ┘
```

stepname
> Job step name (optional).

number
> is the maximum number of dynamically allocated files which can be open at any one time. The number depends on the REXX program being executed, 20 will usually be sufficient.

Example:

JCL statements:

```
//          EXEC PGM=IKJEFT01,DYNAMNBR=20
//SYSEXEC  DD    DSN=T0000.ALPHA.EXEC,DISP=SHR
//SYSTSPRT DD    SYSOUT=A
//SYSTSIN  DD    DSN=T0000.ALPHA.INPUT,DISP=SHR
```

The T0000.ALPHA.EXEC dataset contains member BETA.

The T0000.ALPHA.INPUT dataset contains:

```
EXECUTIL SEARCHDD(YES)
%BETA 12 4
6
```

The TSO commands are read from the SYSTSIN file (T0000.ALPHA.INPUT dataset). The first command, EXECUTIL SEARCHDD(YES), specifies that the SYSEXEC file is to be searched for REXX programs.

The REXX source program BETA is loaded from the SYSEXEC file (T0000.ALPHA.EXEC dataset). Two parameters, 12 and 4, are passed to BETA. BETA fetches one data item with the PARSE PULL instruction, which reads the SYSTSIN file . The result of dividing the product of the two invocation parameters (operand1 and operand2) by the pulled operand (operand3) is displayed with the SAY instruction on the SYSTSPRT file (here assigned to the printer, SYSOUT=A).

14.2.1.3 MVS batch invocation
REXX programs running in MVS batch can use the interpreter IRXJCL, unless TSO facilities are required.

IRXJCL requires the following input:

* EXEC parameter, the name of the member to be executed; additional parameters are passed to the REXX program when it is invoked, i.e. parameters fetched with the PARSE ARG instruction.
* SYSEXEC file (DDname), is the library containing the REXX program to be executed.

- SYSTSPRT file (DDname), is the dataset to contain output produced with the SAY instruction.
- SYSTSIN file (DDname), is the dataset which contains (terminal) input required by the PULL instruction.

```
 ⊷──//┬──────────┬─ EXEC PGM=IRXJCL,PARM='program-name ┬────────────────┬'──⊶
       └ stepname ┘                                      └ argument-string ┘
```

stepname
>   Job step name (optional).

program-name
>   The name of the exec to be executed.

argument-string
>   Arguments to be passed to the program.

Example:

JCL statements:
```
     //          EXEC PGM=IRXJCL,PARM='BETA 12 4'
     //SYSEXEC  DD    DSN=T0000.ALPHA.EXEC,DISP=SHR
     //SYSTSPRT DD    SYSOUT=A
     //SYSTSIN  DD    DSN=T0000.ALPHA.INPUT,DISP=SHR
```

The T0000.ALPHA.EXEC dataset contains member BETA.

The T0000.ALPHA.INPUT dataset contains:
```
     6
```

The REXX source program BETA is loaded from the T0000.ALPHA.EXEC dataset. Two parameters, 12 and 4, are passed to BETA. BETA fetches one data item with the PARSE PULL instruction, which reads the SYSTSIN file (T0000.ALPHA.INPUT dataset). The result of dividing the product of the two invocation parameters (operand1 and operand2) by the pulled operand (operand3) is displayed with the SAY instruction on the SYSTSPRT file (here assigned to the printer, SYSOUT=A).

14.2.2 Linkage to host (MVS-TSO) environment
A REXX exec can link to components from the host environment. The ADDRESS instruction is used to set the host environment, see sections 9.2.2 and 13.2.8.

Example:
```
ADDRESS TSO "TIME";
```
invokes the TSO TIME command.

14.2.3 Linkage to programs

A REXX exec can pass control to a program written in a conventional programming language, such as PL/I or COBOL. The program is invoked with either the ATTACH or LINK host command. The ATTACH command invokes the program asynchronously (i.e. as a separate task), the LINK command invokes the program synchronously. The program is loaded from the program (load) library assigned to the environment.

The program may be passed a single parameter, which may contain subparameters. The invoked program receives two parameters on entry:

- the address of the parameter string;
- the length of the parameter string (full-word).

Note: This is not the standard MVS program linkage convention.

Fig. 14.1 shows the Assembler format for: ADDRESS LINK "BETA 12 4";

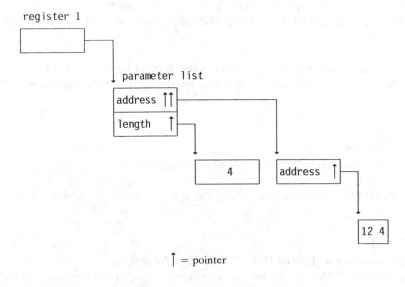

↑ = pointer

Fig. 14.1 - Example of method of passing parameters to a program

Example:
The example shown in Fig. 14.1 links to the program BETA and passes the parameter
"12 4". A sample PL/I program to process a REXX parameter follows. The parameter
and its length are displayed following the text "REXX PARAMETER:".
Note: The maximum length of the parameter passed to a program is 100 characters.

```
BETA: PROC(PARMADDR,PARMLEN) OPTIONS(MAIN);
DCL PARMADDR POINTER;
DCL REXXPARM CHAR(100) BASED(PARMADDR);
DCL PARMLEN FIXED BIN(31);
PUT SKIP LIST ('REXX PARAMETER:',SUBSTR(REXXPARM,1,PARMLEN),PARMLEN);
END BETA;
```

This program would display:
```
REXX PARAMETER:                12 4                              4
```

14.2.4 Interface with ISPEXEC (ISPF Dialog Manager)
REXX execs invoked from the TSO/ISPF environment can use the ADDRESS ISPEXEC
instruction to access ISPEXEC (ISPF Dialog Manager) services. The parameters for
the ISPEXEC service are passed as a normal REXX string, i.e. may be a literal, symbol
or mixture. However, ISPEXEC accepts only upper case characters. The return code
from the ISPEXEC service is set into the RC special variable.

REXX execs and ISPF Dialog Manager share the same function pool, with two
restrictions:

- variable names longer than 8 characters cannot be used in ISPF;
- the VGET and VPUT services cannot be used with compound symbols.

Example:
```
panname = "PAN1";
ADDRESS ISPEXEC "DISPLAY PANEL("panname")";
SAY RC;
```
uses ISPEXEC to display panel PAN1, the return code from the service is displayed.

14.2.5 Interface with ISREDIT (ISPF/PDF Edit macro)
The ISPF/PDF Editor can invoke a procedure to perform processing on a dataset -
this procedure is called an Edit macro and can be a REXX exec. The ADDRESS ISREDIT
instruction invokes Edit macro services. The parameters for the ISREDIT service are

passed as a normal REXX string, i.e. may be a literal, symbol or mixture. The return code from the ISREDIT service is set into the RC special variable.

Edit macros can make full use of REXX facilities. The powerful string processing features of REXX make it an ideal language for the implementation of Edit macros.

Example:

```
1    /* REXX Edit macro */
2    ADDRESS ISREDIT "MACRO (STRING)";
3    ADDRESS ISREDIT "FIND" string "NEXT";
4    IF RC \= 0 THEN SAY "search argument not found";
5    ADDRESS ISREDIT "END";
6    EXIT 0;
```

The line number preceding the REXX statement is not actually part of the Edit macro, and serves only as identification for the following explanation.

2   Macro header. The ISREDIT variable STRING is passed to the macro. *Note*: STRING must be written in upper case, because it is an ISREDIT variable.

3   Invoke the ISREDIT FIND command, string is passed as data and so may be written in lower case.

4   Display the message "search argument not found" if a non-zero return code is passed back from ISREDIT.

5   Terminate ISREDIT.

6   Terminate the REXX exec. This statement is optional.

14.2.6 Interface with DB2 (Database 2)

The TSO DSN command is used in initiate the DB2 session. The DB2 RUN subcommand is used to invoke a program which is to run in the DB2 environment.

The DB2 subcommands to invoke the program, and to terminate the DB2 session, RUN and END, respectively, are set into the stack in the required order before the DB2 session is initiated.

Note: The subcommands cannot be passed directly as is the case with CLISTs.

Example:

```
     /* REXX - DB2 */
     /* set initial parameters for DB2 */
1    QUEUE "RUN PROGRAM(TDB2PGM) PLAN(TDB2PLN)
```

```
                LIB('T0000.RUNLIB.LOAD')";
                /* set final (termination) parameter for DB2 */
        2       QUEUE "END";
                /* invoke DB2 */
        3       ADDRESS TSO "%DSN";
```

1   Set the RUN subcommand at the head of the stack. The subcommand specifies
     the parameters required to invoke the program.

2   Set the END subcommand as second element in the stack. This subcommand is
     required to terminate the DB2 session.

3   Invoke the DB2 session - the subcommands are taken from the stack. If the
     invoked DB2 program makes use of ISPF services then the DSN command
     should be invoked from the ISPF environment rather from TSO, for example
     with the statement: ADDRESS ISPEXEC "SELECT CMD(%DSN)";

14.2.7 Interface with QMF(Query Management Facility)

The invocation of QMF is more involved than invoking DB2 directly. As with the
invocation of QMF from a CLIST, two steps are required:

*   initiate the QMF session (program DSQQMFE), and execute a QMF procedure;
*   this QMF procedure passes control to a REXX exec, which in turn uses the QMF
    Command Interface (CI, program DSQCCI) to process a QMF command.

A full description of the QMF interfaces is beyond the scope of this book. The
appropriate manual or reference book should be consulted for further details.

Note: The general processing is the same as for CLISTs, with the exception that
variable names (and values) cannot be passed with the QMF RUN command. The
QMF SET GLOBAL command can be used to assign values for variables.

The following example uses QMF to run a query, the results of which are displayed
using the ISPF BROWSE service. Dataset names may have to be altered to suit the
requirements of your installation.

Invocation procedure:

```
                /* REXX - QMF invocation */
        1       ADDRESS TSO "ALLOC F(DSQDEBUG) DUMMY";
        2       ADDRESS TSO "ALLOC F(DSQPRINT) DA(QMFOUT.LIST) RECFM(V B) NEW
                  BLKSIZE(10000)";
```

```
3        ADDRESS TSO "ALLOC F(ADMGGMAP) DSN('QMF.TEST.DSQMAPE') SHR";
4        ADDRESS ISPEXEC "SELECT PGM(DSQQMFE) NEWAPPL(DSQE)
         PARM(S=DB2,I=T0000.S6)";
```

1-3   Use TSO to allocate the files need by QMF (DSQDEBUG and ADMGGMAP), and the file need by the command (DSQPRINT).

4   Invoke QMF (DSQQMFE) as sub-environment of ISPF. The QMF procedure T0000.S6 is to be processed.

QMF procedure S6:
```
TSO %S6X
```
This procedure passes control to the TSO command (REXX exec) S6X.

REXX exec S6X:
```
         /* REXX - S6X Procedure */
1        ADDRESS ISPEXEC "SELECT PGM(DSQCCI)
         PARM(SET GLOBAL (PNUM=2222)";
2        ADDRESS ISPEXEC "SELECT PGM(DSQCCI)
         PARM(RUN S6Q)";
3        ADDRESS ISPEXEC "SELECT PGM(DSQCCI)
         PARM(PRINT REPORT(L=CONT))";
4        ADDRESS ISPEXEC "BROWSE DATASET(DB2OUT.LIST)";
5        ADDRESS ISPEXEC "SELECT PGM(DSQCCI) PARM(EXIT)";
6        ADDRESS ISPEXEC "CONTROL DISPLAY REFRESH";
7        EXIT;
```

1   Use the CI to assign the value 2222 to the QMF variable PNUM.

2   Use the CI to invoke the QMF query S6Q.

3   Use the CI to write the report produced by running the query onto the DSQPRINT file, which has been assigned to the DB2OUT.LIST dataset.

4   Use the ISPF BROWSE service to display the contents of the report dataset.

5   Use the CI to terminate QMF session (EXIT command).

6   Restore the display.

7   Terminate the REXX exec.

QMF query S6Q:
```
SELECT * FROM PERS WHERE PNO = &PNUM
```

14.2.8 Interface from programs with REXX
Not only can REXX execs interface with other components, but programs can also make use of REXX services. The program interfaces are described in Chapter 16.

14.3 REXX/2 (OPERATING SYSTEM/2) IMPLEMENTATION

Operating System/2 Version 1.2 supports REXX procedures running in native mode.

14.3.1 REXX/2 invocation
REXX/2 programs are invoked by entering the program name in the OS/2 window or full-screen command line, or directly from the File Manager. REXX/2 programs have .CMD as extension and must have a comment as the first line to distinguish them from normal batch procedures.

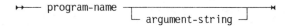

program-name
> The name of the program (together with path information) to be executed. REXX programs have .CMD as extension.

argument-string
> Arguments to be passed to the program.

Example:
> A:\REXXLIB\BETA 12 4

The program BETA.CMD contained in the REXXLIB directory on the A drive is to be invoked. The argument string "12 4" is to be passed to the program.

14.3.2 Linkage to host (OS/2) environment
A REXX exec can link to components from the host environment. The ADDRESS instruction is used to set the host environment, see section 9.2.2.

Example:
```
ADDRESS CMD "TIME";
```
invokes the OS/2 TIME command.

14.4 PERSONAL REXX (DOS) IMPLEMENTATION

The Personal REXX implementation allows a REXX exec to run in the DOS environment on a personal computer (there is also a OS/2 version). The ADDRESS instruction can be used to select the DOS sub-environment for non-REXX statements, e.g. invoke DOS commands.

Personal REXX is comprised of the following major components:

- REXX interpreter (run-time routine);
- REXX interrupt manager;
- REXX stack manager.

The REXX interrupt manager (RXINTMGR) must be resident before REXX programs can be run. The REXX stack manager (STACKMGR) must also be resident if the REXX stack is to be used. The REXX interpreter (REXX) may, optionally, be made resident - this saves time in loading the interpreter if more than one REXX program is to be run. Table 14.1 shows the approximate sizes of these components.

component	approximate size (in Kbytes)
REXX	150
RXINTMGR	2
STACKMGR	10*

* default size, may be increased

Table 14.1 - Approximate size of Personal REXX components

Personal REXX has also a large library of utility functions and commands. For example

- hardware access;
- DOS functions;
- windowing functions.

These extensions are not part of the standard REXX definition and so not discussed in this book.

14.4.1 Personal REXX invocation

REXX execs are executed using the Personal REXX interpreter program. The name of the REXX exec to be executed, together with any parameters, is passed to the REXX interpreter (run-time program).

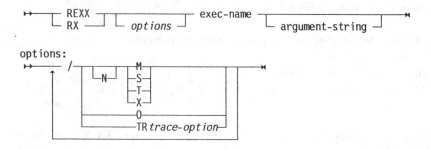

options:

REXX

> The REXX interpreter is to be loaded and invoked.

RX

> The resident REXX interpreter is to be invoked.
> The resident REXX interpreter is loaded with the REXX /R command and unloaded with the RX /U command.

N

> The following option is to be disabled.

M

> Retain statement number tables in storage.

S

> Retain source code in storage.

T

> Include extra object code for tracing.

X

> Use expanded memory (EMS).

O

Process the source exec into internal format and append at the end of the source exec.

Note: No execution is performed when this option is specified.

trace-option

Any option valid for the TRACE instruction.

exec-name

The name of the exec (together with path information) to be executed. REXX execs have .REX as default extension.

argument-string

Arguments to be passed to the exec.

Example:
```
RX /TRA A:\REXXLIB\BETA 12 4
```
The resident REXX interpreter is to invoke the exec BETA.REX contained in the REXXLIB directory on the A drive. The argument string "12 4" is to be passed to the exec. The trace option "A" (ALL) is to be set.

14.4.2 Linkage to host (DOS) environment

A REXX exec can link to components from the host environment. The ADDRESS instruction is used to set the host environment, see section 9.2.2.

Example:
```
ADDRESS DOS "TIME";
```
invokes the DOS TIME command.

14.4.3 Interface from programs to Personal REXX environment

Not only can REXX execs interface with other components, but programs can also make use of Personal REXX services. Such services are:
*   invoke a REXX exec;
*   access REXX variables.

A description of these program interfaces is beyond the scope of this book. The manual *Personal REXX User's Guide* should be consulted for further details, although the general principles discussed in Chapter 16 also apply for the Personal REXX implementation.

15

Worked examples

15.1 INTRODUCTION

This chapter contains two worked examples. The first example uses components belonging to the standard REXX implementation. The second example uses extensions from the MVS-TSO implementation, although equivalent features are available in most implementations.

These worked examples can be used in two ways:

- an exercise with which the reader can test his knowledge and understanding of REXX;
- annotated examples showing the use of REXX in different environments.

Each example is introduced by a specification explaining the exercise to be solved.

15.2 WORKED EXAMPLE 1

This example uses components belonging to the standard REXX implementation. Few non-trivial REXX execs make use of components belonging only to the standard implementation, components from the host environment will normally also be required.

Example 1 uses a subset of REXX to implement additional features. Although this would not be done in practice, the implemented features are themselves part of the standard implementation, it serves as a good example of how the various components fit together.

15.2.1 Specification

Aim: Positive integer multiplication or division of two numbers input on the terminal is to be performed using only repeated addition or subtraction, as appropriate.

Multiplication is done by repeated addition, the multiplicand (first operand) is added to itself the number of times specified by the multiplicator (second operand).

Division is done by repeated subtraction; the divisor (second operand) is repeatedly subtracted from the dividend (first operand), which then yields the new dividend, until this new dividend is less than the divisor - the integer quotient is the number of iterations performed. The individual steps follow.

- Display the message: "enter operand operator (* or /) operand".

- The first operand is to be processed using the second operand according to the specified operation (* represents multiplication, / represents division).
  Example, 7 / 2 would divide 7 by 2 and yield the result 3.

- The non-rounded integer result is to be displayed. The result of a division is to be prefixed with the word "quotient".

- The operator is to be checked for validity, i.e. the message "invalid operator" is displayed if the operator is neither "*" nor "/".

- The operands are to be checked for validity, i.e. the message "invalid operand" (together with the operand in error) is displayed if an operand is non-numeric or the divisor is zero.

- Processing is terminated if an error is encountered.

- Procedures are to be used for the multiplication and division operations. Subroutines are to be used where possible.

REXX exec:

```
1       /* REXX */
2       SAY "enter operand operator (* or /) operand";
3       PARSE PULL operand1 operator operand2
4        CALL CheckOperands;
5       SELECT
6         WHEN operator = '*'
            THEN CALL Multiplication;
7         WHEN operator = '/'
            THEN CALL Division;
8         OTHERWISE
            SAY "invalid operator"
```

```
 9      END;
10      EXIT;
11      CheckOperands:
12        IF \DATATYPE(operand1,'N') THEN CALL ErrorExit 1;
13        IF \DATATYPE(operand2,'N') THEN CALL ErrorExit 2;
14        RETURN;
15      ErrorExit:
16        SAY "invalid operand" ARG(1);
17        EXIT;
18      Multiplication: PROCEDURE EXPOSE operand1 operand2
19        result = 0;
20        DO i = 1 TO operand2;
21          result = result+operand1;
22        END;
23        SAY result;
24        RETURN;
25      Division: PROCEDURE EXPOSE operand1 operand2
26        IF operand2 <= 0 THEN CALL ErrorExit "divisor";
27        n = 0;
28        result = operand1;
29        DO WHILE result >= operand2;
30          n = n + 1;
31          result = result-operand2;
32        END;
33        SAY "quotient" n;
34        RETURN;
```

Explanation:

1　　Comment containing the word REXX must be the first statement of a REXX exec.

2　　Display message to enter input.

3　　Obtain the two operands and the operator from the terminal. The operands are assigned to the variables operand1 and operand2, respectively. The operator is assigned to the variable operator.

4　　The subroutine CheckOperands is called to validate the operands.

5　　Introduce a SELECT-block to validate the operator and to pass control to the appropriate procedure, if the operator is valid.

6　　Pass control to the Multiplication procedure if the operator is "*".

7　　Pass control to the Division procedure if the operator is "/".

8   Introduce the processing to be performed if the operator is neither "*" nor "/" - the message "invalid operator" is displayed.

9   Terminate the SELECT-block and the OTHERWISE clause.

10   Terminate the exec.

11   Introduce the CheckOperands subroutine.

12   Call ErrorExit with parameter 1 if operand1 is not numeric. The DATATYPE function with parameter 'N' returns 0 if the specified variable is numeric. The result is negated, i.e. the returned value changed from 0 to 1, and vice versa, i.e. the value is now either 1 (true) or 0 (false).

13   Call ErrorExit with parameter 2 if operand2 is not numeric.

14   Return to point of invocation if the operand validity checks are satisfied.

15   Introduce the ErrorExit subroutine.

16   Display the message "invalid operand" with the corresponding operand number (1 or 2), respectively.

17   Terminate the exec.

18   Introduce the Multiplication procedure; operand1 and operand2 are exposed, i.e. global variables.

19   Initialise the result work-field.

20   Introduce the DO-loop which performs the number of iterations specified by operand2.

21   Each iteration adds operand1 to a running-counter (result).

22   Terminate the DO-loop. operand1 has been added to itself operand2-times, this accumulation product is in the variable result.

23   Display the result (equivalent to the multiplication of operand1 by operand2).

24   Return to the point of invocation.

25   Introduce the Division procedure.

26   Call ErrorExit with parameter "divisor" if operand2 is either zero or negative.

27   Initialise the n work-field.

28   Initialise the result work-field with operand1.

29   Perform a DO-loop which is terminated when result (the remainder) is smaller than the divisor (operand2); the WHILE condition must be used so that the condition can be checked before each cycle.

30   Increment n (the quotient) for each iteration.

31   Subtract the divisor (operand2) from the remainder (result).

32   Terminate the DO-loop.

33   Display the text "quotient" with the calculated quotient (n).

34   Return to the point of invocation.

15.3 WORKED EXAMPLE 2

This is a more advanced example, which makes use of REXX commands (EXECIO -
read a dataset), TSO commands (ALLOC - allocate a dataset), and ISPF Dialog
Manager services (DISPLAY - display a panel).

15.3.1 Specification

Aim: The contents of a dataset are to be displayed using panel RXPAN. Marked words
in the display are to be converted from lower case to upper case, and vice versa. A
word (in this context) is a series of characters delimited by one or more non-
alphanumeric characters. A word is marked by placing the cursor somewhere in the
word. The conversion function is selected by pressing either the PF5 key (convert to
lower case) or PF6 (convert to upper case). The solution is simplified by not allowing
vertical scrolling.

The name of the dataset to be processed is passed as parameter to the REXX
exec. If the dataset name is not fully qualified (not specified within quotes), then the
current user's TSO prefix is appended at the start of the dataset name.

The data lines in the panel are named: L.1 through L.9. These data lines are filled
with the first 9 records read from the dataset.

For readers not familiar with TSO commands and ISPF Dialog Manager, the salient
points needed for this example are described in the following section.

The TSO ALLOC command allocates a dataset. Allocation here means associate a
dataset name with a file name, which can then be used in the REXX EXECIO
command. The following TSO ALLOC command is needed in this example:

    ALLOC FILE(FILEIN) DSN(dataset-name) SHR REUS

•   The FILE keyword specifies the file name, in this case FILEIN. This file name is used
     by the EXECIO command to access the dataset.

- The DSN keyword specifies the dataset name.

- The SHR keyword specifies that the dataset already exists and can be shared by more than one user. The OLD keyword is required if the dataset cannot be shared by more than one user.

- The REUS keyword specifies that the file allocation is reusable. This means that it can be allocated even if it is already allocated to this user.

The ISPEXEC (ISPF Dialog Manager) DISPLAY command displays a panel. ISPF and REXX share a common pool of variables, i.e. variables having the same names are available to both environments. However, ISPEXEC variable names have a maximum length of eight characters. The variable is the variable name prefixed with an ampersand (&).

```
DISPLAY PANEL(panel-name)
```

- The PANEL keyword specifies the name of the panel to be displayed.

The panel definition for RXPAN is not an essential part of example, this book is primarily concerned with REXX and not with the usage of ISPF Dialog Manager.

This example requires that the two PF keys (PF5 and PF6) are to be processed by the REXX exec. This is done by altering the standard definition for the corresponding system variables for these two keys (ZPF05 and ZPF06, respectively), and by storing these new definitions in the ISPF profile pool, which is done with the VPUT (ZPF05 ZPF06) PROFILE statement. This example assigns the character strings PF05 and PF06 to ZPF05 and ZPF06, respectively.

After the panel has been displayed the pressing of either the PF5, PF6 or the End key will return control to the point of invocation. The panel processing section has set the two variables: &CSRPOS, &CURSOR, to contain the position of the cursor within a line and the name of the line, respectively, i.e. &CSRPOS will contain a number and &CURSOR will contain L.n (n is the line number). The character string (PF05 or PF06) which has been assigned to the pressed PF key is stored in the ZCMD system variable. Pressing the End key (usually PF3) sets the display return code to 8.

Panel definition:

```
 ┌─ RXPAN ──────────────────────────────────────────────────────────────────────
 )ATTR
 $ TYPE(TEXT) INTENS(HIGH)
 # TYPE(TEXT) INTENS(LOW)
 _ TYPE(INPUT) CAPS(ON)
 } TYPE(OUTPUT) INTENS(LOW) JUST(ASIS) CAPS(OFF)
 )BODY EXPAND(//)
 %-/ Dataset Display /-/+
 %COMMAND ===>_ZCMD                                          #SCROLL%===>_SAMT+
 %
 }L.1
 }L.2
 }L.3
 }L.4
 }L.5
 }L.6
 }L.7
 }L.8
 }L.9
 %
 %
 %PF5 make lower case   PF6 make upper case
 )INIT
 &ZCMD = ''
 IF (&SAMT = &Z) &SAMT = 'HALF'
 /* pre-assign function key definitions
 &ZPF05 = 'PF05'
 &ZPF06 = 'PF06'
 VPUT (ZPF05 ZPF06) PROFILE
 )REINIT
 &ZCMD = ''
 REFRESH (ZCMD)
 )PROC
 &CSRPOS = .CSRPOS
 &CURSOR = .CURSOR
 )END
```

REXX exec:

```
1        /* REXX */
         /* Argument: Datasetname */
2        PARSE UPPER ARG dsn;
3        IF SUBSTR(dsn,1,1) \= "'"
           THEN dsn = "'"SYSVAR(SYSPREF)"."dsn"'";
         /* allocate dataset */
4        "ALLOC F(FILEIN) DA("dsn") SHR REUS";
         /* read dataset */
5        "EXECIO * DISKR FILEIN (STEM d. FINIS)"
6        ADDRESS ISPEXEC;
7        nrec = d.0;                          /* no. of records read */
         /* initialisation */
```

```
 8          alpha1 = "abcdefghijklmnopqrstuvwxyz";
 9          alpha2 = "ABCDEFGHIJKLMNOPQRSTUVWXYZ";
10          allcase = alpha1||alpha2||'0123456789';
11          lowercase = alpha1||alpha1||'0123456789';
12          uppercase = alpha2||alpha2||'0123456789';
            /* display loop */
13          DisplayRC = 0;
14          DO WHILE DisplayRC < 8;
15            CALL SetDisplay;
16            IF DisplayRC /= 8 THEN DO;
17              SELECT;
18                WHEN ZCMD = "PF05" THEN CALL MakeLowerCase;
19                WHEN ZCMD = "PF06" THEN CALL MakeUpperCase;
20                OTHERWISE NOP;
21              END;
22            END;
23          END;
            /* rewrite dataset */
24          ADDRESS MVS "EXECIO" nrec "DISKW FILEIN (STEM d. FINIS)";
25          EXIT;                            /* terminate exec */
26          MakeLowerCase:
27            newcase = lowercase;
28            CALL ChangeCase;
29            RETURN;
30          MakeUpperCase:
31            newcase = uppercase;
32            CALL ChangeCase;
33            RETURN;
34          ChangeCase:
            /* change case */
35          PARSE VALUE cursor WITH d '.' lno;
36          ix = csrpos;
37          exp = "line = "cursor;
38          INTERPRET exp;                   /* extract selected line */
39          wk = TRANSLATE(line,,allcase,'0')||' '; /* alphanumeric -> 0 */
40          wk = TRANSLATE(wk,'0','0'XRANGE(),' ');  /* remainder -> ' ' */
            /* <wk> now contains either 0 or ' ' */
            /* locate previous delimiter */
41          iy = LASTPOS(' ',wk,ix);
42          IF iy = ix THEN RETURN;          /* cursor not in a word */
            /* locate following delimiter */
43          iz = POS(' ',wk,iy+1);
44          wd = SUBSTR(line,iy+1,iz-iy-1);  /* extract selected word */
45          wd = TRANSLATE(wd,newcase,allcase,' ');
```

```
46        exp = "d."lno "= OVERLAY(wd,"cursor",iy+1,iz-iy-1)";
47        INTERPRET exp;
48        RETURN;
49     SetDisplay:
50        j = 1;                        /* line index */
51        l. = '';                      /* clear panel lines */
52        DO i = 1 TO 10 WHILE j < nrec; /* set panel lines from buffer */
53          l.i = d.j;
54          j = j+1;
55        END;
56        "DISPLAY PANEL(RXPAN)";
57        DisplayRC = RC;               /* save display return code */
58        RETURN ;
```

Explanation:

1   Comment containing the word REXX must be the first statement of a REXX exec.

2   Fetch parameter (dataset name) passed to exec, store in dsn variable. The UPPER keyword converts any lower case input to upper case.

3   Check whether first character of dsn (dataset name) is "'". If not, prefix with the user's TSO prefix.

4   Use the TSO ALLOC command to allocate the dataset. The allocated dataset is assigned the FILEIN file name.

5   The complete dataset is read into the d. stem variables. The number of records read is stored in the d.0 variable.

6   The environment is set for ISPF Dialog Manager (ISPEXEC). This means that all subsequent REXX commands are passed to ISPEXEC.

7   The number of records read is stored in the nrec variable.

8   Define the variable alpha1 to contain the full set of lower case alphabetic characters (a through z).

9   Define the variable alpha2 to contain the full set of upper case alphabetic characters (A through Z).

10   Define the variable allcase to contain the full set of alphanumeric characters (lower case alphabetic, upper case alphabetic and numerics).

11   Define the variable lowercase to contain the full set of lower case alphanumeric characters (a through z and 0 through 9).

12   Define the variable uppercase to contain the full set of upper case alphanumeric characters (A through Z and 0 through 9).

13   Initialise the DisplayRC variable to zero. DisplayRC is used to contain the return code from the panel display. Panel return code 8 means that the End key has been pressed, which, by convention, indicates that processing is to be terminated.

14   Introduce a DO-loop which is to be performed until the End key is pressed.

15   Invoke the SetDisplay subroutine.

16   Introduce a DO-group to be performed provided that the variable DisplayRC has not been set to 8.

17   Introduce a SELECT-block.

18   Invoke the MakeLowerCase subroutine if the PF5 key has been pressed.

19   Invoke the MakeUpperCase subroutine if the PF6 key has been pressed.

21   If neither key has been pressed, perform no particular processing. The pseudo-instruction NOP is not strictly necessary in the OTHERWISE clause, but it can be used to emphasise that no processing is to be done.

21   Terminate the SELECT-block introduced by statement 17.

22   Terminate the DO-group introduced by statement 16.

23   Terminate the DO-loop introduced by statement 14. This is the end of the display processing, the End key has been pressed.

24   Rewrite the dataset. The ADDRESS MVS clause is required, as the environment has been set to ISPEXEC.

25   Terminate the exec with code 0.

26   Introduce the MakeLowerCase subroutine.

27   Assign the lower case definitions to the newcase variable.

28   Invoke the ChangeCase subroutine to convert the marked word using the translation table contained in newcase.

29   Return to the point of invocation. This is the logical end of the subroutine.

30   Introduce the MakeUpperCase subroutine.

31   Assign the upper case definitions to the newcase variable.

32   Invoke the ChangeCase subroutine to convert the marked word using the translation table contained in newcase.

33   Return to the point of invocation.

34   Introduce the ChangeCase subroutine. The translation table to be used is contained in newcase.

35   Analyse the content of the cursor variable, which contains the name of the marked line. The variable cursor contains an entry of the form: L.n, n being the line number. This line number is assigned with the PARSE instruction to the variable lno. The first operand (.) following the WITH keyword is a placeholder. The second operand ('.') is the delimiter.

36   Set the cursor position (within the line) to the line index ix.

37   Build a statement in exp, which will assign the content of cursor (line) to the variable line.

38   Perform the statement built in the variable exp. This moves the selected display line into the variable line.

39   Translate all alphanumeric characters (a-z, A-Z, 0-9) to '0', and append a single blank character at the end of the transformed data, which is then assigned to wk.

40   Translate all other characters in the transformed data to blank. the variable wk contains only 0's (representing alphanumeric characters) and blanks (representing all other characters, i.e. word delimiters).

41   The first delimiter before the current cursor position (in ix) is determined by searching backwards. This is the position of the delimiter immediately in front of the marked word, it is assigned to iy.

42   If the contents of ix and iy are identical, then the cursor has not been positioned within a word, and no further processing is performed.

43   The position of the next delimiter working forwards is determined and assigned to iz. This is the position of the delimiter immediately following the marked word.

44   The limits (iy + 1,iz-1) of the marked word have now been determined. It is assigned to the variable wd.

45   The contents of wd are translated using the newcase as transformation table.

46   Build a statement in exp, which will overlay the marked line (cursor contains its name) with the transformed marked word.

47   Perform the statement built in the variable exp. This overlays the selected display line with the transformed marked word.

48   Return to point of invocation.

49   Introduce the SetDisplay subroutine.

50   Initialise the line index (j).

51   Initialise l. stem variables. Non-initialised REXX variables are not valid when used in the ISPF environment.

52   Introduce a DO-loop which is performed nine times (the number of panel display lines) provided that the last buffer record (nrec) has not be reached. The control variable (i, the panel display line number) is incremented by one for each iteration through the DO-loop.

53   Move the buffer record line to the corresponding panel display line.

54   Increment the buffer line number.

55   Terminate the DO-loop initiated in statement 52. The control variable (i) is not strictly necessary. It is used to improve the robustness of the exec, i.e. facilitate the detection of misplaced END statements.

56   Display the ISPF Dialog Manager panel RXPAN. The ISPEXEC environment has been set in statement 6.

57   Assign the return code resulting from the panel display in the variable DisplayRC. The RC special variable is set by the invoked command, in this case ISPEXEC DISPLAY PANEL.

58   Return to the point of invocation.

16

System interfaces

16.1 INTRODUCTION

REXX implementations offer many interfaces for using REXX services from programs written in conventional programming languages. This book describes only the interfaces provided in the TSO implementation. However, most implementations provide very similar interfaces, and so the discussions here are generally applicable. Further, this book describes only those interfaces of interest to the applications developer - there are a number of other interfaces which can be used by systems specialists to customise the system.

The interfaces can be grouped into the following categories:

- program invocation of a REXX exec;
- program access to REXX variables;
- stack operations;
- programs as REXX functions (and the grouping of such programs into function packages);
- general service routines.

16.2 GENERAL CONDITIONS

The interfaces are subject to the following conditions:

- Programs using REXX services must use 31-bit addressing (AMODE 31).
- Numeric fields are in binary format, either fullword (4 bytes) or halfword (2 bytes).

- Standard calling conventions are used:
  - register 15 - entry point address;
  - register 14 - return address;
  - register 13 - address of save-area.
- The return code is passed back in register 15 (PLIRETV PL/I variable, RETURN-CODE COBOL special register). Many routines also set an error message in the Environment Block.
- Parameter address lists passed in register 1 must have the high-order bit set in the last address word.
- Standard macros (in the SYS1.MACLIB system macro library) are available for use by Assembler programs to map the more important control blocks. Programs can be written in high-level programming languages (e.g. COBOL, PL/I); however, such programs must themselves define the control block structures - Fig. 16.1 shows the equivalent field types in various programming languages. Not all high-level programming languages provide full support for all the required facilities.

type	Assembler	PL/I	COBOL VS II
address	A	PTR	POINTER
character string	CLn	CHAR(n)	PIC X(n)
fullword	F	FIXED BIN(31)	PIC S9(9) COMP
halfword	H	FIXED BIN(15)	PIC S9(4) COMP
hexadecimal	X	BIT(8)	-

- no exact equivalent

Fig. 16.1 - Equivalent field types

Notes:
1. Only the most important information for the interfaces is described in this chapter - the appropriate manual should be consulted if a more detailed description is required.

2. The entry < symbol > in diagrams denotes that *symbol* is used as prefix to the field names in the corresponding block. The diagrams show only the significant fields. Any fillers at the end of field layout figures are omitted.

16.3 INVOCATION OF A REXX EXEC

There are three ways of invoking a REXX exec:

- using the IRXJCL program;
- using the TSO Service Facility (IJKEFTSR program);
- using the IRXEXEC program.

These three methods are listed in order of ease of use. This is also the order of increasing flexibility, e.g. the IRXEXEC program interface offers more flexibility than the IRXJCL program interface but is more difficult to invoke.

16.3.1 Interface from programs to batch REXX (IRXJCL)

Programs written in a conventional language (PL/I, etc.) can use IRXJCL to invoke a REXX exec. The parameter passed to IRXJCL has the same form as described in section 14.2.1.3; Fig. 16.2 shows the form of the parameter as passed from the invoking program.

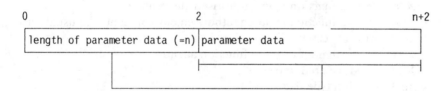

Fig. 16.2 - Format of parameter passed to IRXJCL

Sample program:

```
BETA1: PROC OPTIONS(MAIN);
/* Function: Invoke the REXX exec BETA using IRXJCL */
DCL IRXJCL EXTERNAL OPTIONS(RETCODE,ASSEMBLER,INTER);
DCL PLIRETV BUILTIN;            /* return code */
DCL 1 PARM,
        2 PARM_LEN FIXED BIN(15) INIT(9),
        2 PARM_DATA CHAR(9) INIT('BETA 12 4');
FETCH IRXJCL;              /* load address of entry point */
CALL IRXJCL(PARM);        /* invoke IRXJCL with parameter */
PUT SKIP LIST ('IRXJCL return code:',PLIRETV);
END;
```

This sample program uses IRXJCL to invoke the REXX exec BETA; two parameters, 12 and 4, are passed to the exec.

16.3.2 Invocation of a REXX exec using the TSO Service Facility (IJKEFTSR)
REXX execs can also be invoked from the TSO environment (either dialogue or batch) with the TSO Service Facility (IJKEFTSR program) - the TSO Service Facility has the alias TSOLNK.

Assembler calling sequence:
```
CALL IJKEFTSR,(flags,function_buffer,function_buffer_length,function_rc,
     reason_code,abend_code[,function_parm_list[,cppl]]),VL
```
[ ] indicates an optional entry

flags
>A fullword containing four hexadecimal flag bytes:
>Byte 0 - X'00'.
>Byte 1 - internal processing options flag.
>• X'00' - invoke function from authorised environment.
>• X'01' - invoke function from unauthorised environment (the usual setting).
>Byte 2 - error processing flag.
>• X'00' - force dump if invoked function abends.
>• X'01' - produce no dump.
>Byte 3 - function type flag.
>• X'01' - TSO/E command, REXX exec or CLIST is to be invoked.
>• X'02' - program is to be invoked.
>
>*Note*: High-level languages can set the required flag bits by defining the appropriate binary value: Byte1*65536 + Byte2*256 + Byte3.

function_buffer
>Buffer containing the name of the program, command, REXX exec or CLIST to be invoked. The buffer can contain parameters to be passed to a command, REXX exec or CLIST.

function_buffer_length
>A fullword containing the length of data in **function_buffer**.

function_rc
>A fullword which is set to contain the return code from the invoked function.

reason_code
   A fullword which is set to contain the service routine reason code.

abend_code
   A fullword which is set to contain the abend code if the invoked function ends
   abnormally.

The last two parameters are optional, and are not required for the invocation of a
REXX exec.

Sample program using TSOLNK:

```
BETA2: PROC OPTIONS(MAIN);
DCL 1 PARM1,
       2 PARM11 BIT(8) INIT('00000000'B),  /* reserved */
       2 PARM12 BIT(8) INIT('00000001'B),  /* unauthorised */
       2 PARM13 BIT(8) INIT('00000000'B),  /* no dump */
       2 PARM14 BIT(8) INIT('00000001'B);  /* REXX exec */
DCL 1 PARM2 CHAR(9) INIT('BETA 12 4');  /* command and parameter */
DCL 1 PARM3 FIXED BIN(31) INIT(9);  /* length of command (PARM2) */
DCL 1 PARM4 FIXED BIN(31);  /* command return code */
DCL 1 PARM5 FIXED BIN(31);  /* TSF reason code */
DCL 1 PARM6 FIXED BIN(31);  /* command abend code */
DCL TSOLNK ENTRY
    (1,
       2 BIT(8),   /* reserved */
       2 BIT(8),   /* authorised/unauthorised flag */
       2 BIT(8),   /* dump/no dump flag */
       2 BIT(8),   /* function type flag */
       1 CHAR(*),         /* command and parameter */
       1 FIXED BIN(31),  /* length of command (PARM2) */
       1 FIXED BIN(31),  /* command return code */
       1 FIXED BIN(31),  /* TSF reason code */
       1 FIXED BIN(31)   /* command abend code */
       ) EXTERNAL OPTIONS(RETCODE,ASSEMBLER,INTER);
FETCH TSOLNK;
CALL TSOLNK(PARM1,PARM2,PARM3,PARM4,PARM5,PARM6);
END;
```

This sample PL/I program uses the TSO Service Facility (TSOLNK) to invoke the
REXX exec BETA, which is called with the parameter "12 4". Assembler programs can
also get the address of the TSO Service Facility (IKJEFTSR) from the CVT
(Communications Vector Table). The following Assembler program illustrates the
use of the TSO Service Facility.

Sample program using IKJEFTSR:

```
            TITLE 'USE IKJEFTSR TO INVOKE A REXX EXEC'
            PRINT NOGEN
BETA2       CSECT
* initialise addressing
            STM   R14,R12,12(R13)          save registers
            BALR  R12,0                     base register
            USING *,R12
            LA    R15,SA                    A(save-area)
            ST    R13,4(R15)                backward ptr
            ST    R15,8(R13)                forward ptr
            LR    R13,R15                   A(new save-area)
            L     R15,CVTPTR                A(CVT)
            USING CVT,R15                   address CVT
            L     R15,CVTTVT                A(TSO Vector Table)
            L     R15,TSVTASF-TSVT(R15)     A(TSO Service Facility)
            CALL  (15),(PARM1,PARM2,PARM3,PARM4,PARM5,PARM6),VL
* R15: TSF return code
            L     R13,4(R13)                restore A(old save-area)
            RETURN (14,12),RC=(15)          terminate with return code
SA          DS    18A                       save-area
* symbolic register equates
R12         EQU   12
R13         EQU   13
R14         EQU   14
R15         EQU   15
* parameter definition
PARM1       DS    0XL4
            DC    X'00'                     reserved
            DC    X'01'                     unauthorised
            DC    X'00'                     no dump
            DC    X'01'                     REXX exec
PARM2       DC    C'BETA 12 4'              command and parameter
PARM3       DC    A(L'PARM2)                length of command (PARM2)
PARM4       DS    F                         command return code
PARM5       DS    F                         TSF reason code
PARM6       DS    F                         command abend code
* DSECT definitions
            IKJTSVT
            CVT   DSECT=YES
            END
```

This sample program performs the same processing as the previous PL/I sample program.

16.3.3 Interface from programs to REXX processor (IRXEXEC)

The IRXEXEC routine is the most flexible method of invoking a REXX exec, for example, it is not restricted to passing a single parameter. Fig. 16.3 illustrates the IRXEXEC service.

Assembler calling sequence:
```
CALL IRXEXEC,(addr_execblk,addr_arglist,flags,addr_instblk,addr_cppl,
      addr_workarea_descr,addr_user),VL
```

Note: Register 0 may contain the address of an Environment Block (optional). If register 0 does not point to a valid Environment Block then the Environment Block created for the environment is used.

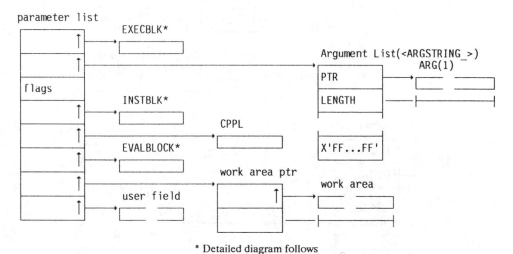

* Detailed diagram follows

Fig. 16.3 - IRXEXEC interface (part 1 of 2)

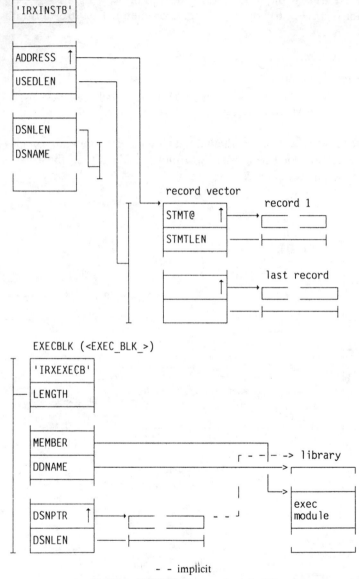

- - implicit

Fig. 16.3 - IRXEXEC interface (part 2 of 2)

addr_execblk

Fullword containing the address of the Exec Block (EXECBLK).
0 if the exec has been preloaded, i.e. **addr_instblk** contains the address of the INSTBLK which describes the exec.

addr_arglist

Fullword containing the address of the Argument List.

flags

Fullword containing four hexadecimal flag bytes:
X'80000000' - exec is being invoked as command.
X'40000000' - exec is being invoked as an external function.
X'20000000' - exec is being invoked as a subroutine.

addr_instblk

Fullword containing the address of the In-storage Control Block (INSTBLK).
0 if the exec has not been preloaded, i.e. the exec will be loaded using information contained in the EXECBLK.

addr_cppl

Fullword containing the address of the TSO CPPL. This parameter is only required for invocation from a TSO address space, and must be 0 for invocation from non-TSO address spaces.

addr_evalblock

Fullword containing the address of the Evaluation Block (EVALBLOCK) which is to contain the result returned by the exec.
0 indicates that no EVALBLOCK is required.

addr_workarea_descr

Fullword containing the address of an 8-byte field which describes a work area to be used by the IRXEXEC routine.
0 indicates that IRXEXEC is to create its own work area.

addr_user

Fullword containing the address of a user field. IRXEXEC does not use this field.
0 indicates that no user field is passed.

Sample program (invoke the REXX exec BETA with parameter "12 4"):

```
BETA3: PROC OPTIONS(MAIN);
/* Function: Invoke the REXX exec BETA using IRXEXEC */
DCL IRXEXEC EXTERNAL OPTIONS(RETCODE,ASSEMBLER,INTER);
DCL 1 P11 PTR INIT(ADDR(EXECBLK));
```

```
DCL 1 P12 PTR INIT(ADDR(ARGLIST));
DCL 1 P13 BIT(32) INIT('1000'B);
DCL 1 P14 FIXED BIN(31) INIT(0);
DCL 1 P15 FIXED BIN(31) INIT(0);
DCL 1 P16 FIXED BIN(31) INIT(0);
DCL 1 P17 FIXED BIN(31) INIT(0);
DCL 1 P18 FIXED BIN(31) INIT(0);
DCL 1 EXECBLK,
      2 EXEC_BLK_ACRYN CHAR(8) INIT('IRXEXECB'),
      2 EXEC_BLK_LENGTH FIXED BIN(31) INIT(48),
      2 EXEC_BLK_RESERV CHAR(4),
      2 EXEC_BLK_MEMBER CHAR(8) INIT('BETA'),
      2 EXEC_BLK_DDNAME CHAR(8) INIT('SYSLIB'),
      2 EXEC_BLK_SUBCOM CHAR(8) INIT(' '),
      2 EXEC_BLK_DSNPTR PTR INIT(ADDR(DUMMY)),
      2 EXEC_BLK_DSNLEN FIXED BIN(31) INIT(0);
DCL 1 ARGLIST,
      2 ARGLIST_ENTRY(2),
        3 ARGSTRING_PTR PTR,
        3 ARGSTRING_LENGTH FIXED BIN(31);
DCL 1 ARG CHAR(4) INIT('12 4'); /* argument for command */
ARGSTRING_PTR(1) = ADDR(ARG);
ARGSTRING_LENGTH(1) = LENGTH(ARG);
ARGSTRING_LENGTH(2) = -1; /* set end-of-list marker */
FETCH IRXEXEC;             /* load address of entry point */
CALL IRXEXEC(P11,P12,P13,P14,P15,P16,P17,P18);
END;
```

16.4 PROGRAM ACCESS TO REXX VARIABLES (IRXEXCOM SERVICE)

Programs running in a REXX environment can use the IRXEXCOM service to access
variables in the environment pool. Fig. 16.4 illustrates the IRXEXCOM service. The sample
function shown in section 16.6 illustrates the use of the IRXEXCOM service. The following functions are available:
- copy value;
- set variable;
- drop variable;
- retrieve symbolic name;
- set symbolic name;
- drop symbolic name;
- fetch next variable;
- fetch user data.

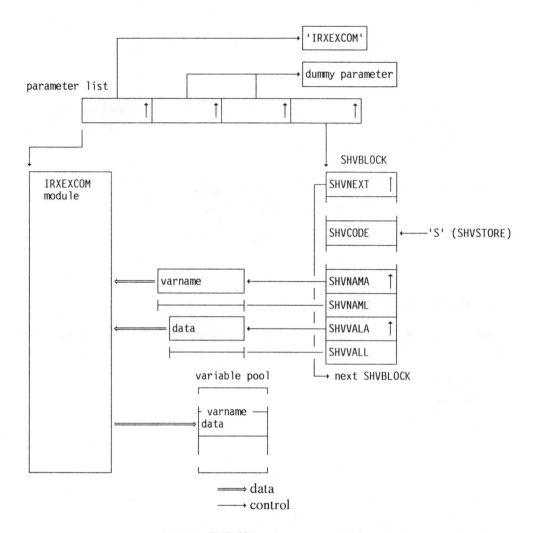

Fig. 16.4 - IRXEXCOM service to store a variable

Assembler calling sequence:

```
CALL IRXEXCOM,(irxexcom_string,dummy_parm,dummy_parm,shvblock),VL
```

irxexcom_string

8-character string 'IRXEXCOM'

dummy_parm
>   The second and third parameters must be identical, their content is not significant - 0 is valid.

shvblock
>   The first of a chain of Shared Variable (Request) Blocks (SHVBLOCK). The SHVBLOCK contains the information to perform the required service (function, variable name, address of data, etc.).

Register 15 is returned with one of the following codes:
  0   complete chain successfully processed;
  -1   at least one error condition detected;
  -2   insufficient main-storage available.

16.5 STACK PROCESSING (IRXSTK SERVICE)

Programs can use the IRXSTK service to perform processing on the current stack. The operations:
- DELSTACK
- DROPBUF
- MAKEBUF
- NEWSTACK
- PULL
- PUSH
- QELEM
- QSTACK
- QUEUE
- QUEUED

have the same function as described in earlier chapters.

The two operations:
- DROPTERM
- MAKETERM

are used by system routines to coordinate stack access from TSO and ISPF. These operations should not be used by application programs.

Assembler calling sequence:
```
CALL IRXSTK,(function,data_ptr,data_len,function_rc),VL
```

function

8-character string designating the function to be performed, DELSTACK, DROPBUF, etc.

data_ptr

pointer to the data element. *Note*: Data in the stack must not be changed.

data_len

fullword containing the length of the data element.

function_rc

fullword returned with the function return code. This field is meaningful only when the service return code (set in register 15) is zero.

The values for the function return code can be obtained from the descriptions for the corresponding operation.

Register 15 is returned with one of the following codes:

0   processing successfully completed;

4   the data stack is empty (PULL function);

Other codes indicate that an error has occurred.

Sample PL/I program:

```
BETA6: PROC OPTIONS(MAIN);
/* Function: retrieve stack element */
DCL IRXSTK EXTERNAL OPTIONS(RETCODE,INTER,ASSEMBLER);
DCL PLIRETV BUILTIN;
DCL 1 FC CHAR(8);              /* function code */
DCL 1 ADDR_ELEM PTR;          /* pointer to data */
DCL 1 LEN_ELEM FIXED BIN(31); /* length of data */
DCL 1 FRC FIXED BIN(31);      /* function return code */
DCL 1 ELEM CHAR(256) BASED(ADDR_ELEM); /* data */
FC = 'PULL';                  /* function */
FETCH IRXSTK;                 /* load address of entry point */
CALL IRXSTK(FC,ADDR_ELEM,LEN_ELEM,FRC);
IF RC = 0 THEN PUT SKIP LIST (SUBSTR(ELEM,1,LEN_ELEM));
END;
```

This PL/I program retrieves and displays the next element from the data stack.

16.6 FUNCTION INTERFACE

Programs written in a conventional programming language (PL/I, COBOL, Assembler, etc.) and stored as a load module in a library can be invoked as external REXX functions (or subroutines). The only difference between a function and a subroutine is that a function must return a value. Fig. 16.5 depicts the function interface.

Entry conditions:

Register 0   Address of an Environment Block (optional). If register 0 does not point to a valid Environment Block then the Environment Block created for the environment is used.

Register 1   Address of the External Function Parameter List (EFPL). The EFPL contains two addresses of direct interest for functions: EFPLARG (the address of the Argument List, which contains the pointers to the parsed arguments) and EFPLEVAL (the address of the pointer to the area which is to be set to contain the result).

Exit conditions:

Register 15   Must contain 0, otherwise the message "IRX0043, Routine not found" will be displayed.

EVALBLOCK   contains the function result.

Sample function program

The function FCONCAT performs the concatenation of the passed arguments. The number of arguments is variable. The result is returned both as function result and as variable CONCAT.

For example,

```
      x = FCONCAT(1,234);
      SAY x CONCAT;
```

displays '1234 1234'.

Coding for this sample function is shown in Assembler, COBOL and PL/I. These sample programs make certain assumptions in order to simplify the coding:
*   the length of an individual argument cannot exceed 256 bytes;
*   the maximum number of arguments for COBOL and PL/I is 10;
*   no check is made as to whether the result fits in the EVALBLOCK.

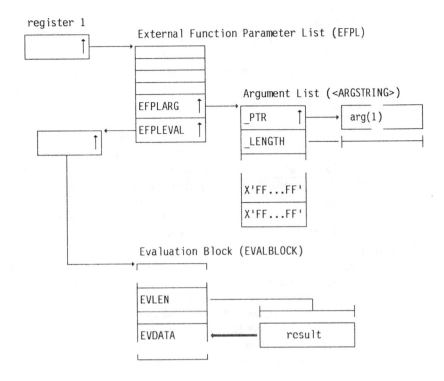

Fig. 16.5 - Function interface

Assembler implementation:

```
          TITLE 'REXX FUNCTION - RETURN CONCATENATED PARAMETERS'
          PRINT NOGEN
FCONCAT   CSECT
* initialise addressing
          STM   R14,R12,12(R13)     save registers
          BALR  R12,0               base register
          USING *,R12
          LA    R15,SA              A(save-area)
          ST    R13,4(R15)          backward ptr
          ST    R15,8(R13)          forward ptr
          LR    R13,R15             A(new save-area)
          USING EFPL,R1
          L     R2,EFPLEVAL         PTR(Evaluation Block)
          L     R11,0(R2)           A(Evaluation Block)
          USING EVALBLOCK,R11
          L     R10,EFPLARG         A(parsed Argument List)
```

```
          USING ARGTABLE_ENTRY,R10
          LA    R9,EVALBLOCK_EVDATA    A(result)
          LA    R8,0                   L(result)
NEXTPARM  LM    R3,R4,ARGTABLE_ARGSTRING_PTR
* R3: A(argument)
* R4: L(argument)
          LTR   R4,R4
          BM    LASTPARM               negative length (=last parameter)
          SH    R4,=H'1'               LengthCode(argument)
          EX    R4,EXMOVE              move argument
          LA    R8,1(R4,R8)            update length accumulator
          LA    R9,1(R4,R9)            update pointer
          LA    R10,ARGTABLE_NEXT-ARGTABLE_ENTRY(R10) next argument
          B     NEXTPARM               get next argument
LASTPARM  ST    R8,EVALBLOCK_EVLEN     entry size
* set data into REXX variable
          LA    R7,IRX_SHVBLOCK
          USING SHVBLOCK,R7            address SHVBLOCK
          MVC   SHVNAML,=A(L'VARNAME)  L(variable name)
          MVC   SHVNAMA,=A(VARNAME)    A(variable name)
          MVI   SHVCODE,SHVSTORE       set STORE function-code
          LA    R0,EVALBLOCK_EVDATA    A(result)
          ST    R0,SHVVALA             A(data)
          ST    R8,SHVVALL             L(data)
          LOAD  EP=IRXEXCOM            load IRXEXCOM
          LR    R15,R0                 entry-point address
          CALL  (15),(IRX_IRXEXCOM,0,0,IRX_SHVBLOCK),VL
          L     R13,4(R13)             restore A(old save-area)
          LA    R15,0                  set zero return code
          RETURN (14,12),RC=(15)
SA        DS    18A                    save-area
* symbolic register equates
R0        EQU   0
R1        EQU   1
R2        EQU   2
R3        EQU   3
R4        EQU   4
R7        EQU   7
R8        EQU   8
R9        EQU   9
R10       EQU   10
R11       EQU   11
R12       EQU   12
R13       EQU   13
```

```
R14        EQU    14
R15        EQU    15
EXMOVE     MVC    0(0,R9),0(R3)              EX-instruction
* data areas
IRX_IRXEXCOM DC CL8'IRXEXCOM'
VARNAME    DC     CL6'CONCAT'               variable name
IRX_SHVBLOCK DC (SHVBLEN)X'0'
           TITLE 'DSECTS'
           IRXEFPL
           IRXEVALB
           IRXARGTB
           IRXSHVB
           END
```

COBOL implementation:

```
       IDENTIFICATION DIVISION.
       PROGRAM-ID. FCONCAT.
       DATA DIVISION.
       WORKING-STORAGE SECTION.
       01 I PIC S9(9) COMP.
       01 J PIC S9(9) COMP.
       01 K PIC S9(9) COMP VALUE 1.
       01 VARNAME PIC X(8) VALUE 'CONCAT'.
       01 DUMMY-PARM PIC X(4).
       01 SHVBLOCK.
         02 SHVNEXT PIC S9(9) COMP VALUE 0.
         02 SHVUSER PIC S9(9) COMP.
         02 SHVCODE PIC X(1).
         02 SHVRET  PIC X(1).
         02 FILLER  PIC X(2).
         02 SHVBUFL PIC S9(9) COMP.
         02 SHVNAMA POINTER.
         02 SHVNAML PIC S9(9) COMP.
         02 SHVVALA POINTER.
         02 SHVVALL PIC S9(9) COMP.
       LINKAGE SECTION.
       01 EFPLCOM  PIC X(4).
       01 EFPLBARG PIC X(4).
       01 EFPLEARG PIC X(4).
       01 EFPLFB   PIC X(4).
       01 EFPLARG.
         02 ARGTABLE-ENTRY OCCURS 10.
           03 ARGSTRING-PTR POINTER.
```

```
        03 ARGSTRING-LENGTH PIC S9(9) COMP.
01 EFPLEVAL POINTER.
01 ARGSTRING.
   02 ARGSTRING-CHAR OCCURS 256.
      03 ARGSTRING-SINGLE-CHAR PIC X(1).
01 EVALBLOCK.
   02 EVALBLOCK-EVPAD1 PIC X(4).
   02 EVALBLOCK-EVSIZE PIC S9(9) COMP.
   02 EVALBLOCK-EVLEN  PIC S9(9) COMP.
   02 EVALBLOCK-EVPAD2 PIC X(4).
   02 EVALBLOCK-EVDATA.
      03 RESULT-ENTRY OCCURS 256.
         04 RESULT-CHAR PIC X(1).
PROCEDURE DIVISION
      USING EFPLCOM EFPLBARG EFPLEARG EFPLFB EFPLARG EFPLEVAL.
*     get next Argument List entry
      SET ADDRESS OF EVALBLOCK TO EFPLEVAL
      PERFORM
       VARYING I FROM 1 BY 1
        UNTIL ARGSTRING-LENGTH(I) = -1
          SET ADDRESS OF ARGSTRING TO ARGSTRING-PTR(I)
*         concatenate result
          PERFORM
           VARYING J FROM 1 BY 1
            UNTIL J > ARGSTRING-LENGTH(I)
              MOVE ARGSTRING-SINGLE-CHAR(J) TO RESULT-CHAR(K)
              ADD 1 TO K
          END-PERFORM

      END-PERFORM
      MOVE K TO EVALBLOCK-EVLEN
*     set REXX variable
      MOVE 'S' TO SHVCODE
      CALL 'SETPTR' USING VARNAME SHVNAMA
      MOVE 6 TO SHVNAML
      CALL 'SETPTR' USING EVALBLOCK-EVDATA SHVVALA
      MOVE K TO SHVVALL
      CALL 'IRXEXCOM' USING BY CONTENT 'IRXEXCOM'
       BY REFERENCE DUMMY-PARM DUMMY-PARM SHVBLOCK.
      STOP RUN.


*     subprogram to set pointer
IDENTIFICATION DIVISION.
PROGRAM-ID. SETPTR.
```

```
DATA DIVISION.
LINKAGE SECTION.
01 VAR-DATA PIC X(8).
01 VAR-PTR POINTER.
PROCEDURE DIVISION
    USING VAR-DATA VAR-PTR.
    SET  VAR-PTR TO  ADDRESS OF VAR-DATA
    GOBACK.
  END PROGRAM SETPTR.

END PROGRAM FCONCAT.
```

PL/I implementation:

```
FCONCAT: PROC(EFPLCOM,EFPLBARG,EFPLEARG,
 EFPLFB,EFPLARG,EFPLEVAL) OPTIONS(MAIN,NOEXECOPS);
DCL IRXEXCOM EXTERNAL OPTIONS(RETCODE,ASSEMBLER,INTER);
DCL 1 EFPLCOM FIXED BIN(31); /* reserved */
DCL 1 EFPLBARG FIXED BIN(31); /* reserved */
DCL 1 EFPLEARG FIXED BIN(31); /* reserved */
DCL 1 EFPLFB FIXED BIN(31);  /* reserved */
DCL 1 ARGTABLE BASED(P),
      2 ARGTABLE_ENTRY(10),
        3 ARGSTRING_PTR PTR,    /* address of argument */
        3 ARGSTRING_LENGTH FIXED BIN(31); /* length of argument */
DCL 1 EFPLEVAL PTR; /* pointer to address of EVALBLOCK */
DCL 1 EVALBLOCK BASED(EFPLEVAL),
      2 EVALBLOCK_EVPAD1 FIXED BIN(31),
      2 EVALBLOCK_EVSIZE FIXED BIN(31),
      2 EVALBLOCK_EVLEN FIXED BIN(31),
      2 EVALBLOCK_EVPAD2 FIXED BIN(31),
      2 EVALBLOCK_EVDATA CHAR(256);
DCL 1 ARGSTRING CHAR(256) BASED(ARGSTRING_PTR(I));
DCL 1 SHVBLOCK,                  /* Shared Variable Request Block */
      2 SHVNEXT FIXED BIN(31) INIT(0), /* pointer to next SHVBLOCK */
      2 SHVUSER FIXED BIN(31),        /* used during "FETCH NEXT" */
      2 SHVCODES,
        3 SHVCODE CHAR(1),        /* function code - type of variable
                                     access request */
        3 SHVRET BIT(8),          /* return codes */
        3 SHVRSV FIXED BIN(15),   /* reserved */
      2 SHVBUFL FIXED BIN(31),    /* length of fetch value buffer */
      2 SHVNAMA PTR,              /* address of variable name */
      2 SHVNAML FIXED BIN(31),    /* length of variable name */
```

```
           2 SHVVALA PTR,                 /* address of value buffer */
           2 SHVVALL FIXED BIN(31);       /* length of value buffer */
   DCL 1 VARNAME CHAR(8) INIT('CONCAT');  /* variable name */
   DCL 1 RESULT CHAR(256) BASED(ADDR_EVDATA);           /* result data */
   DCL 1 DUMMY_PARM CHAR(1);
   DCL 1 P PTR;
   DCL 1 ADDR_EVDATA PTR;
   DCL 1 I FIXED BIN(31);
   DCL 1 J FIXED BIN(31);
   DCL 1 K FIXED BIN(31) INIT(1);
   ADDR_EVDATA = ADDR(EVALBLOCK_EVDATA);
   P = ADDR(EFPLARG);
   DO I = 1 BY 1 WHILE(ARGSTRING_LENGTH(I) > 0);
     J = ARGSTRING_LENGTH(I);
     SUBSTR(RESULT,K,J) = SUBSTR(ARGSTRING,1,J);
     K = K + J;
   END;
   EVALBLOCK_EVLEN = K;
   SHVCODE = 'S';
   SHVNAMA = ADDR(VARNAME);
   SHVNAML = 6;
   SHVVALA = ADDR(RESULT);
   SHVVALL = K;
   FETCH IRXEXCOM;                /* load address of entry point */
   CALL IRXEXCOM('IRXEXCOM',DUMMY_PARM,DUMMY_PARM,SHVBLOCK);
   END;
```

16.7 FUNCTION PACKAGE

For reasons of efficiency functions can be grouped together as a **function package** - function packages are searched before the other libraries. Three classes of function package can be defined:

- user function package;
- local function package;
- system function package.

The system support personnel will usually be responsible for the local and system function packages, and so they will not be discussed in this book, although the general logic is the same as for the user function package.

A function package consists of a **function package directory** and functions, as described in the previous section. The function package directory is a load module contained in the load library - IRXFUSER is the standard name for the load module defining the user function package. This name can be changed in the Function Package Table. Fig. 16.7 shows the diagrammatic representation of a function package.

The function package directory contains the names of the functions (subroutines) as invoked from a REXX exec and a pointer to the appropriate load module. This pointer can have one of two forms:

- The address of a load module which has been linkage edited together with the function package directory - such load modules must be serially reusable, as they are loaded only once.
- The name of a load module which will be loaded from the specified load library.

16.7.1 Function Directory

The Function Directory defines the functions contained in a function package. The Function Directory consists of a header and one entry for each function contained in the Function Directory. Fig. 16.6 shows the mapping of the Function Directory fields. The Function Directory is mapped with the IRXFPDIR macro.

displ	field name	type	description
-	FPCKDIR_HEADER	DSECT	REXX Function Package Directory Header
0	FPCKDIR_ID	CL8	'IRXFPACK' character id
8	FPCKDIR_HEADER_LENGTH	F	length of directory header
12	FPCKDIR_FUNCTIONS	F	number of functions
16	-	F	reserved
20	FPCKDIR_ENTRY_LENGTH	F	length of directory entry
	FPCKDIR_ENTRY	DSECT	REXX Function Package Directory Entry
+0	FPCKDIR_FUNCNAME	CL8	name of function or subroutine
+8	FPCKDIR_FUNCADDR	A	address of the routine entry point
+12	-	F	reserved
+16	FPCKDIR_SYSNAME	CL8	name of the entry point
+24	FPCKDIR_SYSDD	CL8	DD name of load file
	FPCKDIR_NEXT		next FPCKDIR entry

Fig. 16.6 - Function Package Directory fields

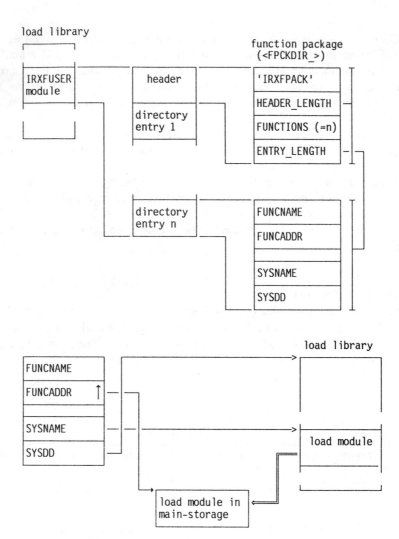

Fig. 16.7 - Diagrammatic representation of a function package

Function Package Directory Header:

FPCKDIR_ID
 'IRXFPACK' character identifier.

FPCKDIR_HEADER_LENGTH
 Length of the directory header (24 bytes).

FPCKDIR_FUNCTIONS
Number of functions in the package.

FPCKDIR_ENTRY_LENGTH
Length of a directory entry (32 bytes).

Function Package Directory Entry:

FPCKDIR_FUNCNAME
Name of function or subroutine as invoked.
Blank = ignore entry.

FPCKDIR_FUNCADDR
Address of the entry point of the routine.
0 = load module from the load library specified by FPCKDIR_SYSDD.

FPCKDIR_SYSNAME*
Name of the entry point (module name in the load library).

Sample Function Package Directory:
```
IRXFUSER CSECT
         DC    CL8'IRXFPACK'     identifier
         DC    AL4(SOD-IRXFUSER) length of header
         DC    AL4(ND)           no. of entries in directory
         DC    FL4'0'            zero
         DC    AL4(LDE)          entry length
     SOD EQU   *                 start of directory (first entry)
         DC    CL8'FDIGIT'       function name
         DC    VL4(FDIGIT)       address
         DC    FL4'0'            reserved
         DC    CL8' '            name of entry point
         DC    CL8' '            DD-name of load library
     LDE EQU   *-SOD             length of directory entry
* next entry
         DC    CL8'FGEDATE'      function name
         DC    AL4(0)            address, 0 = load from library
         DC    FL4'0'            reserved
         DC    CL8'FGEDATE'      name of entry point
         DC    CL8'ISPLLIB'      DD-name of load library
     EOD EQU   *                 end of directory
     ND  EQU   (EOD-SOD)/LDE     no. of directory entries
         END
```

This sample Function Package Directory contains two functions:
*   FDIGIT - linkage edited with the Function Package Directory;
*   FGEDATE - to be loaded from the ISPLLIB library.

16.8 LOAD ROUTINE - IRXLOAD SERVICE

The load routine (IRXLOAD) can be used in several ways:

*   load an exec into main-storage - this creates the In-storage Control Block for the exec;
*   check whether an exec is currently loaded in main-storage;
*   free an exec;
*   close a file from which execs have been loaded.

IRXLOAD is also used when the language processor environment is initialised and terminated. This book describes only the load function. Fig. 16.8 illustrates the IRXLOAD service.

Entry conditions:

Register 0   Address of an Environment Block (optional).

Register 1   Address of the parameter list.

Assembler calling sequence:
         CALL IRXLOAD,(function,addr_exec_block,addr_in-storage_control_block),VL

function
         8-byte character field containing the function to be performed: 'LOAD   '

addr_exec_block
         The address of the Exec Block (EXECBLK). The EXECBLK describes the exec to be loaded.

addr_in-storage_control_block
         The address of the allocated (and filled) In-storage Control Block (INSTBLK) is set into this address word.

Register 15 is returned with one of the following codes:
         0   processing completed successfully;

-3   the exec could not be located.

Other codes indicate a processing error.

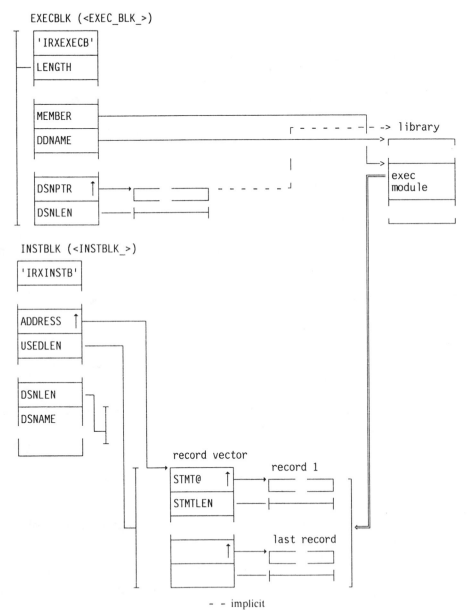

- - implicit

Fig. 16.8 - IRXLOAD interface

16.9 INITIALISATION ROUTINE - IRXINIT SERVICE

The initialisation routine (IRXINIT) can be used in two ways:

* initialise a new environment;
* obtain the address of the current Environment Block.

The first function is only used by system specialists, and so is not discussed in this book. The second function is used principally to access an error message which has been set by a service routine.

Entry conditions:

Register 0   Address of an Environment Block (optional).

Register 1   Address of the parameter list.

Return conditions:

Register 0   Address of the Environment Block; 0 indicates that the Environment Block could not be located.

Register 15   Return code. 0 or 4 indicates successful completion.

Assembler calling sequence:
```
CALL IRXINIT,(function,blank_name,0,0,0,addr_env_block,reason_code),VL
```

function
> The character string 'FINDENVB' indicates that the address of the current Environment Block is to be returned.

blank_name
> The string of 8 blanks indicates that no Parameter Module is to be used.

addr_env_block
> The fullword is returned with the address of the Environment Block; the address is also returned in register 0.

reason_code
> The fullword is returned with the reason code for an unsuccessful completion.

Sample (PL/I) coding to retrieve the current Environment Block and display the error message:

```
/* Function: Display message from Environment Block */
DCL IRXINIT EXTERNAL OPTIONS(RETCODE,ASSEMBLER,INTER);
DCL 1 ENVBLOCK BASED(ADDR_ENVB),    /* REXX Environment Block */
        2 ENVBLOCK_ID CHAR(8),          /* identifier 'ENVBLOCK'*/
        2 ENVBLOCK_VERSION CHAR(4),     /* version number */
        2 ENVBLOCK_LENGTH FIXED BIN(31), /* length of ENVBLOCK */
        2 ENVBLOCK_PARMBLOCK PTR,       /* address of the PARMBLOCK */
        2 ENVBLOCK_USERFIELD PTR,       /* address of the user field */
        2 ENVBLOCK_WORKBLOK_EXT PTR,    /* address of current WORKBLOK_EXT */
        2 ENVBLOCK_IRXEXTE PTR,         /* address of IRXEXTE */
        2 ENVBLOCK_ERROR,               /* error information */
          3 ERROR_CALL@ PTR,            /* address of the first caller */
          3 RSVR FIXED BIN(31),         /* reserved */
          3 ERROR_MSGID CHAR(8),        /* message id used by the first caller */
          3 PRIMARY_ERROR_MESSAGE CHAR(80), /* primary error message */
          3 ALTERNATE_ERROR_MSG CHAR(160); /* supplementary error msg */
DCL 1 ADDR_ENVB PTR;
DCL 1 RC FIXED BIN(31);
CALL IRXINIT('FINDENVB','        ',0,0,0,ADDR_ENVB,RC);
PUT SKIP LIST ('MESSAGE',PRIMARY_ERROR_MESSAGE);
```

16.10 GET RESULT - IRXRLT SERVICE

The get result routine (IRXRLT) can be used in two ways:

- fetch result set by an exec invoked with the IRXEXEC service;
- allocate an Evaluation Block of the specified size.

Entry conditions:

Register 0   Address of an Environment Block (optional).

Register 1   Address of the parameter list.

Return conditions:

Register 15   Return code.

    0   successful completion; however, the GETRLT result may have been truncated (if EVLEN is negative).

Other codes indicate that an error has occurred.

Assembler calling sequence:
```
CALL IRXRLT,(function,addr_evalblock,data_length),VL
```

function

The 8-character string which indicates the function to be performed.

'GETRLT   ' - obtain the result from the last exec invoked in this environment. This function is only valid when no exec is currently executing. EVLEN is set to the negative length of the result if it does not fit in the Environment Block (the return code is set to 0).

'GETBLOCK' - obtain an Evaluation Block for the current external function or subroutine. This function may only be invoked from an external function or subroutine.

addr_evalblock

Address of the Evaluation Block to be used (for GETRLT) or returned (for GETBLOCK).

data_length

Fullword containing the length (in bytes) of the data area in the new Evaluation Block which is to be allocated. This parameter is not used for the GETRLT function.

Sample program:
```
BETA5: PROC OPTIONS(MAIN);
/* Function: Allocate a new Evaluation Block */
DCL IRXRLT EXTERNAL OPTIONS(RETCODE,ASSEMBLER,INTER);
DCL 1 EVALBLOCK BASED(ADDR_EVALBLOCK),
      2 EVPAD1 FIXED BIN(31),
      2 EVSIZE FIXED BIN(31),
      2 EVLEN  FIXED BIN(31),
      2 EVPAD2 FIXED BIN(31),
      2 EVDATA CHAR(1);
DCL 1 ADDR_EVALBLOCK PTR;
DCL 1 LEN FIXED BIN(31) INIT(800);
FETCH IRXRLT;            /* load address of entry point */
CALL IRXRLT('GETBLOCK',ADDR_EVALBLOCK,LEN);
PUT SKIP LIST ('EVSIZE:',EVSIZE*8+16);
END;
```
This sample PL/I program allocates a new Evaluation Block having a maximum data length of 800 bytes. The total length of the allocated Evaluation Block is displayed.

16.11 CONTROL BLOCKS

This section describes the most important control blocks used by the REXX interfaces described in this chapter. The control blocks are listed in alphabetic sequence.

16.11.1 Argument List

The Argument List describes the input arguments passed to a function. Each argument passed to the function has one Argument List entry (consisting of two words) in the Argument List. The Argument List is terminated with two words each containing binary -1 (X'F...F'). Fig. 16.9 shows the mapping of the Argument List fields. The Argument List is mapped with the IRXARGTB macro.

displ	field name	type	description
–	ARGTABLE_ENTRY	DSECT	REXX Argument Table Entry (ARGTABLE)
+0 +4	ARGTABLE_ARGSTRING_PTR ARGTABLE_ARGSTRING_LENGTH	A F	address of the argument length of the argument
+8	ARGTABLE_NEXT	–	next ARGTABLE entry

Fig. 16.9 - Argument List fields

ARGTABLE_ARGSTRING_PTR
    Address of the argument.

ARGTABLE_ARGSTRING_LENGTH
    Length of the argument.

16.11.2 EFPL - External Functions Parameter List

The EFPL describes the external arguments for a function; the pointer to the input arguments and to the result field. The input arguments are defined in the Argument List. The result is defined in the EVALBLOCK (Evaluation Block). Fig. 16.10 shows the mapping of the EFPL fields. The EFPL is mapped with the IRXEFPL macro.

displ	field name	type	description
-	EFPL	DSECT	External Functions Parameter List (EFPL)
0	EFPLCOM	A	reserved
4	EFPLBARG	A	reserved
8	EFPLEARG	A	reserved
12	EFPLFB	A	reserved
16	EFPLARG	A	address of the Argument List
20	EFPLEVAL	A	pointer to address of EVALBLOCK

Fig. 16.10 - EFPL fields

EFPLARG
> Address of the Argument List. The Argument List is a table containing the address and length of each parsed argument passed to the function.

EFPLEVAL
> Pointer to a full-word containing the address of the EVALBLOCK. The EVALBLOCK contains the result returned by the function.

16.11.3 ENVBLOCK - Environment Block
The ENVBLOCK describes the REXX operating environment. An ENVBLOCK is automatically created when the REXX environment is initiated. The ENVBLOCK is principally used by the application developer to obtain error messages. Fig. 16.11 shows the mapping of the ENVBLOCK. The ENVBLOCK is mapped with the IRXENVB macro.

ENVBLOCK_ID
> Block identifier 'ENVBLOCK'.

ENVBLOCK_VERSION
> Version number.

ENVBLOCK_LENGTH
> Length of ENVBLOCK (288 bytes).

ENVBLOCK_PARMBLOCK
> Address of the PARMBLOCK.

displ	field name	type	description
-	ENVBLOCK	DSECT	REXX Environment Block
0	ENVBLOCK_ID	CL8	'ENVBLOCK' character id
8	ENVBLOCK_VERSION	CL4	version number
12	ENVBLOCK_LENGTH	F	length of ENVBLOCK
16	ENVBLOCK_PARMBLOCK	A	address of the PARMBLOCK
20	ENVBLOCK_USERFIELD	A	address of the user field
24	ENVBLOCK_WORKBLOK_EXT	A	address of current work-block extension
28	ENVBLOCK_IRXEXTE	A	address of IRXEXTE
32	ENVBLOCK_ERROR	-	error information
32	ERROR_CALL@	A	address of error routine
36	-	F	reserved
40	ERROR_MSGID	CL8	message identifier (first message)
48	PRIMARY_ERROR_MESSAGE	CL80	first error message
128	ALTERNATE_ERROR_MSG	CL160	supplementary error message

Fig. 16.11 - ENVBLOCK fields

ENVBLOCK_USERFIELD
Address of the user field.

ENVBLOCK_WORKBLOK_EXT
Address of the current WORKBLOK_EXT (Work Block extension).

ENVBLOCK_IRXEXTE
Address of IRXEXTE - vector of external subroutine addresses.

ENVBLOCK_ERROR
Start of error information.

ERROR_CALL@
Address of the routine which caused the error.

ERROR_MSGID
Message identifier of first message.

PRIMARY_ERROR_MESSAGE
First error message.

ALTERNATE_ERROR_MSG
Supplementary error message.

16.11.4 EVALBLOCK - Evaluation Block

The EVALBLOCK describes the result passed back from a function. Fig. 16.12 shows the mapping of the EVALBLOCK fields. The EVALBLOCK is mapped with the IRXEVALB macro.

displ	field name	type	description
–	EVALBLOCK	DSECT	REXX Evaluation Block (EVALBLOCK)
0	EVALBLOCK_EVPAD1	F	reserved - set to binary zero
4	EVALBLOCK_EVSIZE	F	size of EVALBLOCK (in double words)
8	EVALBLOCK_EVLEN	F	length of data
12	EVALBLOCK_EVPAD2	F	reserved - set to binary zero
16	EVALBLOCK_EVDATA	0C	start of data

Fig. 16.12 - EVALBLOCK fields

EVALBLOCK_EVPAD1

Reserved - set to binary zero.

EVALBLOCK_EVSIZE

Size of EVALBLOCK (in double words, 8-byte units).

EVALBLOCK_EVLEN

Length of data. This value is set to the negative length if the data do not fit in the Evaluation Block. The maximum length of the data which can be stored in the EVALBLOCK is EVALBLOCK_EVSIZE*8-16 bytes.

EVALBLOCK_EVPAD2

Reserved - set to binary zero.

EVALBLOCK_EVDATA

Start of data. The IRXRLT (Get Result) routine can be used to retrieve the complete result, even if it cannot be stored in the EVALBLOCK, or to allocate a new Evaluation Block of the required size.

16.11.5 EXECBLK - Exec Block

The EXECBLK describes an external exec. Fig. 16.13 shows the mapping of the EXECBLK fields. The EXECBLK is mapped with the IRXEXECB macro.

displ	field name	type	description
-	EXECBLK	DSECT	REXX EXEC Block (EXECBLK)
0	EXEC_BLK_ACRYN	CL8	block identifier 'IRXEXECB'
8	EXEC_BLK_LENGTH	F	length of EXECBLK
12	-	F	reserved
16	EXEC_MEMBER	CL8	member name of exec.
24	EXEC_DDNAME	CL8	DD name for the dataset
32	EXEC_SUBCOM	CL8	initial subcommand environment name
40	EXEC_DSNPTR	A	address of PARSE SOURCE dataset name
44	EXEC_DSNLEN	F	length of EXEC_DSNPTR dataset name
	EXECDLEN	EQU	length of EXECBLK

Fig. 16.13 - EXECBLK fields

EXEC_BLK_ACRYN
>   Block identifier 'IRXEXECB'.

EXEC_BLK_LENGTH
>   Length of EXECBLK (48 bytes).

EXEC_MEMBER
>   Member name of exec, if partitioned dataset; blank if sequential dataset.

EXEC_DDNAME
>   DD name for the dataset from which the exec is to be loaded ('LOAD') or to be closed ('CLOSEDD'). This entry is not used if an INSTBLK has been defined. Blank means that the exec is loaded from the file defined by the LOADDD entry in the Module Name table - default is SYSEXEC.

EXEC_SUBCOM
>   Name of the initial subcommand environment.

EXEC_DSNPTR
>   Address of the dataset name to be returned by the PARSE SOURCE instruction; the dataset name may specify a member name within parentheses.
>   0 = no entry.

EXEC_DSNLEN
>   Normalised length of dataset name pointed to by EXEC_DSNPTR.
>   0 = no entry.

16.11.6 INSTBLK - In-storage Control Block

The INSTBLK describes (address and length) the individual records (lines) of a REXX exec contained in main-storage. The IRXLOAD service can be used to build the INSTBLK. Fig. 16.14 shows the mapping of the INSTBLK fields. The INSTBLK is mapped with the IRXINSTB macro.

displ	field name	type	description
-	INSTBLK	DSECT	REXX In-storage Control Block
0	INSTBLK_HEADER	-	In-storage Block Header
0	INSTBLK_ACRONYM	CL8	block identifier 'IRXINSTB'
8	INSTBLK_HDRLEN	F	length of INSTBLK header
12	-	F	reserved
16	INSTBLK_ADDRESS	A	address of first INSTBLK_ENTRY
20	INSTBLK_USEDLEN	F	total length of INSTBLK_ENTRYs
24	INSTBLK_MEMBER	CL8	member name of loaded exec
32	INSTBLK_DDNAME	CL8	DD-name of dataset of loaded exec
40	INSTBLK_SUBCOM	CL8	name of subcommand environment
48	-	F	reserved
52	INSTBLK_DSNLEN	F	length of dataset name
56	INSTBLK_DSNAME	CL54	dataset name
-	INSTBLK_ENTRY	DSECT	REXX In-storage Block Entry
+0	INSTBLK_STMT@	A	address of REXX statement
+4	INSTBLK_STMTLEN	F	length of REXX statement

Fig. 16.14 - INSTBLK fields

INSTBLK_HEADER (In-storage Block Header):

INSTBLK_ACRONYM
> Block identifier 'IRXINSTB'

INSTBLK_HDRLEN
> Length of the INSTBLK header (128 bytes).

INSTBLK_ADDRESS
> Address of first INSTBLK entry.

INSTBLK_USEDLEN
> Total length of INSTBLK entries. The number of entries (rows in the REXX

exec) can be determined by dividing this total length by the size of each entry
(= 8).

INSTBLK_MEMBER
Name of member of the partitioned dataset from which the exec was loaded -
blank if loaded from a sequential dataset.

INSTBLK_DDNAME
Name of the DD statement which identifies the dataset from which the exec
was loaded.

INSTBLK_SUBCOM
Name of initial subcommand environment under which exec is run.

INSTBLK_DSNLEN
Normalised length of dataset name (INSTBLK_DSNAME). The normalised length is
the length excluding blanks.

INSTBLK_DSNAME
Dataset name from which exec was loaded.

INSTBLK_ENTRIES
Start of the array of INSTBLK (data) entries. The INSTBLK_ENTRY DSECT maps
each INSTBLK entry.

INSTBLK_STMT@
Address of REXX statement in main-storage.

INSTBLK_STMTLEN
Length of the REXX statement.

16.11.7 SHVBLOCK - Shared Variable (Request) Block
The SHVBLOCK describes the variable to be accessed from the variable pool.
SHVBLOCKs can be chained together. Fig. 16.15 shows the mapping of the
SHVBLOCK fields. The SHVBLOCK is mapped with the IRXSHVB macro.

displ	field name	type	description
–	SHVBLOCK	DSECT	REXX Shared Variable Request Block
0	SHVNEXT	A	address of next SHVBLOCK in chain.
4	SHVUSER	F	used during "FIND NEXT" processing
8	SHVCODE	CL1	function type
9	SHVRET	XL1	return code flags
10	–	H	reserved
12	SHVBUFL	F	length of the fetch value buffer
16	SHVNAMA	A	address of the variable name
20	SHVNAML	F	length of the variable name
24	SHVVALA	A	address of the data value
28	SHVVALL	F	length of the data value

Fig. 16.15 - SHVBLOCK fields

SHVNEXT

Address of the next SHVBLOCK in chain.

0 = end of chain.

SHVUSER

is used during "FIND NEXT" processing to contain the length of the buffer pointed to by SHVNAMA.

SHVCODE

Function type:
- 'D' (SHVDROPV) - drop variable;
- 'd' (SHVSYDRO) - drop symbolic name;
- 'F' (SHVFETCH) - copy value of shared variable;
- 'f' (SHVSYFET) - retrieve symbolic name;
- 'N' (SHVNEXTV) - fetch "next" variable (the repetitive use of this function retrieves successive variables);
- 'P' (SHVPRIV) - fetch private (user) information;
- 'S' (SHVSTORE) - store value for variable;
- 's' (SHVSYSET) - set symbolic name.

The parenthesised name is the EQU-name defined by the IRXSHVB macro.

Note: The variable name is interpreted as being a symbol for lower case function codes.

SHVRET

Return code flags:
- X'00' (SHVCLEAN) - execution completed successfully;
- X'01' (SHVNEWV) - variable did not exist;
- X'02' (SHVLVAR) - last variable transferred ("N" processing);

SHVBUFL

Length of value buffer used for fetch processing.

SHVNAMA

Address of the variable name.

SHVNAML

Normalised length (without blanks) of the left-justified variable name.

SHVVALA

Address of the data value. The data are usually in character format.

SHVVALL

Length of the data value.

16.11.8 VEEP - Vector of External Entry Points

The VEEP contains the addresses of the external REXX service routines - both standard and replaceable routines. Fig. 16.16 shows the mapping of the standard VEEP fields, the addresses of the replaceable routines have been omitted. The VEEP is mapped with the IRXEXTE macro.

displ	field name	type	description
-	IRXEXTE	DSECT	REXX Vector of External Entry Points (VEEP)
0	IRXEXTE_ENTRY_COUNT	F	number of entry points in the VEEP (=20)
4	IRXINIT	A	IRXINIT - initialisation routine
12	IRXLOAD	A	IRXLOAD - load exec routine
16	IRXEXCOM	A	IRXEXCOM - variable access routine
20	IRXEXEC	A	IRXEXEC - run exec routine
28	IRXINOUT	A	IRXINOUT - Input/Output routine
32	IRXJCL	A	IRXJCL - run JCL routine
36	IRXRLT	A	IRXRLT - get result routine
44	IRXSTK	A	IRXSTK - data stack processing routine
48	IRXSUBCM	A	IRXSUBCM - subcommand service routine
52	IRXTERM	A	IRXTERM - termination routine
56	IRXIC	A	IRXIC - immediate commands routine
64	IRXMSGID	A	IRXMSGID - message routine
72	IRXUID	A	IRXUID - userid routine
76	IRXTERMA	A	IRXTERMA - abnormal termination routine

Fig. 16.16 - Vector of External Entry Points fields

Appendix A

REXX instructions syntax summary

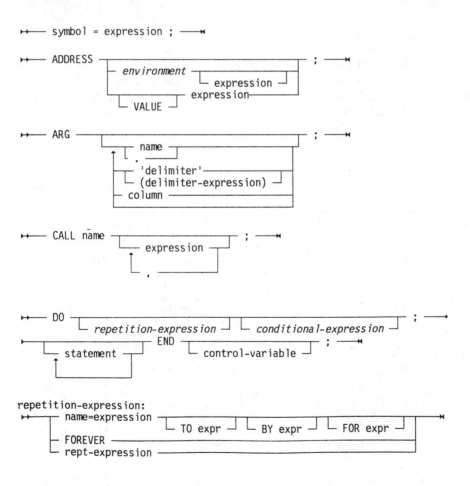

```
►►─── symbol = expression ; ───►◄

►►─── ADDRESS ──────────────────────────────────── ; ───►◄
              ┌─ environment ──────────────┐
              │              └─ expression ─┘
              │              expression
              └─ VALUE ─┘

►►─── ARG ──────────────────────────────────── ; ───►◄
          ┌─────── name ──────────────────┐
          │   └─ . ─┘                      │
          │   ┌─ 'delimiter' ──────────┐   │
          │   └─ (delimiter-expression) ─┘ │
          └─ column ──────────────────────┘

►►─── CALL name ─────────────────── ; ───►◄
               ┌─ expression ─┐
               └──────────────┘
                    └─ , ─┘

►►─── DO ─────────────────────────────────────────────── ; ───►◄
        └─ repetition-expression ─┘ └─ conditional-expression ─┘
►─────────────────────── END ──────────────── ; ───►◄
    └─ statement ─┘          └─ control-variable ─┘

repetition-expression:
►►─┬─ name=expression ─────────────────────────────────────────────────►◄
   │                 └─ TO expr ─┘ └─ BY expr ─┘ └─ FOR expr ─┘
   ├─ FOREVER ────────────────────────────────────────────────
   └─ rept-expression ────────────────────────────────────────
```

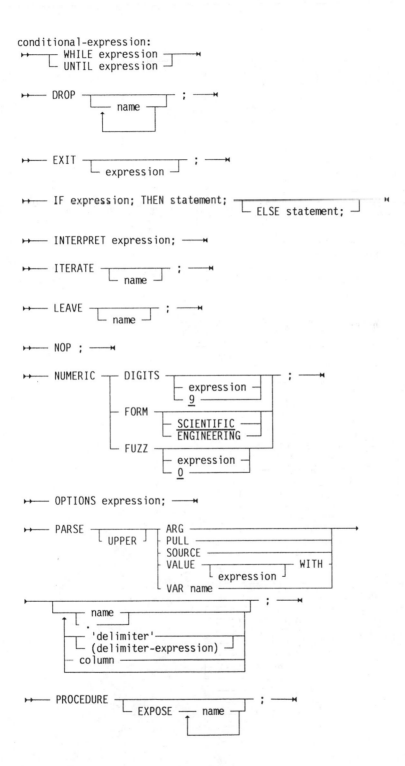

```
conditional-expression:
►►─┬─ WHILE expression ─┬─►◄
    └─ UNTIL expression ─┘


►►── DROP ─┬─────────────┬─ ; ─►◄
           │  ┌────────┐ │
           └──┤  name  ├─┘
              └────────┘


►►── EXIT ─┬──────────────┬─ ; ─►◄
           └─ expression ─┘


►►── IF expression; THEN statement; ─┬──────────────────┬─►◄
                                     └─ ELSE statement; ─┘


►►── INTERPRET expression; ──►◄


►►── ITERATE ─┬────────┬─ ; ─►◄
              └─ name ─┘


►►── LEAVE ─┬────────┬─ ; ─►◄
            └─ name ─┘


►►── NOP ; ──►◄


►►── NUMERIC ─┬─ DIGITS ─┬──────────────┬─┬─ ; ─►◄
             │          ├─ expression ─┤ │
             │          └─ 9 ──────────┘ │
             ├─ FORM ─┬──────────────┬───┤
             │        ├─ SCIENTIFIC ─┤   │
             │        └─ ENGINEERING ┘   │
             └─ FUZZ ─┬──────────────┬───┘
                      ├─ expression ─┤
                      └─ 0 ──────────┘


►►── OPTIONS expression; ──►◄


►►── PARSE ─┬─────────┬─┬─ ARG ──────────────────────┬─►
            └─ UPPER ─┘ ├─ PULL ─────────────────────┤
                        ├─ SOURCE ───────────────────┤
                        ├─ VALUE ─┬──────────────┬─ WITH ─┤
                        │         └─ expression ─┘        │
                        └─ VAR name ─────────────────────┘

►─┬─ name ────────────────────────────┬─ ; ─►◄
  ├─ . ─┬─ 'delimiter' ─────────────┬─┤
  │     └─ (delimiter-expression) ─┘ │
  └─ column ──────────────────────────┘


►►── PROCEDURE ─┬───────────────────────┬─ ; ─►◄
               └─ EXPOSE ─┬─ name ─┬────┘
                          └────────┘
```

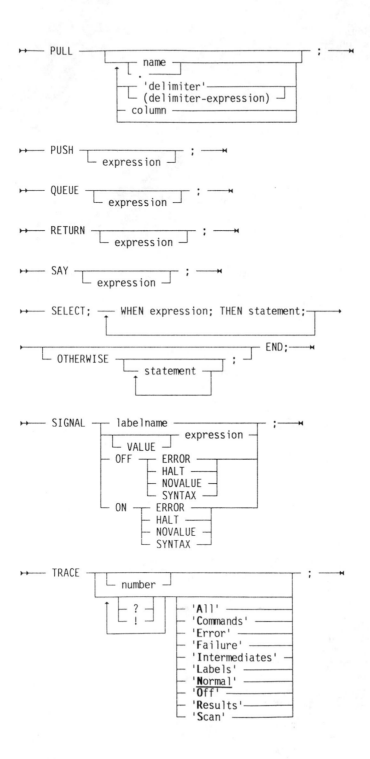

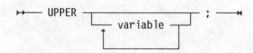

Appendix B

REXX built-in functions syntax summary

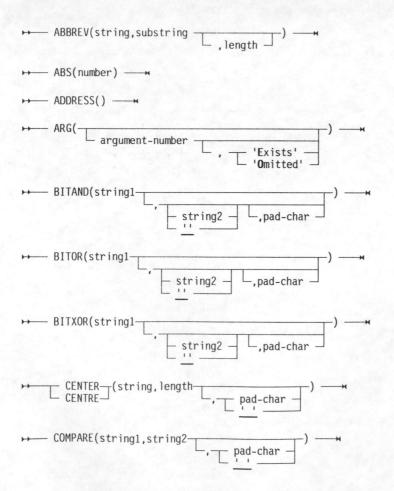

```
►►── ABBREV(string,substring ─┬──────────┬─) ──►◄
                             └─ ,length ─┘


►►── ABS(number) ──►◄

►►── ADDRESS() ──►◄

►►── ARG(─┬─────────────────────────────────────────┬─) ──►◄
          └─ argument-number ─┬──────────────────┬─┘
                              └─,─┬─ 'Exists' ──┬─┘
                                  └─ 'Omitted' ─┘


►►── BITAND(string1─┬──────────────────────────────┬─) ──►◄
                    └─,─┬─ string2 ─┬─┬─ ,pad-char ─┬┘
                        └─  ''  ───┘ └────────────┘


►►── BITOR(string1─┬──────────────────────────────┬─) ──►◄
                   └─,─┬─ string2 ─┬─┬─ ,pad-char ─┬┘
                       └─  ''  ───┘ └────────────┘


►►── BITXOR(string1─┬──────────────────────────────┬─) ──►◄
                    └─,─┬─ string2 ─┬─┬─ ,pad-char ─┬┘
                        └─  ''  ───┘ └────────────┘


►►─┬─ CENTER ─┬─(string,length─┬─────────────────┬─) ──►◄
   └─ CENTRE ─┘                └─,─┬─ pad-char ─┬─┘
                                   └─   ''   ──┘


►►── COMPARE(string1,string2─┬─────────────────┬─) ──►◄
                            └─,─┬─ pad-char ─┬─┘
                                └─   ''   ──┘
```

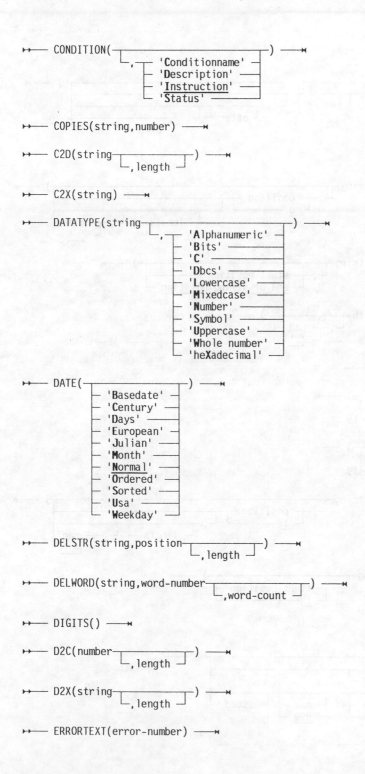

```
►►── CONDITION(─┬─────────────────────────┬─)──►◄
               └─,─┬─'Conditionname'─┬────┘
                   ├─'Description'───┤
                   ├─'Instruction'───┤
                   └─'Status'────────┘

►►── COPIES(string,number) ──►◄

►►── C2D(string─┬──────────┬─)──►◄
               └─,length──┘

►►── C2X(string) ──►◄

►►── DATATYPE(string─┬─────────────────────────┬─)──►◄
                    └─,─┬─'Alphanumeric'──┬────┘
                        ├─'Bits'──────────┤
                        ├─'C'─────────────┤
                        ├─'Dbcs'──────────┤
                        ├─'Lowercase'─────┤
                        ├─'Mixedcase'─────┤
                        ├─'Number'────────┤
                        ├─'Symbol'────────┤
                        ├─'Uppercase'─────┤
                        ├─'Whole number'──┤
                        └─'heXadecimal'───┘

►►── DATE(─┬──────────────┬─)──►◄
           ├─'Basedate'───┤
           ├─'Century'────┤
           ├─'Days'───────┤
           ├─'European'───┤
           ├─'Julian'─────┤
           ├─'Month'──────┤
           ├─'Normal'─────┤
           ├─'Ordered'────┤
           ├─'Sorted'─────┤
           ├─'Usa'────────┤
           └─'Weekday'────┘

►►── DELSTR(string,position─┬──────────┬─)──►◄
                           └─,length──┘

►►── DELWORD(string,word-number─┬──────────────┬─)──►◄
                               └─,word-count──┘

►►── DIGITS() ──►◄

►►── D2C(number─┬──────────┬─)──►◄
               └─,length──┘

►►── D2X(string─┬──────────┬─)──►◄
               └─,length──┘

►►── ERRORTEXT(error-number) ──►◄
```

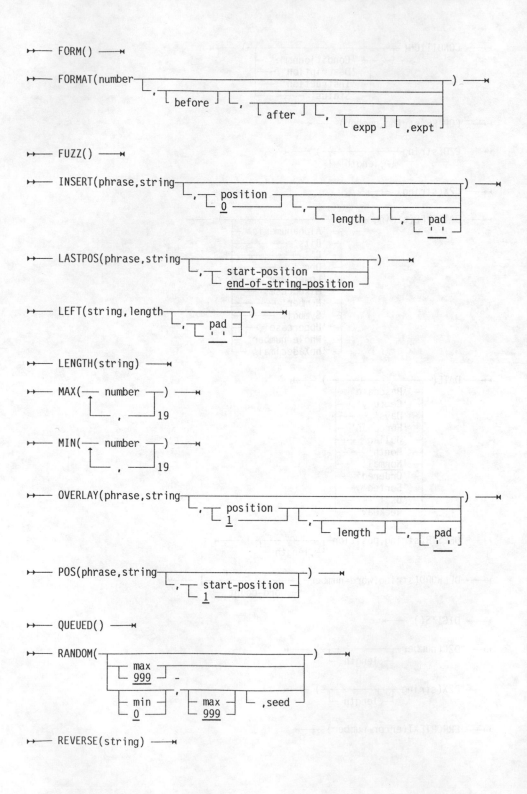

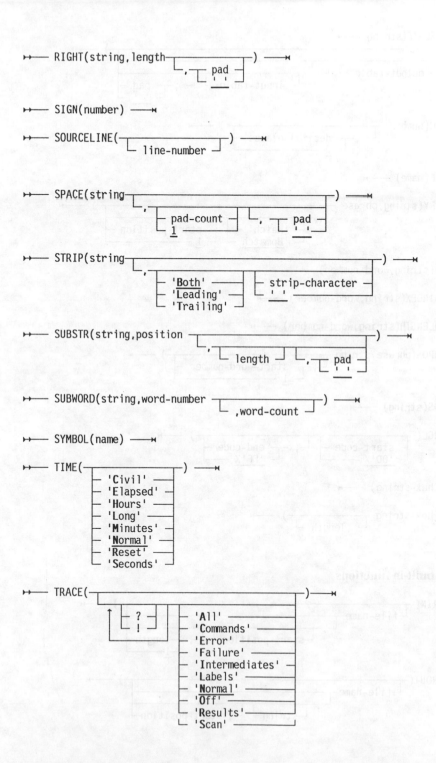

```
►►─── RIGHT(string,length─┬──────────┬─)─── ►◄
                         └─,─┬─pad─┬─┘
                            └──' '──┘

►►─── SIGN(number)───►◄

►►─── SOURCELINE(─┬──────────────┬─)───►◄
                 └─ line-number ─┘

►►─── SPACE(string─┬───────────────────────────────────────┬─)───►◄
                  └─,─┬─pad-count─┬──┬───┬─┬─────┬─┘
                      └────1──────┘  └─,─┘ └─pad─┘
                                           └' '┘

►►─── STRIP(string─┬─────────────────────────────────────┬─)───►◄
                  └─,─┬─ 'Both' ────┬──┬─ strip-character ─┬─┘
                      ├─ 'Leading' ─┤  └────' '────────────┘
                      └─ 'Trailing' ┘

►►─── SUBSTR(string,position ─┬──────────────────────┬─)───►◄
                             └─,─┬─ length ─┬─┬───┬─┬─┘
                                 └──────────┘ └─,─┘ └─pad─┘
                                                    └' '┘

►►─── SUBWORD(string,word-number ─┬──────────────┬─)───►◄
                                 └─,word-count ──┘

►►─── SYMBOL(name)───►◄

►►─── TIME(─┬─────────────┬─)───►◄
           ├─ 'Civil' ────┤
           ├─ 'Elapsed' ──┤
           ├─ 'Hours' ────┤
           ├─ 'Long' ─────┤
           ├─ 'Minutes' ──┤
           ├─ 'Normal' ───┤
           ├─ 'Reset' ────┤
           └─ 'Seconds' ──┘

►►─── TRACE(─┬─────────────────────────────────┬─)───►◄
            │  ┌─────┐  ┌─ 'All' ───────────┐  │
            ├──┤ ? ├──┤  ├─ 'Commands' ──────┤  │
            │  └─ ! ─┘  ├─ 'Error' ─────────┤  │
            │           ├─ 'Failure' ───────┤  │
            │           ├─ 'Intermediates' ─┤  │
            │           ├─ 'Labels' ────────┤  │
            │           ├─ 'Normal' ────────┤  │
            │           ├─ 'Off' ───────────┤  │
            │           ├─ 'Results' ───────┤  │
            │           └─ 'Scan' ──────────┘  │
```

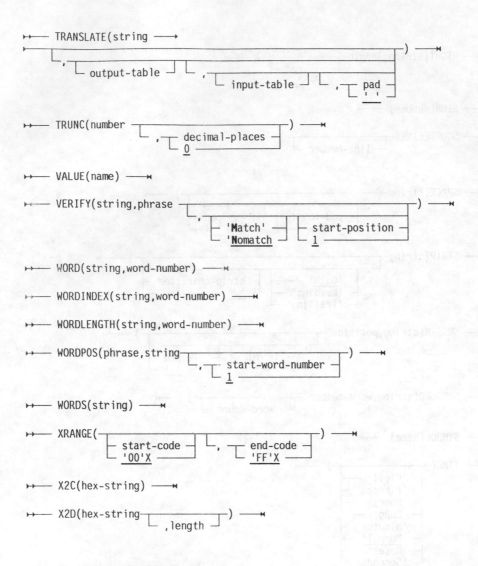

Non-SAA built-in functions

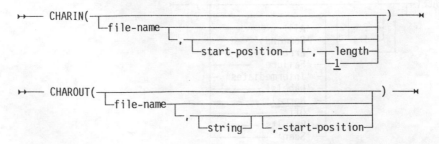

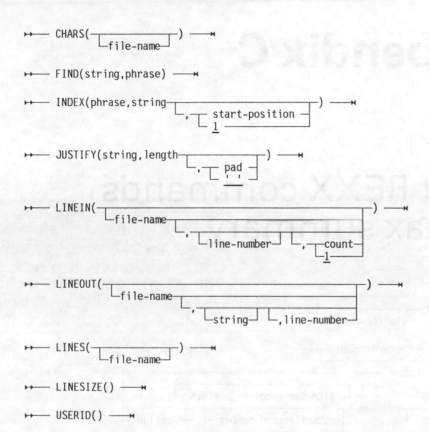

Appendix C

Host REXX commands syntax summary

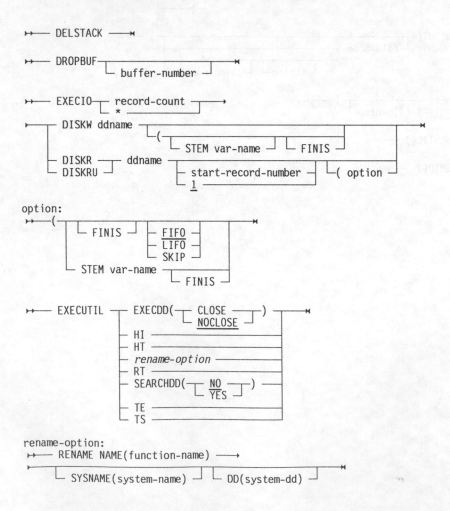

▸▸── HI ──▸

▸▸── HT ──▸

▸▸── MAKEBUF ──▸

▸▸── NEWSTACK ──▸

▸▸── QBUF ──▸

▸▸── QELEM ──▸

▸▸── QSTACK ──▸

▸▸── RT ──▸

▸▸── SUBCOM *environment* ──▸

▸▸── TE ──▸

▸▸── TS ──▸

Appendix D

MVS command functions syntax summary

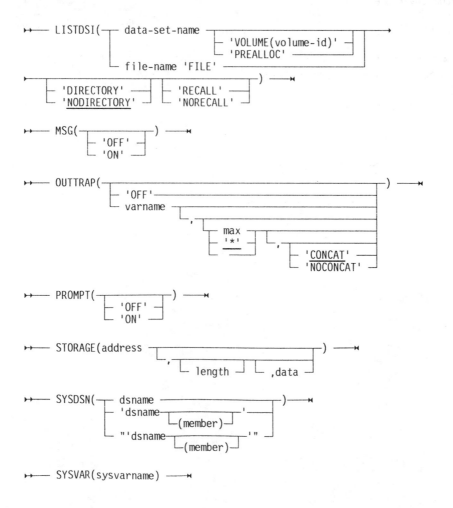

Appendix E

Syntax notation

Syntax diagram

This book makes use of syntax diagrams to describe the syntax of expressions. Syntax diagrams are read left to right, top to bottom.

⊢—— indicates the beginning of the statement

——⊣ indicates the end of the statement

——→ indicates that the statement is continued

⊢—— indicates the continuation of the statement

⊢⊤ indicates a junction (branch-point). The principal path is the horizontal.

• Mandatory items cannot be branched around.

    Example:

    "mandatory" must be selected - it is on the horizontal path and cannot be branched around. At the following junction either the horizontal path (containing no entries) or the branch containing the entry optional can be taken - as there is a choice of paths the entry is optional.

• If **one** of a number of mandatory items *must* be selected, then these items appear in a vertical stack.

Example:

```
├──┬─ mandatory1 ─┬──►
   └─ mandatory2 ─┘
```

Either "mandatory1" or "mandatory2" must be selected. The first junction offers two paths, one path with mandatory1 and one path with mandatory2 - each path contains an entry, and so one of the entries is mandatory.

• Multiple options appear in a vertical stack, **one** of the specified options *may* be selected.

Example:

```
├────────────────►
  ├─ option1 ─┤
  └─ option2 ─┘
```

Either "option1" or "option2" may be selected. The first junction offers three paths: the horizontal path has no entry; the other two paths have the entries option1 or option2, respectively. Because the paths containing option1 and option2 need not be taken, these entries are optional.

• Repetition is indicated by the following constructions:

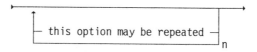

```
├────────────────────────────────────►
    ┌─ this option may be repeated ─┐
    └───────────────────────────────┘ n
```

n at the right, if present, specifies the maximum number of times that the item *may* be repeated; the default value is unlimited.

Example:

```
├────────────────────►
   ┌─ alpha ─┐
   └─────────┘ 2
```

In this case the first junction is at the right-hand side of the diagram. This junction offers two paths, one horizontal to the end of the statement and one vertical. This vertical path has two subsequent paths, which contain either alpha or no entry. The value 2 indicates that up to two repetitions may be made. This means that either no entry, one alpha entry or two alpha entries may be specified.

```
 ┌─────────────────────────────────┐
─┤                                 ├─►
 n│
  └─ this option must be repeated ─┘
```

n at the left, if present, specifies the number of times that the item *must* be repeated.

Example:

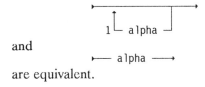

Again the first junction is at the right-hand side of the diagram. The value 3 indicates that three repetitions must be made, i.e. three alpha entries must be specified.

The repetition value 1 is a special case, and is indicates a mandatory item. For example

```
 ┌──────────┐
─┤          ├─►
 1└─ alpha ─┘
```

and

```
►── alpha ──►
```

are equivalent.

•   If the repeat path contains an item, then this item is mandatory for repetitions.

Example:

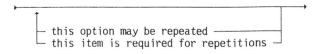

•   An item written in upper case must be spelled exactly as shown, an item written in lower case is replaced by a valid entry (described in the text). An underlined entry is the default value.

Example:

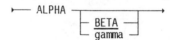

The first item is mandatory and must be ALPHA; the second item is optional, the default value is BETA. If an item is selected, then it must be a valid value for gamma.

•   If an item is written italicised, then this is a parameter, the definition of which follows.

Example:

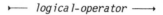

logical-operator:

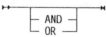

The parameter "logical-operator" may be replaced by one of the optional values: AND or OR.

A syntax diagram is formed by combining the simple elements defined above.

Font

The sans serif font is used to depict commands, keywords or data set names.

Example:
The statement TSO DELETE is a command which invokes the TSO component DELETE.

Appendix F

Bibliography

Systems Application Architecture

SAA Common Programming Interface Procedures Language Reference
Describes the SAA definition of the REXX language.

MVS-TSO/E Implementation

TSO/E Version 2 REXX User's Guide
Contains short code examples on the use of REXX in the MVS-TSO/E implementation.

TSO/E Version 2 REXX Reference
Describes the MVS-TSO/E REXX implementation - syntax and semantics. This manual includes the descriptions of the system interfaces.

TSO/E Programming Services
Describes the TSOLNK service.

VM/SP Implementation

VM/SP System Product Interpreter User's Guide

VM/SP System Product Interpreter Reference

OS/2 Implementation (REXX/2)

OS/2 Procedures Language 2/REXX User's Guide
Contains examples on the use of REXX in the OS/2 implementation.

OS/2 Procedures Language 2/REXX Reference
Describes the OS/2 REXX implementation - syntax and semantics. This manual includes the descriptions of the system interfaces.

Personal REXX

Personal REXX User's Guide (Mansfield Software Group, Inc.)
Describes the Personal REXX implementation.

REXX Language

M.F.Cowlishaw *The REXX Language, A Practical Approach to Programming*, Prentice-Hall, 1985.
Describes the REXX language elements.

My books in the Ellis Horwood series on computers and their applications:

ISPF (Interactive System Productivity Facility)

Practical Usage of ISPF Dialog Manager, Ellis Horwood, 1989.
Describes how to use the ISPF Dialog Manager elements to create dialogue applications.

Database2 (DB2) and Query Management Facility (QMF)

Implementing Practical DB2 Applications, Ellis Horwood, 1990.
Describes how DB2 and QMF are used to implement applications. The book includes detailed descriptions of the interfaces (program and file) to these products.

Appendix G

Glossary

address space   The virtual storage allocated to a task. An **address space** accommodates a batch job, TSO user, etc.

alphabetic   The set of characters containing the lower and upper case letters together with the three national characters: #, @ and $.

alphameric   The **alphabetic** characters together with the ten numeric digits: 0 through 9.

alphanumeric   The same as **alphameric.**

ASCII   American Standard Code for Information Interchange. The data code used primarily on personal computers. Appendix H contains the codes for the ASCII alphameric characters.

clause   In the REXX sense, a sub-expression.

CLIST   Command List. Procedure consisting of TSO commands and subcommands and control statements. CLISTs are also known as **command procedures**.

CMS   Conversational Monitor System. VM's user interface - functionally similar to TSO.

command procedure   See CLIST.

compiler   A software component which converts a source program into an object module.

CVT   Communications Vector Table. Operating system table (starting at absolute address 16) which can be used in read-only mode to obtain the addresses of routines and storage areas.

data base   See database.

database   A logically related set of named data elements. Database systems largely isolate users from the physical data storage.

DATABASE2^{TM} IBM relational data base, usually known as DB2.

dataset   Synonymous term for a file.

DBCS   Double-Byte Character Set. A set of pairs of characters used to represent characters in Far-East languages (Chinese, Japanese, Korean, etc.).

DBMS   Database Management System. A program to control the use of a database.

DB2^{TM} DATABASE2. IBM relational database.

DD   Data Definition. The JCL statement used to assign the physical data (dataset, printer output class, etc.) to the logical dataset defined in the program. The **ddname** links the logical dataset to the JCL DD statement.

Dialog Manager   ISPF component which administers dialogue facilities. Dialog Manager is usually synonymous with ISPF.

dialogue   Man-machine interaction using a terminal directly attached to computer. Various levels of program systems (application program, terminal monitor program, etc.) control the dialogue.

DOS   Disk Operating System - the generic name for the two operating systems (MS-DOS and PC-DOS) used for the IBM Personal Computer and compatibles.

DSORG   Dataset organisation. The organisation of information in a dataset.

EBCDIC   Extended Binary Coded-Decimal Interchange Code. The data code used primarily on IBM mainframe computers. Appendix H contains the codes for the EBCDIC alphameric characters.

edit macro   A procedure (REXX or CLIST) invoked from (or with) the ISPF/PDF Editor to perform a predefined series of operations on the current dataset. An edit macro combines the facilities offered by procedures and the Editor.

EMS   Expanded Memory Specification. PC memory usable above the 640K boundary.

EXEC   Execute program or procedure. The JCL statement used to invoke a program or JCL procedure.

exec   synonymous with a REXX program.

FIFO   First-in/First-out. Storage management concept where the elements are retrieved in the same order as which they were inserted - this is also known as **queue processing**.

file   A collection of data (= dataset). With regard to TSO it is equivalent to the JCL DD statement.

filename   The identifier of the **file**. In TSO it is equivalent to the **ddname**. In the PC environment it is the fully qualified name of the file, i.e. contains the drive (unit) identifier, path name as well as the name in the directory.

GDDM^{TM}   Graphic Data Display Manager. IBM product consisting of basic subroutines for processing and displaying graphic data.

help environment   Sub-environment used to provide on-line assistance.

help panel   Panel which is used for display or data entry within the help environment.

hexadecimal   Coding scheme which uses sixteen as base. The decimal values 10, 11, 12, 13, 14 and 15 are represented by A, B, C, D, E and F, respectively. One byte (8 bits) in hexadecimal notation can be presented by 2 digits, 00 through FF. The prefix or suffix operator X is used to denote a hexadecimal value, for example, '10'x represents decimal 16.

IBM^{TM}   International Business Machines Corporation, supplier of ISPF, PDF, MVS, etc. licensed products.

interpreter   A software component which directly executes a source program without producing an intermediate object module. An interpreter offers more flexibility than a compiler and usually has better diagnostics (the complete source code is available). However, this flexibility is bought at the cost of increased resource usage at run-time.

ISPEXEC   ISPF component which provides dialogue services for CLISTs and REXX programs.

ISPF   Interactive System Productivity Facility, IBM programming system to provide dialogue facilities. ISPF requires TSO.

ISPLINK   ISPF component which provides dialogue services for programs.

ISPSTART   ISPF component which invokes the ISPF environment.

ISREDIT   ISPF component which makes available ISPF/PDF Editor services. Such services can be used to implement so-called edit macros.

JCL   Job Control Language. The statements used to control the processing of a batch job. The principal JCL statements are: DD and EXEC.

library   A partitioned dataset.

LIFO   Last-in/First-out. Storage management concept where the elements are retrieved in the reverse order as which they were inserted - this is also known as **push-down stack processing**.

Linkage Editor   IBM program to combine one or more object modules into an executable load module.

link list   System programs (e.g. compilers) which can be invoked without having to specify from which library they come.

load module Machine-readable Linkage Editor output in a form suitable for loading into virtual storage for execution.

LRECL Logical record length. The number of characters forming a record.

member Independent part of a partitioned dataset. A member can be directly accessed and processed as if were a sequential dataset.

MS-DOS^{TM} Microsoft^{TM} Disk Operating System - functionally equivalent to IBM's PC-DOS. These two operating systems are generically known as DOS (Disk Operating System) and are the principal operating systems for the IBM Personal Computer and compatibles.

MVS^{TM} Multiple Virtual Systems operating system.

object module Machine-readable compiler output.

Operating System/2^{TM} also known as OS/2. The operating system originally announced for IBM PS/2 computers. There are two versions; Standard Edition and Extended Edition. Standard Edition is available from both IBM and Microsoft. Extended Edition is available only from IBM and provides additional features, for example, Database Manager.

OS/2^{TM} See Operating System/2.

panel Form with which data is to be displayed on a VDU.

partitioned dataset A data set comprising of members. Each member can be accessed directly by means of its (member) name. A partitioned dataset is also called a **library**.

PC-DOS^{TM} IBM Personal Computer Disk Operating System - functionally equivalent to Microsoft's MS-DOS. These two operating systems are generically known as DOS (Disk Operating System) and are the principal operating systems for the IBM Personal Computer and compatibles.

PDF Program Development Facility, IBM dialogue utility package to assist the programmer in program development. PDF is an ISPF application.

Personal REXX Mansfield Software Group implementation of the REXX language for personal computers (DOS and OS/2 software environments).

phrase In the REXX sense, one or more characters. A phrase is usually used as argument for a longer string.

PL/I Modern high-level structured programming language combining many of the features of COBOL and FORTRAN.

profile pool The pool of dialogue variables belonging to a particular application. The profile pool is retained across ISPF/TSO sessions.

QMF^{TM} Query Management Facility. End-user interface to DB2.

RACF   Resource Access Control Facility; IBM security package.

REXX   Restructured Extended Executor. REXX is a high-level programming language functionally similar to CLIST. The REXX language is more powerful and efficient than the CLIST language.

REXX/2   IBM's implementation of the REXX language for the OS/2 environment - available for OS/2 Version 1.2.

SAA^{TM} Systems Application Architecture^{TM}. SAA is an IBM concept designed to provide a standard interface to the user (application developer).

SBCS   Single-Byte Character Set. The standard character set where one byte represents one character, see also **DBCS**.

session   The dialogue environment for the current user. TSO is the lowest level session.

shared pool   The pool of dialogue variables belonging to the current ISPF session.

source program   Input to a compiler. A source program constitutes the "computer instructions" produced by the programmer. Source programs can exist in a number of levels of detail. **Low-level** languages (e.g. Assembler) require that the programmer has an intimate knowledge of the machine instructions available on the computer on which his program will run. **High-level** languages (e.g. PL/I) remove much of this burden from the programmer and enable him to be more concerned with the procedure required to solve his problem; such languages are often referred to as **procedure oriented** languages. So called **4th generation** languages (REXX offers certain features) are **problem oriented**. Modern high-level languages offer structuring facilities.

string   In the REXX sense, one or more characters.

TSO   Time Sharing Option, programming system to provide users with on-line access to computing system. TSO is now a standard MVS component.

user id   The unique code for the user when he logs onto the TSO system.

VDU   Visual Display Unit. Terminal unit with TV-like display.

VM^{TM} Virtual Machine. Mainframe operating system which supports the concurrent operation of multiple operating systems. CMS is VM's user interface.

word   In the REXX sense, one or more non-blank characters.

word-list   In the REXX sense, one or more **words** separated by blanks.

Appendix H

Alphanumeric code table

Decimal	Hexa-decimal	ASCII	EBCDIC
48	30	0	
49	31	1	
50	32	2	
51	33	3	
52	34	4	
53	35	5	
54	36	6	
55	37	7	
56	38	8	
57	39	9	

Decimal	Hexa-decimal	ASCII	EBCDIC
65	41	A	
66	42	B	
67	43	C	
68	44	D	
69	45	E	
70	46	F	
71	47	G	
72	48	H	
73	49	I	
74	4A	J	

Decimal	Hexa-decimal	ASCII	EBCDIC
75	4B	K	
76	4C	L	
77	4D	M	
78	4E	N	
79	4F	0	
80	50	P	
81	51	Q	
82	52	R	
83	53	S	
84	54	T	
85	55	U	
86	56	V	
87	57	W	
88	58	X	
89	59	Y	
90	5A	Z	
97	61	a	
98	62	b	
99	63	c	
100	64	d	
101	65	e	
102	66	f	
103	67	g	
104	68	h	
105	69	i	
106	6A	j	
107	6B	k	
108	6C	l	
109	6D	m	
110	6E	n	
111	6F	o	
112	70	p	
113	71	q	
114	72	r	
115	73	s	
116	74	t	
117	75	u	
118	76	v	
119	77	w	
120	78	x	
121	79	y	
122	7A	z	

Decimal	Hexa-decimal	ASCII	EBCDIC
129	81		a
130	82		b
131	83		c
132	84		d
133	85		e
134	86		f
135	87		g
136	88		h
137	89		i
145	91		j
146	92		k
147	93		l
148	94		m
149	95		n
150	96		o
151	97		p
152	98		q
153	99		r
162	A2		s
163	A3		t
164	A4		u
165	A5		v
166	A6		w
167	A7		x
168	A8		y
169	A9		z
193	C1		A
194	C2		B
195	C3		C
196	C4		D
197	C5		E
198	C6		F
199	C7		G
200	C8		H
201	C9		I
209	D1		J
210	D2		K
211	D3		L
212	D4		M
213	D5		N
214	D6		O
215	D7		P
216	D8		Q
217	D9		R

Decimal	Hexa-decimal	ASCII	EBCDIC
226	E2		S
227	E3		T
228	E4		U
229	E5		V
230	E6		W
231	E7		X
232	E8		Y
233	E9		Z

Decimal	Hexa-decimal	ASCII	EBCDIC
240	F0		0
241	F1		1
242	F2		2
243	F3		3
244	F4		4
245	F5		5
246	F6		6
247	F7		7
248	F8		8
249	F9		9

Appendix I

Compatibility

This appendix summarises the features available in various implementations. The
following legend is used in the tables:

    s   SAA specification

    r   REXX language definition (superset of the SAA specification)

    x   extension for the implementation

    +   additional feature

    ( )   implementation dependent

    -           not available.

REXX Instructions

	MVS/TSO-E	VM/CMS	REXX/2	Personal REXX
=	S	S	S	S
ADDRESS	S	S	S	S
ARG	S	S	S	S
CALL	S+	S	S	S
DO	S	S	S	S
DROP	S	S	S	S
EXIT	S	S	S	S
IF	S	S	S	S
INTERPRET	S	S	S	S
ITERATE	S	S	S	S
LEAVE	S	S	S	S
NOP	S	S	S	S
NUMERIC	S	S	S	S
OPTIONS	(S)	(S)	(S)	(S)
PARSE	S+	S	S	S
PROCEDURE	S	S	S	S
PULL	S	S	S	S
PUSH	S	S	S	S
QUEUE	S	S	S	S
RETURN	S	S	S	S
SAY	S	S	S	S
SELECT	S	S	S	S
SETLOCAL	–	–	X	–
SIGNAL	S+	S	S	S
TRACE	S	S	S	S
UPPER	X	X	–	–

Host REXX commands (TSO implementation)

	MVS/TSO-E	VM/CMS*	REXX/2*	Personal* REXX
DELSTACK	X	–	–	–
DROPBUF	X	–	–	X
EXECIO	X	X	–	X
EXECUTIL	X	–	–	–
HI	X	X	–	–
HT	X	–	–	–
MAKEBUF	X	–	–	X
NEWSTACK	X	–	–	–
QBUF	X	–	–	–
QELEM	X	–	–	–
QSTACK	X	–	–	–
RT	X	–	–	–
SUBCOM	X	X	–	–
TE	X	X	–	–
TS	X	X	–	–

* The REXX commands from the MVS/TSO implementation are used as reference, other implementations may have their own commands.

Built-in functions (SAA), part 1 of 2

	MVS/TSO-E	VM/CMS	REXX/2	Personal REXX
ABBREV	S	S	S	S
ABS	S	S	S	S
ADDRESS	S	S	S	S
ARG	S	S	S	S
BITAND	S	S	S	S
BITOR	S	S	S	S
BITXOR	S	S	S	S
CENTRE (CENTER)	S	S	S	S
COMPARE	S	S	S	S
CONDITION	S	-	S	S
COPIES	S	S	S	S
C2D	S	S	S	S
C2X	S	S	S	S
DATATYPE	S	S	S	S
DATE	S	S	S	S
DELSTR	S	S	S	S
DELWORD	S	S	S	S
DIGITS	S	-	S	S
D2C	S	S	S	S
D2X	S	S	S	S
ERRORTEXT	S	S	S	S
FORM	S	-	S	S
FORMAT	S	S	S	S
FUZZ	S	-	S	S
INSERT	S	S	S	S
LASTPOS	S	S	S	S
LEFT	S	S	S	S
LENGTH	S	S	S	S
MAX	S	S	S	S
MIN	S	S	S	S
OVERLAY	S	S	S	S
POS	S	S	S	S
QUEUED	S	S	S	S
RANDOM	S	S	S	S
REVERSE	S	S	S	S
RIGHT	S	S	S	S
SIGN	S	S	S	S
SOURCELINE	S	S	S	S
SPACE	S	S	S	S
STRIP	S	S	S	S
SUBSTR	S	S	S	S
SUBWORD	S	S	S	S
SYMBOL	S	S	S	S
TIME	S	S	S	S
TRACE	S	S	S	S
TRANSLATE	S	S	S	S
TRUNC	S	S	S	S
VALUE	S	S	S	S
VERIFY	S	S	S	S
WORD	S	S	S	S
WORDINDEX	S	S	S	S
WORDLENGTH	S	S	S	S

Built-in functions (SAA), part 2 of 2

	MVS/TSO-E	VM/CMS	REXX/2	Personal REXX
WORDPOS	s	–	s	s
WORDS	s	s	s	s
XRANGE	s	s	s	s
X2C	s	s	s	s
X2D	s	s	s	s

Built-in functions (non-SAA)

	MVS/TSO-E	VM/CMS	REXX/2	Personal REXX
BEEP	–	–	x	–
B2X	–	–	x	–
CHARIN	–	–	r	r
CHAROUT	–	–	r	r
CHARS	–	–	r	r
DIRECTORY	–	–	x	–
ENDLOCAL	–	–	x	–
EXTERNALS	–	x	–	–
FILESPEC	–	–	x	–
FIND	x	x	–	x
INDEX	x	x	–	x
JUSTIFY	x	x	–	–
LINEIN	–	–	r	r
LINEOUT	–	–	r	r
LINES	–	–	r	r
LINESIZE	r	r	–	r
SETLOCAL	–	–	x	–
STREAM	–	–	x	–
USERID	x	x	–	x
X2B	–	–	x	–

Index

!, 74
%, 30
&&, 32
&, 32
&LASTCC, 189
**, 30
*, 30
-, 76
+++, 76
+, 30
-, 30
/, 30
//, 30
/=, 31
/==, 31
<, 31
<<, 31
<<=, 31
<=, 31
<>, 31
= (assignment), 86
= (comparison), 31
>, 31
>.>, 76
><, 31
>=, 31
>>, 31
>>=, 31
>>>, 76

>C>, 76
>F>, 76
>L>, 76
>O>, 76
>P>, 76
>V>, 76
?, 74, 76
\, 31
|, 32
||, 29
¬, 31

ABBREV, 115
ABS, 115
abuttal, 24
add, 30
address space, 273
ADDRESS, 86, 116
addressing, 31-bit, 217
All, 73, 74
alphabetic, 273
alphameric, 273
alphanumeric, 273
ALTERNATE_ERROR_MSG, 247
AMODE 31, 217
And, 32
ARG, 89, 116
Argument List, format, 245
arguments, 47

array, 26
ASCII, 273
Assembler, function implementation, 231
assignment (=), 41, 58
attribute, 26

BITAND, 117
BITOR, 118
BITXOR, 119
built-in functions, *see* functions

C2D, 122
C2X, 123
CALL, 56, 90
CENTER, 119
CENTRE, 119
CHARIN, 70, 159
CHAROUT, 70, 160
CHARS, 70, 161
clause, 273
CLIST, 273
    statements, 178
CMS, 273
COBOL, function implementation, 233
command functions, host environment, 18
command procedure, 273
command processor, 60
command, data returned by, 178
Commands, 73, 74
commands, native, 88
communication, program, 59
COMPARE, 120
compatibility, 83
compiler, 273
concatenation operator, explicit (| |), 29
concatenation, 29
CONDITION, 121
condition, iteration, 50, 52
conditions, exception, 73
control blocks, definitions, 245
control variable, 50, 51
COPIES, 122
current buffer, 61
current position pointer, 70

current stack, 61
CVT, 273

D2C, 129
D2X, 130
data base, 273
data buffering, 69
data files, opening and closing, 69
data, passing between programs, 63
database, 274
DATABASE2, 274
dataset, 274
DATATYPE, 124
DATE, 125
DB2, 274
    interface with, 197
    subcommands, 197
DBCS, 274
DBMS, 274
DD, 274
debug, interactive, 78
debugging, 41, 63, 72
    example, 79
    terminate, 78
DELSTACK, 70, 168
DELSTR, 127
DELWORD, 128
Dialog Manager, 274
dialogue, 274
DIGITS, 128
divide, 30
DO, 91
Do,
    endless, 51
    repetitive, 51
    simple, 51
Do-group, 49
    nested, 49
Do-loop, 49
    processing within , 53, 54
DOS, 274
    linkage to, 203
DROP, 93
DROPBUF, 168

DSN command, 197
DSORG, 274
DSQCCI, 198
DSQQMFE, 198

EBCDIC, 274
edit macro, 274
EFPL, 230, 245
    format, 246
EFPLARG, 246
EFPLEVAL, 246
EMS, 274
End value, 50
entry point addresses, 253
ENVBLOCK, 223, 230, 240, 242, 243, 246
    address of, 242
    format, 247
    obtain, 242
ENVBLOCK_ERROR, 247
ENVBLOCK_ID, 246
ENVBLOCK_IRXEXTE, 247
ENVBLOCK_LENGTH, 246
ENVBLOCK_PARMBLOCK, 246
ENVBLOCK_USERFIELD, 247
ENVBLOCK_VERSION, 246
ENVBLOCK_WORKBLOK_EXT, 247
Environment Block, *see* ENVBLOCK
environment,
    initialise , 242
    standard, 42
equal, 31
error processing, 41
Error, 73, 74
ERROR_CALL@, 247
ERROR_MSGID, 247
ERRORTEXT, 130
EVALBLOCK, 245, 248
    allocate, 243
    format, 248
EVALBLOCK_EVDATA, 248
EVALBLOCK_EVLEN, 248
EVALBLOCK_EVSIZE, 248
Evaluation Block, *see* EVALBLOCK
examples, worked, 205-216

Exclusive Or, 32
Exec Block, *see* EXECBLK
EXEC parameter, 193
EXEC, 274
exec,
    check whether loaded, 240
    invocation of,
        MVS-TSO, 191-194, 219-224
        Personal REXX, 200
        REXX/2, 202
    load into main-storage, 240
EXEC_BLK_ACRYN, 249
EXEC_BLK_LENGTH, 249
EXEC_DDNAME, 249
EXEC_DSNLEN, 249
EXEC_DSNPTR, 249
EXEC_MEMBER, 249
EXEC_SUBCOM, 249
EXECBLK, 248
    format, 249
EXECIO, 70, 168
execs, 18
executable load module, 275
EXECUTIL, 171
EXIT, 78, 93
exponent, 66
expression, conditional, 50, 52
external functions, 42
External Functions Parameter List, *see* EFPL
external routines, 46

Failure, 73, 74
false, 30
field types, 218
FIFO, 60, 274
file buffer, 59, 63
file, 274
filename, 275
FIND, 161
FINIS, 69
FORM, 131
FORMAT, 131
format, default, 22
FPCKDIR_ENTRY_LENGTH, 239

FPCKDIR_FUNCADDR, 239
FPCKDIR_FUNCNAME, 239
FPCKDIR_FUNCTIONS, 239
FPCKDIR_HEADER_LENGTH, 238
FPCKDIR_ID, 238
FPCKDIR_SYSNAME, 239
function, 45
  external, 42
  interface, 230, 231
  invocation, 46
  internal, 42
  non-SAA, 18, 42
    CHARIN, 159
    CHAROUT, 160
    CHARS, 161
    FIND, 161
    INDEX, 161
    JUSTIFY, 162
    LINEIN, 163
    LINEOUT, 164
    LINES, 165
    LINESIZE, 165
    USERID, 166
  parameters, maximum, 47
  recursive, 45
  SAA, 113
    ABBREV, 115
    ABS, 115
    ADDRESS, 116
    ARG, 116
    BITAND, 117
    BITOR, 118
    BITXOR, 119
    C2D, 122
    C2X, 123
    CENTER, 119
    CENTRE, 119
    COMPARE, 120
    CONDITION, 121
    COPIES, 122
    D2C, 129
    D2X, 130
    DATATYPE, 124
    DATE, 125

DELSTR, 127
DELWORD, 128
DIGITS, 128
ERRORTEXT, 130
FORM, 131
FORMAT, 131
FUZZ, 132
INSERT, 132
LASTPOS, 133
LEFT, 133
LENGTH, 134
MAX, 135
MIN, 135
OVERLAY, 136
POS, 137
QUEUED, 138
RANDOM, 138
REVERSE, 139
RIGHT, 139
SIGN, 140
SOURCELINE, 141
SPACE, 141
STRIP, 142
SUBSTR, 143
SUBWORD, 144
SYMBOL, 144
TIME, 145
TRACE, 147
TRANSLATE, 149
TRUNC, 151
VALUE, 151
VERIFY, 152
WORD, 153
WORDINDEX, 153
WORDLENGTH, 154
WORDPOS, 154
WORDS, 155
X2C, 156
X2D, 157
XRANGE, 155
function definitions,
  non-SAA, 158
  SAA, 113
Function Directory, 237

function implementation, sample, 235
Function Package Directory,
    Entry, 239
    format, 237
    Header, 238
    sample, 239
Function Package Table, 237
function package, 46, 236
    diagram, 238
    directory, 237
    local, 236
    system, 236
    user, 236
function pool, restrictions, 196
FUZZ, 132

GDDM, 275
greater than or equal, 31
greater than, 31

Halt, 73
help environment, 275
help panel, 275
hexadecimal, 275
HI, 173
hierarchy level, 49
hierarchy, 49
host commands,
    DELSTACK, 168
    DROPBUF, 168
    EXECIO, 168
    EXECUTIL, 171
    HI, 173
    HT, 173
    MAKEBUF, 173
    NEWSTACK, 174
    QBUF, 174
    QELEM, 175
    QSTACK, 175
    RT, 175
    SUBCOM, 176
    suppress execution of , 74
    TE, 177
    TS, 177

HT, 173

IF, 94
IJKEFTSR, 220
IKJEFT01, 192
In-storage Control Block, see INSTBLK
Inclusive Or, 32
increment, 50
INDEX, 161
information hiding, 44
initial value, 50
initialisation routine - IRXINIT service, 242
input/output, 68
INSERT, 132
INSTBLK, 240, 250
    format, 250
INSTBLK_ACRONYM, 250
INSTBLK_ADDRESS, 250
INSTBLK_DDNAME, 251
INSTBLK_DSNAME, 251
INSTBLK_DSNLEN, 251
INSTBLK_ENTRIES, 251
INSTBLK_HDRLEN, 250
INSTBLK_HEADER, 250
INSTBLK_MEMBER, 251
INSTBLK_STMT@, 251
INSTBLK_STMTLEN, 251
INSTBLK_SUBCOM, 251
INSTBLK_USEDLEN, 250
instructions, keyword, 18
interactive debugging, invoke, 74
interactive tracing, terminate, 78
interface,
    Personal REXX environment, 203
    with DB2, 197
    with ISPEXEC, 196
    with ISREDIT, 196
    with QMF, 198
    with REXX, 200
Intermediate, 73, 75
INTERPRET, 95
interpreter, 275
IRXEXCOM, 226
IRXEXEC, 223, 224

IRXEXTE, 247, 253
IRXJCL, 193, 219
IRXLOAD, 240, 241
IRXRLT, 243, 248
IRXSTK, 228
ISPEXEC, 275
    interface with, 196
ISPF, 275
ISPLINK, 275
ISPSTART, 275
ISREDIT, 275
    interface with, 196
ITERATE, 53, 95

JCL, 275
    statements, 193, 194
JUSTIFY, 162

Labels, 73, 75
LASTPOS, 133
LEAVE, 54, 96
LEFT, 133
LENGTH, 134
less than or equal, 31
less than, 31
library, 275
LIFO, 59, 275
LINEIN, 70, 163
LINEOUT, 70, 164
LINES, 70, 165
LINESIZE, 165
link list, 276
Linkage Editor, 275
linkage,
    to host (DOS) environment, 203
    to host (MVS-TSO) environment, 194
    to host (OS/2) environment, 200
    to programs, 195
LISTDSI, 180
literal, 23
    continuation, 24
    hexadecimal, 23
    maximum length, 23
load module, 276

logical operation, bit-by-bit, 32
LRECL, 276

macro,
    IRXARGTB, 245
    IRXEFPL 245
    IRXENVB, 246
    IRXEVALB, 248
    IRXEXECB, 248
    IRXEXTE, 253
    IRXFPDIR, 237
    IRXINSTB, 250
    IRXSHVB, 251
maintainability, 83
MAKEBUF, 173
mantissa, 66
MAX, 135
member, 276
MIN, 135
MS-DOS, 276
MSG, 182
multiply, 30
MVS, 276
    batch invocation, 193
    command function calls, 178
    host environment commands, 178
MVS-TSO,
    implementation, 191
    linkage to, 194

NEWSTACK, 174
No value, 73
NOP, 96
not equal, 31
number, 22
numbers, floating-point, 22
NUMERIC, 97

object module, 276
Operating System/2, 276
operations,
    character-mode, 70
    file-mode, 70
    line-mode, 70

sequence of, 66
operator, 26
   priority, 33
   suffix, 23
operators,
   arithmetic, 30
   character, 29
   comparison, 30
   logical (Boolean), 32
   prefix, 30, 74
OPTIONS, 98
OS/2, 276
   linkage to, 200
OUTTRAP, 183
OVERLAY, 136

panel, 276
parameters, 47
parentheses, 33, 67
PARSE, 98
parsing of arguments, 39
parsing of characters, 36
parsing, 35, 41
   at delimiter, 37
   at position, 36
   at words, 38
   composite, 40
   dynamic, 40
   placeholders, 39
   relative, 39
partitioned dataset, 276
   member of, 191
PC-DOS, 276
PDF, 276
performance, 84
Personal REXX, 276
   implementation, 201
   interface with, 203
   invocation, 202
phrase, 276
PL/I, 276
   sample function, 235
   sample using,
      IRXEXCOM, 235

IRXEXEC, 225
IRXJCL, 219
IRXRLT, 244
IRXSTK, 229
TSOLNK, 221
placeholder, 35, 39
PLIRETV (PL/I), 218
POS, 137
power, 30
precision, 22, 65
   default, 22
PRIMARY_ERROR_MESSAGE, 247
PROCEDURE, 101
procedure, 44
   invocation, 46
profile pool, 277
programming, practices, 81
programs, linkage to, 195
PROMPT, 185
PULL, 69, 102
PUSH, 69, 103

QBUF, 174
QELEM, 175
QMF, 277
   interface with, 198
QSTACK, 175
queue, 59
QUEUE, 69, 104
QUEUED, 138
quotes, delimiting, 23

RACF, 277
RANDOM, 138
RC, 63
readability, 82
repetitive Do, controlled , 52
Restructured Extended Executor, 15
result, get (IRXRLT service), 243
RESULT, 63
Results, 73, 75
RETURN, 104
RETURN-CODE (COBOL), 218
REVERSE, 139

REXX, 277
  application areas, 17
  components, 18
  features, 16
  host command definitions, 167
  interface with, 200
  invocation, 191
  items, 20
  syntax, 27
REXX commands, host, 18
REXX exec,
  identification, 191
  invocation, 34
REXX implementation, scope of, 16
REXX instructions, 85
  = - assignment, 86
  ADDRESS, 86
  ARG, 89
  CALL, 90
  DO, 91
  DROP, 93
  EXIT, 93
  IF, 94
  INTERPRET, 95
  ITERATE, 95
  LEAVE, 96
  NOP, 96
  NUMERIC, 97
  OPTIONS, 98
  PARSE, 98
  PROCEDURE, 101
  PULL, 102
  PUSH, 103
  QUEUE, 104
  RETURN, 104
  SAY, 104
  SELECT, 105
  SIGNAL, 106
  TRACE, 109
  UPPER, 111
REXX invocation parameter, sample PL/I
  program to process, 196
REXX language, implementations, 190
REXX variables, program access to, 226

REXX's origin, 16
REXX/2, 277
  implementation, 200
  invocation, 200
RIGHT, 139
routine, 42
  internal, 46
  external, 46
routines, use of RETURN, 48
RT, 175
RXINTMGR, 201

SAA, 277
  procedural language (REXX), 15
SAY, 69, 104
SBCS, 277
search order, 46
SELECT, 55, 105
sequence control, 41
session, 277
shared pool, 277
Shared Variable (Request) Block, see
  SHVBLOCK
SHVBLOCK, 251
  format, 252
SHVBUFL, 253
SHVCODE, 252
SHVNAMA, 253
SHVNAML, 253
SHVNEXT, 252
SHVRET, 252
SHVUSER, 252
SHVVALA, 253
SHVVALL, 253
SIGL, 63
SIGN, 140
SIGNAL, 57, 73, 106
  used as GoTo, 108
single-stepping, 78
source program, 277
SOURCELINE, 141
SPACE, 141
special variables, 63
  RC, 63

RESULT, 63
SIGL, 63
stack, 69
    used as terminal input buffer, 60
    used to pass data between programs, 61
stack (queue) processing, 41, 59, 228
    program services, 228
    MVS-TSO, 62
STACKMGR, 201
statement format, 18
status code, 178
stem, 25
STORAGE, 186
strictly equal, 31
strictly greater than or equal, 31
strictly greater than, 31
strictly less than or equal, 31
strictly less than, 31
strictly not equal, 31
string, 277
STRIP, 142
structured programming constructions, 41
SUBCOM, 176
subroutine, 43
    control and invocation, 41, 46
SUBSTR, 143
subtract, 30
SUBWORD, 144
SYMBOL, 144
symbol, 24
    compound, 25
    data, length of, 26
    declaration of, 26
    name, maximum length, 24
    simple, 25
Syntax, 73, 75
syntax, conventions, 267-270
SYSDSN, 186
SYSEXEC, 192, 193
SYSPROC, 192
Systems Application Architecture, 15
SYSTSIN, 192, 194
SYSTSPRT, 192, 194
SYSVAR, 187

TE, 177
template, 35
terminal input buffer, 59
terminal operations, 69
TIME, 145
trace,
    data prefixes, 76
    intermediate data prefixes, 76
    options, 73
    output, 75
        example, 76
TRACE, 109, 147
TRANSLATE, 149
true, 30
TRUNC, 151
TS, 177
TSO, 277
    batch invocation, 192
    commands,
      MSG, 182
      OUTTRAP, 183
      PROMPT, 185
      STORAGE, 186
      SYSDSN, 186
      SYSVAR, 187
    invocation of, 188
TSO/ISPF, invocation, 191
TSOLNK, 220, 221

unequal, 31
UPPER, 111
user id, 277
USERID, 166

VALUE, 151
variable pool, 251
variables,
    global, 44
    program access, 226
VDU, 277
Vector of External Entry Points, *see* VEEP
VEEP, 253
VERIFY, 152

VGET, 196
VM, 277
VPUT, 196

WORD, 153
word, 277
word-list, 277
WORDINDEX, 153
WORDLENGTH, 154
WORDPOS, 154
WORDS, 155
words, 35
    processing of, 35

X2C, 156
X2D, 157
XRANGE, 155

ELLIS HORWOOD SERIES IN COMPUTERS AND THEIR APPLICATIONS
Series Editor: IAN CHIVERS, Senior Analyst, The Computer Centre, King's College, London, and formerly Senior Programmer and Analyst, Imperial College of Science and Technology, University of London

Rahtz, S.P.Q.	INFORMATION TECHNOLOGY IN THE HUMANITIES
Ramsden, E.	MICROCOMPUTERS IN EDUCATION 2
Rubin, T.	USER INTERFACE DESIGN FOR COMPUTER SYSTEMS
Rudd, A.S.	PRACTICAL USAGE OF ISPF DIALOG MANAGER
Rudd, A.S.	PRACTICAL USAGE OF REXX
Rudd, A.S.	IMPLEMENTING PRACTICAL DB2 APPLICATIONS
de Saram, H.	PROGRAMMING IN MICRO-PROLOG
Savic, D.	OBJECT-ORIENTED PROGRAMMING WITH SMALLTALK/V
Schirmer, C.	PROGRAMMING IN C FOR UNIX
Schofield, C.F.	OPTIMIZING FORTRAN PROGRAMS
Sharp, J.A.	DATA FLOW COMPUTING
Sherif, M.A.	DATABASE PROJECTS
Smith & Sage	EDUCATION AND THE INFORMATION SOCIETY
Smith, J.M & Stutely, R.	SGML
Späth, H.	CLUSTER ANALYSIS ALGORITHMS
Späth, H.	CLUSTER DISSECTION AND ANALYSIS
Stratford-Collins, P.	ADA
Teunissen, W.J. & van den Bos, J.	3D INTERACTIVE COMPUTER GRAPHICS
Tizzard, K.	C FOR PROFESSIONAL PROGRAMMERS
Turner, S.J.	AN INTRODUCTION TO COMPILER DESIGN
Tsuji, T.	OPTIMIZING SCHEMES FOR STRUCTURED PROGRAMMING LANGUAGE PROCESSORS
Wexler, J.	CONCURRENT PROGRAMMING IN OCCAM 2
Whiddett, R.J.	CONCURRENT PROGRAMMING FOR SOFTWARE ENGINEERS
Whiddett, R.J., Berry, R.E., Blair, G.S., Hurley, P.N., Nicol, P.J. & Muir, S.J.	UNIX
Xu, Duan-Zheng	COMPUTER ANALYSIS OF SEQUENTIAL MEDICAL TRIALS
Yannakoudakis, E.J. & Hutton, P.J.	SPEECH SYNTHESIS AND RECOGNITION SYSTEMS
Zech, R.	FORTH FOR THE PROFESSIONAL

Computer Communications and Networking

Currie, W.S.	LANS EXPLAINED
Deasington, R.J.	A PRACTICAL GUIDE TO COMPUTER COMMUNICATIONS AND NETWORKING, 2nd Edition
Deasington, R.J.	X.25 EXPLAINED, 2nd Edition
Henshall, J. & Shaw, S.	OSI EXPLAINED, 2nd Edition
Kauffels, F.-J.	PRACTICAL LANS ANALYSED
Kauffels, F.-J.	PRACTICAL NETWORKS ANALYSED
Kauffels, F.-J.	UNDERSTANDING DATA COMMUNICATIONS
Muftic, S.	SECURITY MECHANISMS FOR COMPUTER NETWORKS